Russia 1917

Workers' Revolution and the
Festival of the Oppressed

Dave Sherry

About the Author

Dave Sherry is a retired housing worker and trade union activist in Glasgow. He is the author of *John MacLean: Red Clydesider* (Bookmarks, 1998, republished 2014), *Occupy! A Short History of Workers' Occupations* (Bookmarks, 2010) and *Empire and Revolution: A Socialist History of the First World War* (Bookmarks, 2014). He is a member of the Socialist Workers Party.

Russia 1917

Workers' Revolution and the Festival of the Oppressed

Dave Sherry

Bookmarks Publications

Russia 1917:
Workers' Revolution and the Festival of the Oppressed
By Dave Sherry

Published 2017
© Bookmarks Publications
c/o 1 Bloomsbury Street, London WC1B 3QE
Designed and typeset by Peter Robinson
Cover design Ben Windsor
Printed by Melita Press

ISBN 78-1-910885-40-6 (pbk)
978-1-910885-41-3 (Kindle)
978-1-910885-42-0 (ePub)
978-1-910885-43-7 (PDF)

Contents

Foreword   7

1   Introduction   11

2   Context: Russia at the start of the 20th century   21

3   1905: Russia's great dress rehearsal and the years of reaction   51

4   The outbreak of war and the collapse of official socialism   75

5   February 1917: Soviets and the Provisional government   91

6   April 1917: Re-arming the party   111

7   The Kornilov coup and the road to workers' power   139

8   War and Revolution: The international impact   166

9   Achievements of the Revolution   181

10   Consolidating Soviet power   197

11   Revolution under siege and how it was lost   214

12   Conclusion: When all things are possible   241

Endnotes   257
Further reading   265
Bibliography   270
Index   274

Foreword

Names, dates and places

Russia

There is a problem about what to call Russia in the 20th Century. Before 1917 it was the Romanov Empire: what Lenin called "a prison house of nations". It stretched from Finland, the Baltic States, Poland and Ukraine through the Caucasus and Central Asia to the nomadic tribes of Siberia in the far north and the Pacific Ocean in the far east. Centuries of imperial conquest by the Tsars had created a multinational state in which "Great Russians" were only 43 percent of its 150 million people.

From the 1920s to 1991 it was officially known as the Soviet Union or the USSR (Union of Socialist Soviet Republics). But by 1930 it was an empire under the control of a new autocracy—Stalin's ruling bureaucracy in Moscow. By then it had ceased to be a federation of free republics and certainly not a workers' state, let alone a socialist state. This was one of the reasons it broke apart in 1991.

The disintegration of this system in the late 1980s and its subsequent transition after 1991 has not been as fundamental as many commentators have suggested. Russia has shifted away from state capitalism towards a more market form of capitalism.

By the mid 1920s there were no soviets as there had been during the 1905 revolution and again from the moment the Tsar was toppled in early 1917 until after the end of the civil war in the early 1920s. With the triumph of Stalin, the Supreme Soviet and other bodies in Russia that included the word soviet in their official title, were in no way elected organs of workers' power, unlike the workers', soldiers' and peasants' councils' that had triumphed in October 1917. I have therefore tried to avoid using the terms Soviet Union and USSR, unless appropriate, to reflect the reality of the situation.

Stalinism

In using this term I am in full agreement with Alex Callinicos's defini-
tion, in *The Revenge of History*: "By 'Stalinism' I mean, not one person's
rule or even a body of beliefs, but the whole system of social power
crystallised in the USSR in the 1930s, exported to Eastern Europe in the
second half of the 1940s, and that survived till the late 1980s when it
began to collapse; a system characterised by the hierarchically organised
control of all aspects of social life, political, economic, and cultural, by
a narrow oligarchy seated at the apex of the party and state apparatus—
the nomenklatura".[1]

Petrograd/St Petersburg

The capital of Tsarist Russia is called St Petersburg when referring to the
period before August 1914. Tsar Peter the Great founded the city in 1703
as his imperial capital. When Russia went to war with Germany in August
1914, Peter's descendant Tsar Nicholas II had its German-sounding name
changed to Petrograd during an outburst of anti-German hysteria.

British royalty responded in a similar fashion. King George V was a
cousin of both Tsar Nicholas II and Kaiser Wilhelm. In 1917 he changed
the family name from the German Saxe-Coburg and Gotha to Windsor;
these are the royals and their acolytes who thunder on about "our scep-
tered isle" and "Britishness". Queen Victoria's parents were German: she
was the Kaiser's granny. In contrast the internationalist and anti-war
Bolsheviks defied national chauvinism in 1914 by insisting on retaining
the title of their 'Petersburg Committee'.

After Lenin's death in 1924 Petrograd was renamed Leningrad in
honour of his role in the revolution. The embalmed Lenin would have
been spinning in his tomb; he detested the cult of personality that was
to become such a key feature of Stalinism and marked a sharp break
from the revolutionary spirit of Bolshevism. In 1991 the city's original
name was restored. By then Lenin's reputation had nosedived because
of the deliberate distortions promoted by the American secret intelligence services and by what passed for Western bourgeois scholarship:
often the two were indistinguishable.

This, combined with the personality cult created by the Russian
bureaucracy after his death, meant Lenin was posthumously and unjustly

---

1 A Callinicos, *The Revenge of History* (London, 1991), p15.

linked to the hideous crimes of Stalinism and the state capitalist regime that continued after the dictator's death in 1953. Lenin's fate must rank among the worst-ever cases of guilt by association.

Whites and Reds
In the civil war from the end of 1917 until the end of 1920, the counter-revolutionary forces backed by world capitalism were known as "the Whites" or "the White Terror".

Dates
Until February 1918 Russia used the Julian or Byzantine calendar, which was 13 days behind the Gregorian calendar in the West. This is why the two revolutions of 1917 are referred to by the months of February and October. According to the Western or Gregorian calendar they took place in March and November. In this book the dates for the events of 1917 and early 1918 are the Julian ones used in Russia at the time. As Trotsky explained in his epic *History of the Russian Revolution*: "The October revolution happened according to European reckoning in November... The reader will be kind enough to remember that before overthrowing the Byzantine calendar, the revolution had to overthrow the institutions that clung to it".[2]

This is a fairly chronological history, aiming to give a clear account with a discussion of context and politics as the revolution proceeds. It concludes with why the Russian Revolution matters today. Out of the bloodbath of the First World War, it opened up the prospect of a better world. Its message of international solidarity and working class self-emancipation sped round the globe. It showed that the highest ideals of humanity were practical and that the movement for achieving them had begun. Those prospects lasted far into the following decade and although destroyed under Stalinism, they still illuminate what's possible.

1917 is a portrait of ordinary women and men striving to end war and achieve human liberation. It serves to remind us—at a time when we need reminding—of what can happen in times of revolution, when the local and the immediate become merged with the national and the international, when people are filled with hope that all things are possible, not just for themselves, but for all humanity.

---

2   Trotsky, *The History of the Russian Revolution*, Volume I, (London, 1967), pp19, 20.

Acknowledgements

Sally Campbell encouraged and guided me, organising the editing and production of this book along with Eileen Short and Carol Williams and I thank them for all their work. Martin Empson and Joseph Choonara read my initial draft and made a number of comments and criticisms from which the book has benefitted. Its shortcomings are mine, not theirs and I appreciate their help.

Thanks to Helen Blair and Kathleen Sherry for their comments and suggestions on Bolshevik women and the role of women workers throughout 1917, and to Julie Sherry for putting up with me and listening to my sounding off on the revolution.

I owe a great deal to Tony Cliff, Duncan Hallas, Paul Foot, Chris Harman and Harry McShane: five remarkable socialists who enlivened the international socialist tradition for thousands of people like me in the early 1970s and for many others before and since. They would have had a lot to say had they been around for the centenary of 1917. I was fortunate to have been around when they did have their say.

Finally the book is dedicated to the memory of Liam Currie, a fine young comrade who died at the end of December 2016 and is sadly missed by those who knew him.

Introduction

On the morning of International Women's Day, Thursday, 23 February 1917,[3] thousands of angry women workers streamed out of the textile plants in Petrograd, the imperial capital of Russia and fifth biggest city in Europe. They were joined by women workers from the Vasilev Island tram terminus who had already visited the neighbouring barracks of the 180th Infantry Regiment to win the soldiers' promise not to shoot if they came out on strike.

Although they did not yet know it, their strikes would ignite the second Russian Revolution in twelve years. Unlike its 1905 predecessor, this uprising would topple the Tsarist autocracy, open up the road to a revolutionary workers' government in Russia, and to a Europe-wide revolt that would topple three other great Empires and end the First World War.

The women who were about to change history, many with husbands conscripted in the Tsar's army on the Eastern front, were in a militant mood; not just the strikers but also the masses of women forced to queue for hours in cold, wintry Petrograd for bread and fuel. Together they took over the streets, defying Cossack cavalry armed with sabres and whips. They stopped any trams still running and by noon 50,000 other workers had joined them in an angry protest on Sampsonevsky Prospekt, one of the main thoroughfares. The striking women marched through the factory districts, calling on the predominantly male workers in the big engineering plants to down tools and join them. A young metalworker from the Nobel factory said:

> We could hear women's voices: 'Down with high prices! Down with the war! Down with hunger! Bread for the workers!' Masses of women

---

3   7 March according to the Western Calendar. Until 1918 Russia used the Julian calendar, 13 days behind the Gregorian calendar used in the West.

workers filled the factory lane. Those who caught sight of us began to wave their arms, shouting 'Come out! Stop work!' Snowballs were fired through the windows. We decided to join the revolution.[1]

The women went far beyond what the local revolutionaries and the leaders of the skilled male workers thought feasible in the circumstances. It was the women who took the lead in approaching the troops to persuade them not to fire on or charge the demonstrators.

The world was into the third year of the greatest mass slaughter ever seen and there was no end in sight. The relentless profiteering of the rich and the one-sided sacrifices imposed on the poor brought strikes, food riots and demonstrations to every major European power. Resentment and resistance had spread to the trenches. Mutiny, desertions and a readiness to fraternise with the enemy meant disruption and class war at the front. Something had to give and Tsarist Russia was the weakest link.

War was capital's response to its deepening crisis of profits and competition. Suddenly in August 1914 the economic rivalry of the great imperial powers shifted onto the battlefield. As always the workers and the poor became its cannon fodder. War lasted four years taking 20 million lives, with another 35 million maimed or wounded. With the exception of the Bolsheviks, the Serbian and Bulgarian socialists and some brave souls elsewhere, the leaders of the European labour movement capitulated to patriotism in 1914, abandoning their fine talk of internationalism to back the war and their own ruling class. Behind the lie of a "war for democracy" the ruling classes of Britain, France, Russia and Italy had secretly colluded on how they would divide the spoils of war once they defeated Germany and her allies. In 1917 the USA joined them.

Lenin, founding member of the Russian Social-Democratic Labour Party (RSDLP)[2] and leader of the Bolsheviks, mocked their hypocrisy: "The bourgeoisie of each country is claiming it is out to defeat the enemy not for plunder and the seizure of territory, but for the liberation of all other peoples except its own".[3]

Russia: the weak link

Everything written about the horrors of the Western front applied to the Eastern front and then some. In the first ten months Russia's armies lost 300,000 men a month, either dead, wounded or taken prisoner. By 1916 Russia's autocracy was finding the task of fighting a full-scale modern war impossible. The brittle, stupid Romanov regime was cracking under the pressure.

In Petrograd the events begun by the women on 23 February triggered strikes and demonstrations that quickly brought the city to a standstill. The Tsar's troops, when ordered to fire on the demonstrators, ignored their commanders and sided with the protests. Some young soldiers even shot their officers.

Within days the entire city was on strike and mutiny had engulfed the troops garrisoning it. Soldiers stormed the jails releasing the Tsar's political prisoners. Loyal regiments sent back from the front to restore order joined the revolution. A similar pattern of events followed in Moscow and other Russian towns and cities. As the troops switched allegiance, the Tsarist regime fell apart. On 2 March Tsar Nicholas reluctantly abdicated in favour of his brother, the Grand Duke Mikhail. Next day the Grand Duke had to abdicate too, making his the shortest reign in world history. Tsarism was ended and the revolution announced by radio to a startled world.

The casualties in those February days were considerable. The Tsar's secret police machine-gunned the crowds from the rooftops and some of them were beaten or killed in retaliation. But the new Russia was born in jubilation. The old authorities collapsed, the Tsar's secret police disappeared overnight and ecstatic crowds of citizens and soldiers joined symbolic marches and enormous public meetings to mark the change. For the first time socialist parties could operate freely and people looked forward to the prospect of democratic elections.

One of the socialist newspapers outlawed from the start of the war, and now selling widely, cautioned, "the yellow press now calls itself non-party socialist while the banks try to protect themselves by raising the red banner of revolution over their buildings".[4]

The Romanov dynasty that had ruled Russia since 1613 was blown away in eight days. Weeks before it had seemed all-powerful; now it had fallen to a spontaneous, popular revolution—but February was only the start.

With Tsarism gone an unelected Provisional government, committed to modernising Russia along the lines of Western capitalism, filled the vacuum at the top of society. Led by a Prince Lvov and dominated by landowners and industrialists, it contained only one figure with any left-wing credentials, the socialist lawyer Kerensky: he would prove to be a renegade.

Posing as defenders of the revolution, privately the new government thought that in getting rid of the Tsar the revolution had gone far enough; some thought too far. It was desperate to restore order and keep Russia in the war. It was immediately recognised by the allied powers of France, Britain and the US, who were determined to achieve the same outcome. But from the bottom of society came an alternative, parallel form of government: councils (soviets in Russian) of workers', peasants' and soldiers' deputies. First seen in the 1905 revolution, these soviets were directly elected by the people and governed from below. Unlike parliament, delegates to the soviet were unpaid and subject to immediate recall by the voters.

Within weeks of the February overthrow there was no town in Russia without a soviet. In shaping events the working class was creating the machinery of an embryonic form of self-government and beginning the process of its own emancipation. While the new government pulled in one direction, the masses that had made the revolution were pushing in the opposite. The gap between them grew with every passing day. Lenin, exiled abroad in Switzerland, called this strange, dynamic state of affairs "dual power". Often workers and soldiers would refuse instructions from the Provisional Government unless the soviets signed off the decision.

The Provisional government was not strong enough to either suppress the soviets or to ignore them. A real test of strength was inevitable at some point in the future. The revolution that had begun spontaneously could not end spontaneously.

Lenin's *April Theses*

With the war and the hardships that produced the February protest continuing, and poor peasants denied the land they were promised, the Provisional government became weaker and more unpopular, despite changing personnel and co-opting a few moderate socialists. The real question was: would it be overthrown and replaced by a right-wing military dictatorship, or by a socialist revolution?

The only party to see a clear way forward was the Bolsheviks. Their perspectives crystallised in April, when Lenin returned from exile to challenge the party leadership over its "critical support" for the Provisional government. Instead Lenin insisted it must openly oppose what was a "government of the bourgeoisie" and stand on the most radical wing of soviet democracy under the slogan "All power to the soviets—down with the war".

The leaders of the other socialist parties, the Mensheviks and the Socialist Revolutionary Party (SRs), who held a majority in the soviets at this point, were aghast at Lenin's attack on the Provisional government and his call for a second revolution. Most of the other Bolshevik leaders also thought an out of touch Lenin had lost the plot. But Lenin's *April Theses* made sense to many unhappy with their leadership's support for a pro-war government. By the end of the month Lenin had won the great majority of the party to the call for a second revolution against the Provisional government.

Leon Trotsky, a former Menshevik who had come to this same view long before Lenin, in May arrived back in Petrograd from exile and began working with the Bolsheviks. Joining them in July he played a leading role alongside Lenin in the fight for workers' power.

By May 1917 there were 300 soviets; by August 600; by October 900. In June after another botched war offensive ended in huge casualties, soldiers deserted the front in droves. In July the anger of the workers and soldiers boiled over into a near spontaneous uprising in Petrograd: "more than a demonstration and less than a revolution" in Lenin's words.

The immediate consequence of the events, that became known as the July Days, was not to increase support for the Bolsheviks: they were accused of being "German agents and spies". Although the Bolsheviks had not summoned the uprising, the Provisional government and its moderate supporters blamed them for it. As the movement retreated the forces of reaction, confident the moderates were as fearful of the masses as they were, seized their chance. General Kornilov, commander-in-chief of the army, convinced that the weak regime now led by Kerensky could never curb the soviets and restore order, launched a military coup in late August. The persecuted Bolsheviks were able to play a crucial role in developing a united front of factory committees, trade unions, soviets and the other socialist groups to decisively defeat the attempted coup. Their reputation among the masses soared as a result.

At times the mass of the workers and soldiers were ahead of the Bolshevik leadership and they shaped the party as much as it shaped them. In the eight months from February to October it grew from 23,000 members to a mass party of 400,000.[5] Building a broad movement in opposition to war, oppression and capitalism among the different parts of Russian society demanded patience, clarity and organisation. Links had to be made between the soviets in the various urban centres, and with the peasants seizing the land and the soldiers rebelling at the front.

Across the Empire oppressed nationalities and persecuted religious minorities, now suddenly free of the Tsar, were demanding autonomy and democratic rights that Kerensky's government could not or would not concede. Now there was a concerted fight to win over sections of workers imbued with chauvinist attitudes, to support national and religious struggles and in particular to combat anti-semitism. The revolutionary ferment also brought dramatic challenges to the age-old norms of family life: against patriarchy, sexism, misogyny, homophobia and religious superstition.

The October insurrection and the Soviet government

By September the Bolsheviks had won majorities in all the key soviets around their slogan "Peace, Land and Bread—All Power to the Soviets". When the first All-Russian Congress of Soviets convened in June, they were still a minority; by the time of the bigger Second Congress in October, a majority supported the Bolsheviks.

With the support of the workers, the soldiers and poor peasants, the Bolsheviks were able to lead a victorious insurrection and topple the Provisional government. The soviets took power on 25 October and the new government offered an immediate armistice to all states at war with Russia, pending a permanent peace based on no annexations and no indemnities. It also made public all the secret treaties behind the war and renounced the former Tsar's colonial possessions.

But by early 1918 Soviet Russia was up against it. On top of the suffering and economic dislocation caused by three and a half years of war, the regime now faced civil war, an international blockade and military invasion launched by pro-monarchist, anti-semitic forces funded by the USA and backed by an invasion of 14 capitalist armies. The White Russian counter-revolutionaries and Western capitalism combined in an attempt to crush the Reds and re-impose a military dictatorship. Through armed force they set up puppet regimes in former Tsarist territories, which attracted the revolution's opponents.

Yet Soviet democracy was able at first to endure and deliver real change, especially to the poor and the oppressed. The first few years saw an amazing social transformation: workers' control over production; the division of the rich landowners' property among the poor landless peasants; self-determination for the oppressed nationalities of the old Russian Empire; and an ending of state discrimination against Jews, Muslims and other persecuted minorities.

Arguably the most impressive achievements came from the concerted attempt to end women's oppression. There was a flood of social reforms far in advance of anything in even the most advanced capitalist countries of the time. These won women the vote, legalised divorce and established state run crèches, nurseries, communal laundries and restaurants. Russia became the first country in the world to legalise abortion and make abortion and contraception safe and freely available. A whole host of provisions for pregnant and nursing mothers was introduced and made freely available. This was not really about reforms from above; women had started the revolution and remained prominent throughout 1917.

Russia underwent a genuine, if unfinished, sexual revolution. We can look back to that era with real pride, as an example of the gains that can be won for genuine equality and sexual liberation through class struggle—gains that far outstripped anything available to women or LGBT+ people in the "advanced" states of Europe or the USA.

Under the Tsars less than 20 percent of Russia was literate. In a concerted drive to make education free to all, the new government revolutionised and expanded the education system, massively increasing the number of schools, libraries and cultural institutions and providing adult education and free maintenance for all students. These changes were implemented not just in metropolitan Russia but in every corner of the land. Russia saw mass literacy campaigns alongside a ferment of innovation and experiment in literature, painting, cinema, photography, music, drama and architecture.

Unlike its later demise under Stalin, the new Soviet government rejected the notion that social and economic progress should come at the expense of the natural world. One of Russia's oldest nature reserves in the Volga delta owes its origins to the Russian Revolution, when in 1919 scientists convinced Lenin of the need to protect its wildlife.[6] In 1920 the government created a nature reserve in the Urals, the first "anywhere by a government exclusively aimed at the scientific study of nature".[7]

Spreading the revolution

Marx and Engels had insisted a socialist society could only be built once advanced capitalism was established, and until February 1917 Lenin and the Bolsheviks had argued against any notion that the coming revolution in Russia could be a socialist revolution. After all it was a backward country, a long way short of advanced capitalism. There were pockets of the most advanced industry and a powerful, militant working class. Yet four fifths of its people still lived off the land in virtually medieval conditions with minimal literacy and no knowledge of the world outside a thirty-mile radius. But Lenin and the Bolsheviks changed their minds about what was possible after February 1917. They quickly grasped that the unfolding revolution was an integral part of a wave of revolt that could spread across Europe, a process Trotsky, who came to the idea in 1905, called "permanent revolution".[8]

The leaders of the October Revolution insisted from the start that an isolated Russian Revolution was doomed: "Either the Russian revolution will raise the whirlwind of struggle in the West, or the capitalists of all countries will stifle our struggle".[9] European revolution was not a crazy dream and the October Revolution did raise a whirlwind: the three great empires straddling most of Europe and the Middle East all collapsed after 1917. It was a period that saw workers' councils rule in Berlin, Vienna and Budapest as well as Moscow and Petrograd. It saw some of the biggest strikes in British history, a guerrilla war and a civil war in Ireland, the first great national liberation movements in the Middle East, India and China, the occupation of factories and land seizures in Italy, bloody industrial struggles in Barcelona and general strikes in North America, South America and Australia.

But it was a period that ended with capitalist rule intact everywhere except Russia. It was not inevitable this should happen, but it did and it undercut the premise on which the revolution could survive. Europe came very close on several occasions but Russia was the only country where workers' revolution triumphed. By the end of 1921 the European crisis had eased, capitalism had temporarily stabilised and the workers' councils outside Russia were defeated.

It was not that workers in the West were immune to revolutionary ideas but the leaders of the various social democratic[10] and Labour parties most certainly were. Terrified of revolution, they worked with capitalist governments and the military authorities to maintain order. "I hate revolution like the plague," said social democratic leader Ebert, chairman of the Peoples' Commissars in 1918 and President of the German Republic in 1919. Not all counter-revolutions are led by arch-reactionaries. Some are carried out in the name of democracy and led by people who call themselves socialists. Instead of European revolution coming to the aid of the beleaguered Russian workers' republic, the leaders of European social democracy gave new life and hope to the forces intent on crushing it.

By 1921 the Soviet government was isolated in a hostile world. The revolutionaries in Russia tried to keep the beacon alight, but the final defeat of the German Revolution at the end of 1923 followed by Lenin's death in 1924 sealed its fate.

Incredibly it survived the civil war, won against all the odds by the Red army, but at a terrible cost. Unimaginable economic devastation led to the closure of all the major factories, bringing hardship, starvation and disease to city and country alike. It led to the atomisation and disintegration of the industrial working class that had made the revolution. Devastation brought bureaucracy into the party and then a new bureaucratic dictatorship. The Soviet regime, the rule of the working class through democratic workers' councils, had finally perished by 1928 under Stalin's dictatorship and the rise of state capitalism in Russia.

The story of how this happened is told in Chapter 11. But the return of exploitation and oppression under Stalin was inseparable from the isolation of the revolution not, as historians with a conservative agenda like to tell us, the product of human nature or of some inherent flaw in the revolution or in Bolshevism itself. Stalin was neither the continuation of Lenin nor the rightful heir of the October Revolution; he was its nemesis. The living revolution and what it achieved in its early years was strangled, but no one should blame the revolution for the abomination it became.

Out of the bloodbath of 1914 had come the real possibility of a new world. The message of October sped around the globe: that the highest ideals of humanity were practical and that the movement for their achievement had begun.

That possibility continued into the mid 1920s but the subsequent defeat of the Russian Revolution was a terrible setback, not just for the left but all humanity. Its defeat led to the barbarisms of the 1930s and 1940s: the swastika, the holocaust, Stalin's labour camps, the Second World War, the atom bomb, Hiroshima and the Cold War.

There have been many revolutions since 1917. Revolutions that are defeated are soon forgotten, but not the Russian Revolution. No one can make sense of our world without understanding it. Everything that happened since has been influenced by it. It remains the biggest social movement the world has seen; the most successful anti-war movement ever built. It wrote a new chapter in human history that shows working people can indeed change the world.

This is why the centenary matters. It takes place against a backdrop as grim and terrifying as the world Russia's workers rose up against: imperialist war, an intractable global recession, an unparalleled refugee crisis and impending ecological catastrophe. Modern capitalism reproduces the horrors of war, the threat of nuclear annihilation, climate chaos and famine. It will continue like this until we replace it with a sustainable, socialist society where human need and concern for the natural world, not profit, becomes the driving force.

The purpose of this book is to celebrate the making of the Russian Revolution and the astonishing achievements of its early years. It also aims to show that what began in 1917 is unfinished business. In that sense, the Russian Revolution, the revolution they can't forget, lights the present and the future as well as our past.

Context: Russia at the start of the 20th century

> Although compelled to follow the advanced countries, a backward country does not take things in the same order. The privilege of historic backwardness—and such a privilege exists—permits, or rather compels, the adoption of whatever is ready in advance of any specified date, skipping a whole series of intermediate stages. Savages throw away their bows and arrows for rifles all at once, without travelling the road that lay between those two weapons in the past. The European colonists in America did not begin history all over again.[11]
>
> —*Trotsky*

In the 16th and 17th centuries a great power began to emerge in eastern Europe, outside the area shaped by the Renaissance and the Reformation. A succession of rulers began to transform the old duchy of Muscovy into a centralised Russian state and then an empire that spread out across the whole of northern Asia and encroached into Poland in the west. At the beginning of the 19th century with Turkey's vast Ottoman Empire increasingly under pressure, Tsarist Russia conquered much of the Caucasus and the Black Sea coast and set its sights on Istanbul, the Ottoman capital.

Turkish expansion had reached the walls of Vienna but after the failure of the second siege in 1683, its Ottoman Empire was driven back. By the 19th century various European powers were coveting Turkish possessions in the Balkans. When the Serbs rebelled against Turkish rule they were able to set up an autonomous kingdom in 1815. Fighting for independence from the Ottoman Empire, the Greeks too carved out their own state in the 1820s, with Russian and British help. The Tsars encouraged similar movements in the region, posing as the protectors of ethnic groups speaking languages like their own and belonging to the same Orthodox branch of Christianity. Tsarism aimed to rule over fellow Slavs across the region.

Russian ambition began to frighten the rulers of western Europe, even when they still depended, as Austria and Prussia did, on the Tsar's armies to crush democratic stirrings in their own lands. Russia had been a centre of counter-revolution ever since its role in helping resurrect the old regimes in western Europe after Napoleon's defeat in 1814-15. The Russian monarchy used its wealth and military might as a battering ram, against attempts to create parliamentary democracies and later against revolutionary movements of workers throughout Europe. Even moderate liberals regarded Russia as an abomination.

The rulers of western Europe—Britain in particular—were concerned to maintain the ailing Ottoman Empire as a barrier to Russian expansion and this led to the Crimean War between Russia on one side and Britain, France and Turkey on the other. Although its outcome checked Russian ambitions for the time being, these concerns continued to dominate European diplomacy right up until 1914.

In 1878 at the Congress of Berlin, Britain, Germany and Austria were granted various "spheres of influence" over Ottoman possessions. British governments were at the forefront of these manoeuvres. Propping up the Ottoman Empire allowed them not only to check Russian power, which they saw as threatening British rule in northern India, but also ensured British goods got free access to key markets in the Middle East and the Balkans.

The prison house of nations

By the end of the 19th century a new Tsar, Nicholas II, ruled over an empire that included Finland, the Baltic States, most of Poland and all of the Ukraine. It stretched through the Caucasus and Central Asia to the Arctic and the Pacific.

Lenin described the Romanov Empire as "the prison house of nations". Imperial conquest had created a multinational state with Russians only 43 percent of its population. National oppression of non-Russian peoples was extreme with native Russians feared and hated as colonists and oppressors. The national question was an explosion waiting to happen.

Many on the left, including the revolutionary left, failed to understand the tremendous force of anti-imperialist nationalism, which began to awaken in eastern Europe and right across the Russian Empire in the early twentieth century. Following Marx, Lenin believed the only way workers in imperialist countries could be won away from national chauvinism was if they identified with the struggle of those nations oppressed by their own ruling class: under Tsarism it was essential for workers belonging to the Great Russian nation to support the demand, for example, of the Finns or the Poles for national independence.

This didn't imply endorsement of nationalism, but by seeing the rights of oppressed nations Russian workers could be won to revolutionary internationalism. It was only by advocating, fighting for and guaranteeing self-determination, up to and including the right of separation, that Lenin and the Bolsheviks won the confidence of the small and oppressed nationalities of Tsarist Russia. This confidence ultimately proved decisive in the later battle against counter-revolution during the civil war. Championing the right to national self-determination led not to the disintegration of the revolutionary forces, as Rosa Luxemburg and others feared, but to their victory within the oppressed nations as well as in Greater Russia itself.

Finland was a province of the Russian Empire, a territory snatched by the Tsars at the start of the 19th century. In 1898 the new Tsar Nicholas II annulled Finland's constitution, passing the death sentence on its hopes for independence. Ever since Tsar Alexander I turned it into a Grand Duchy of Russia, Russian officials ran the country treating Finns with arrogance and brutality. According to her biographer Cathy Porter, Bolshevik Alexandra Kollontai was a frequent visitor to Finland, in her youth, and later as an exiled clandestine revolutionary, smuggling Marxist literature and correspondence into and out of Tsarist Russia via Finland.

Kollontai remembered how the wealthy Russians with their dachas on the Finnish border would flog and bully Finns working for them and how any resistance would be reported in the Russian press as "Finnish independence riots". In 1899 with another Russian bully called General Bobrikov appointed governor-general, the Finnish language was replaced by Russian, the Finnish army disbanded, freedom of speech and free assembly banned, and the Finnish parliament, the Seim, reduced to a powerless consultative assembly. "Finland was reduced to the status of a Russian serf, without a voice or rights",[12] wrote Kollontai. Immediately after the October Revolution, in January 1918, there was a revolutionary uprising in Finland.

Anti-Semitism

At the turn of the century a crude and brutal system of anti-semitism was run from Moscow. For more than a hundred years Jews had been forced to live within the so-called Pale of Settlement, stretching from Crimea in the south to the Baltic coast in the north-east. Forbidden to own land or practice the professions, Jews were forced to live in small towns called *shtetls* or in the worst of the city slums. In the main they spoke Yiddish, worked long hours in small workshops and developed an urban culture based on self-help and the *kehilla*, the religious council that ran every Jewish community.

Most educated Russians assumed that as the Russian economy modernised, anti-semitism, the Pale, the *kehilla* and Yiddish would die out. But when industrialisation really took off in the 1880s, anti-semitism was deliberately intensified. Tsarist police organised racist mobs to rampage through Jewish areas, killing and maiming at random. Residency laws were tightened and the Tsar expelled the Jews from Moscow and St Petersburg. Jews who wanted to live in either city had to have written permission from the Tsar. This enforced migration of over one million people doubled the population of some of the small towns within the Pale.

The factory system was growing rapidly in the cities but Jewish workers were generally excluded. They tended to work in smaller factories, not the big engineering plants. In 1897, the year that the Bund was founded (the socialist, All-Jewish Workers' League of Poland, Lithuania and Russia), Jews made up 58 percent of the urban population in the area that is now Poland, Latvia, Lithuania and Belarus. "About ninety percent of the whole Jewish population come near to being a proletariat," wrote the Tsar's official sociologist.[13] This increasing oppression and growing urbanisation gave birth to a new national consciousness. Paul Mason writes:

> In the same year as the Bund, the World Zionist Organisation was founded. Its leader, Hertzl argued that given the upsurge of racist violence, Jews could not survive within Gentile society and that

emigration to a new Jewish state in Palestine was the only future. For its part the Bund rejected Zionism as an ideology and emigration as a strategy. Its slogan was "Our home is here!" And while the Zionists remained uneasy about the secular lifestyle of young Jews, the Bund, as orthodox Marxists, revelled in it.[14]

For centuries the Tsars had ruled their vast empire virtually unchallenged. There were liberal circles and peasant rebellions but these were always crushed. In 1861 Tsar Alexander II felt compelled to end serfdom but gave half the land to the old feudal class and left the peasantry very much at its mercy. At the end of the 19th century the Romanov dynasty, with its courtiers, nobility and priests, ruled in much the same medieval way as its feudal predecessors.

But in western Europe a new system was developing that would undermine Tsarism. It had developed furthest and fastest in Britain, France, Germany and the USA, with a different, more powerful dynamic than the feudal societies that preceded it. As Western industrial economies grew in competition with each other, so they were forced to look beyond their borders and overseas for new markets, raw materials and for new opportunities to profit and expand. The age of empire saw native industries destroyed, as great swathes of the world were colonised by the superpowers.

They used their capacity to produce ever more deadly weaponry to threaten and impose their rule abroad. This pre-supposed an arms race, for while imperialism implies the dominance of the stronger nation states over weaker ones, its key focus was and still is on the struggle for dominance, "a struggle between the strongest in which the less developed countries figure primarily as passive battle grounds, not as active participants".[15] These were the years when imperialist icon Cecil Rhodes boasted: "I contend we are the first race in the world and that the more of the world we inhabit the better it is for the human race. If there be a God, I think he would like me to paint as much of the map of Africa British red as possible. I would annex the planets if I could".[16]

In these years European and US capitalism underwent profound structural changes. Laissez-faire capitalism was giving way to monopoly capitalism. A handful of Western states ran much of the world through colonial administrations subservient to monarchs and politicians in the Western capitals. British governments ruled an empire covering a quarter of humanity, on which "the sun never set" and where, according to Chartist and socialist Ernest Jones, "the blood never dried".[17]

Holland, the first bourgeois republic, ruled the East Indies archipelago: modern day Indonesia. France ran half of Africa and King Leopold of Belgium somehow personally owned the Congo, a vast territory comprising the bulk of central Africa. The USA had seized the Philippines and Puerto Rica and used military invasions, or threatened them, to dictate to supposedly independent governments in Cuba and Central America. At the same time the semi-feudal monarchies based in Vienna, St Petersburg and Constantinople ruled over most of central, eastern and south eastern Europe, the Middle East and North Africa: in Russia's case a huge territory to the east, west and south of Russia proper, all the way to the Indian border and to the Pacific port of Vladivostok.

China remained nominally independent but throughout the second half of the 19th century the Western imperialist powers, along with the newest imperial power Japan, seized many of China's key cities as concessions—enclaves of direct colonial rule. Russia had imperial designs there too. The Tsar's troops occupied parts of northern China in a drive east towards the Pacific, a drive that would lead them into direct conflict with Japan's drive west.

As each of these empires expanded they began to collide. Germany, the fastest growing industrial power in Europe, was virtually without an empire and sections of German capital were demanding one. They looked to the German state to help them carve out overseas markets and establish military outposts. But wherever Germany's empire-builders turned they rubbed up against their rivals: the Russians in the Balkans; the British in the Middle East and east Africa; the French in north Africa. In China they encountered all of them, plus Japan, another newly industrialising power in search of empire.

Russia: uneven and combined development

At the start of the 20th century Russia as a whole was still backward. The great mass of its people tilled the land using methods scarcely changed since the late middle ages. Tsarism was based on the aristocracy, not the weak Russian capitalist class.

Russia entered the 20th century without having shaken off feudalism. Before the First World War Lenin argued that the era of the bourgeois revolution in Russia had started with Tsar Alexander II's agrarian reforms of 1861, and would only be completed by the working class. Bourgeois revolutions are bourgeois not because they are led by the bourgeoisie—the capitalists—but because they make possible the development of a bourgeois society on the basis of the capitalist mode of production. It is the outcome that is important, not necessarily the leading personnel.

But aspects of bourgeois culture and industrial capitalism were grafted onto Russia's archaic state structure as it came under pressure from the capitalist West and this had important consequences. Forced to begin a rapid industrialisation financed by foreign capital, Tsarism at the end of the 19th century ruled over a society where the traditional conflicts between landlord and peasant, intelligentsia and state, were supplemented and intensified by the conflict between capital and labour. At the end of the 19th century Tsarist Russia exemplified what Leon Trotsky called "uneven and combined development", a concept vividly captured in his following sentence:

> Within this vast space every epoch of human culture is to be found: from the primeval barbarism of the northern forests, where people eat raw fish and worship blocks of wood, to the modern social relations of the capitalist city, where socialist workers consciously recognise themselves as participants in world politics.[18]

Before 1917 most Marxists did not believe that a workers' revolution was possible in any but the most advanced countries; they thought countries would achieve workers' power in strict conformity with the stage to which they had advanced technologically. Orthodox Marxism, as represented in the parties of European social democracy that in 1889 established the Second International, assumed Russia's revolution would have a similar goal and outcome to the English Revolution of the 17th century and the French Revolution of the late 18th century but in a 20th century setting: a bourgeois, parliamentary republic.

This implied a stages theory: that only after industrial development and transition through a capitalist parliamentary regime could the working class mature sufficiently to be capable of socialist revolution. All the Russian Social Democrats, Bolshevik as well as Menshevik, were convinced Russia was heading for its bourgeois revolution, resulting from the conflict between the productive forces of capitalism and the Tsarist autocracy and the other surviving relics of feudalism. Marxists saw their task as supporting and pushing the liberal bourgeoisie in the coming Russian revolution. Lenin and the Bolsheviks also agreed the revolution would be bourgeois in character but they would disagree with the Mensheviks over what class would lead it.

Trotsky broke from this view during the 1905 revolution and anticipated what would transpire in 1917. He began to form the theory of permanent revolution when the mass workers' strikes of 1905 gave birth to the first Petrograd Soviet. Marx's analysis of the 1848 revolution in the *Communist Manifesto*, predicted that because of the "developed proletariat" of Germany, "the bourgeois revolution in Germany" would be "but the prelude to an immediately following proletarian revolution".[19] After the fiasco of the 1848 revolution Marx concluded that, faced with the unwillingness of the 19th century bourgeoisie to carry through the anti-feudal revolution, the working class had to struggle for the growth of the bourgeois revolution into the proletarian revolution and of the national revolution into the international revolution. In his address to the Communist League in 1850 Marx wrote:

> While the democratic petit bourgeois wish to bring the revolution to a conclusion as quickly as possible, our interest and our task consist in making the revolution permanent, until the possessing classes are removed from authority, until the proletariat wins state power, until the union of the proletarians—not only in one country but in all the leading countries of the world—is sufficiently developed to end competition between the proletarians of these countries, and until at the very least the main productive forces are in the hands of the proletarians... The workers' battle cry must be: 'permanent revolution'.[20]

It was not until the revolution of February 1917 that Lenin really discarded the old orthodoxy that the Russian Revolution would be a bourgeois revolution. In September 1914 he was still writing that the Russian Revolution must limit itself to three fundamental tasks: "the establishment of a democratic republic in which equality of rights and full freedom of self-determination would be granted to all nationalities; confiscation of the estates of the big landlords; and the application of the eight-hour day".[21]

Yet Lenin differed fundamentally from the Mensheviks in his insistence on the independence of the workers' movement from the bourgeoisie and the need to carry the bourgeois revolution through to victory against its resistance. Instead of the Menshevik alliance with the bourgeoisie, Lenin called for an alliance of the workers and peasants.

The Tsarist state was forced by its military rivalry with the more advanced West to encourage pockets of large-scale capitalism to produce, notably, arms and railways. The process transformed millions of Russian peasants into industrial workers. This would impact on the nature of the coming revolutions. After 1880 Russian industry was expanded massively but the main driving force was not native private capital. Foreign industry provided most of the plant and machinery and foreign banks most of the capital. Beside them stood the Tsarist state, providing additional capital, placing huge orders for years in advance, tightly controlling the new workforce and acting as both guarantor and enforcer for the German textile magnates and the French stock exchange.

One example was the rapid creation of a massive steel complex in the Ukraine to exploit the coal and iron ore of the Donets basin. Started by a Welshman called Hughes and named Yuzovka after him, it soon became a colossal state of the art industrial complex, financed and run by foreign capital. Nikita Khrushchev, the son of poor peasants who became the leader of the USSR in the 1950s, started work at the Yuzovka complex as a lad of 15:

> I worked at a factory owned by Germans, in pits owned by the French and at a chemical plant owned by Belgians. I discovered something about capitalists; they are all alike, whatever their nationality. All they wanted from me was the most work for the least money that would keep me alive.[22]

In the 1890s Russia's annual rate of economic growth at over eight percent was the highest in the world and continued at over six percent, the highest in Europe, until 1914. Although the Russian economy was still forging ahead on the eve of the First World War, its historic backwardness meant it was still well behind the more slowly advancing West. In a sense Tsarist Russia was like an early form of state capitalism. The historian Bertram Wolfe claimed that even before the 1917 revolution "the Russian state became the biggest landowner, the largest trader, the largest owner of capital in Russia, or in the world".[23]

The native Russian bourgeoisie was characterised from the outset by its secondary role in the country's development and by its dependence on foreign and state capital. This meant it clung to the apron strings of Tsarism and never broke away. As the 1898 Manifesto, drawn up for what turned out to be the abortive First Congress of Russia's Social Democrats, famously declared:

> The farther east one goes in Europe, the more the bourgeoisie becomes in the political respect weaker, more cowardly and meaner, and the larger are the cultural and political tasks, which fall to the proletariat. On its strong shoulders the Russian working class must bear and will bear the task of winning political liberty.[24]

This notion is what historian Neil Harding called the "orthodoxy of Russian Marxism".[25] The Congress was a small gathering, with only nine delegates from a few localities and different groupings. Its only achievements were issuing the Manifesto and the election of a central committee of three. All but one of the delegates and two of the three elected committee members were arrested and incarcerated by the Tsar's secret police days after the meeting. Lenin, exiled in Siberia and under police surveillance, could not attend this Minsk Congress. The outcome convinced him that building a national organisation to lead Russian social democracy out of its crisis demanded a more systematic preparation.

The cowardice of the Russian bourgeoisie was not the result of geography. The rise of the industrial working class, the necessary concomitant of the rise of capitalism, made the 19th century bourgeoisie everywhere a timid and conservative class. Russia could expect no modern Cromwell or Robespierre. Ending Russia's feudal autocracy would need a different leadership with different objectives.

The peasantry

By far the largest group that stood to gain from ending Tsarist feudalism was the peasantry. The "freedom" they were granted in 1861, when serfdom was abolished, soon proved a Tsarist con, and it came at a terrible cost: the exorbitant rents they were forced to pay for tiny plots of subsistence land; the enormous debts they still owed for the right to work on them; and the long hours they were obliged to work to benefit a landowning nobility that ground them into the dirt. Yet they deferred to Tsarism, the very power that held them down. Most peasants had been brought up to believe Tsars were fair to rich and poor alike, and tended to blame their oppression on the Tsar's bad advisors, corrupt local administrators or bad priests.

The Russian Orthodox Church was a very powerful component of Tsarist ideology. The extreme subordination of women, vicious anti-semitism, racism and national oppression were all sponsored and promoted by the Tsar, his courtiers and the men who ran his empire— but the Orthodox Church and its religious hierarchy provided the ideological glue that held it all together.

In pre-industrial societies the producers, whether serfs or free peasants, worked in small groups, isolated from similar groups dotted throughout the countryside. Although brutally exploited and oppressed, it was extremely difficult for them to think and act as a class. Writing about the French peasantry Marx explained:

> Insofar as millions of families live under economic conditions of existence that divide their mode of life from that of other classes and put them in hostile contrast to the latter, they form a class. Insofar as there is merely a local interconnection among these small peasants, and the identity of their interests begets no unity, no national union and no political organisation, they are not a class. They are consequently incapable of enforcing their own interests. They cannot represent themselves, they must be represented.[26]

In Russian history there were moments when the poor peasants could and did revolt. Sporadic peasant unrest often took the form of violent attacks on the landlords and demands that the land stolen from them when they were released from serfdom in 1861 be returned. Certainly they could burn down the big houses and kill the rich land-owners. What they could not do, except for very short periods and in very exceptional circumstances, was to impose their rule as a class. Either the old rulers regained control or new ones took their place, for sooner or later the peasants had to disperse and head back to their plots, cultivate them and bring in the harvest, or they would starve.

Meanwhile around the major towns and cities new industrial suburbs were sprouting up and in them lived and worked the new factory proletariat. Their living conditions were primitive even by Dickensian standards. Recruited straight from the countryside, the new workforce was raw, unskilled, uneducated and without organisation. It was young and included large numbers of peasant women. Some socialists of the time claimed this combination was unorganisable, but perceived weaknesses would turn out to be assets—another aspect of the "process of combined and uneven development" described by Trotsky.

Although the new workforce had little or no trade union experience, it certainly wasn't held back by the conservative tradition of craftism and sectionalism, as were its British and German counterparts. And although it formed only a small minority, around three percent of a large Russian population, it would hold the key to the coming revolution.

The People's Will

The Russian autocracy had always aroused opposition and the early 1860s saw the beginnings of an organisation with socialist aspirations. For a period it would dominate the opposition to Tsarism among the radical intelligentsia. Launched as the Land and Freedom party it became Narodnaya Volya, which means The People's Will or The People's Freedom. Its followers were called Narodniks or populists. Their vision of socialism was based on the peasantry, rather than the tiny emerging working class. It was from this tradition of peasant socialism that the Socialist Revolutionary Party (the SRs) later emerged in 1901, claiming, with some justice, to be the inheritors of The People's Will.

The Narodniks were influenced by European socialism and a limited knowledge of Marxism. But they insisted the transformation of Russia into an industrialised, capitalist economy like Britain or Germany was a disaster to be avoided at all costs. Instead they argued agrarian, feudal Russia would sidestep the evils of modern industrialism and achieve a socialist order based on the Mir or Obshchina, the primeval community of land that survived in the Russian countryside. On this basis the party's young, student-based support was dispatched into the countryside to preach rebellion against the Tsar. By and large the peasantry was underwhelmed, greeting its would-be liberators with indifference, mistrust and sometimes hostility. "Going to the People" failed to produce any results so The People's Will turned to terrorism. Engels explained this odd combination of Narodnism and Marxism in a letter written before his death in 1895:

> In a country like yours, where modern industry has been grafted onto
> the primitive peasant commune and where all the intermediate stages

of civilisation co-exist with each other; in a country which, in addition to this, has been enclosed by despotism with an intellectual Chinese wall—in the case of such a country one should not wonder at the emergence of the most incredible and bizarre combination of ideas.[27]

Having failed to arouse the peasantry against the autocracy, the Narodniks tried to overthrow it by individual terror. Because they believed agrarian socialism was already virtually in existence, hidden under the hard crust of a feudal aristocracy, it was in their view just a simple matter of smashing the crust: "If the peasants are not ready to act, the revolutionaries will act on their behalf." Zhelyabov, their leader, insisted the people's revolutionaries were "giving history a push" by physically destroying an autocracy that was blocking the path to socialism.[28] Intended to galvanise the masses, the tactic led instead to apathy and despair. Isaac Deutscher described the Narodniks as: "men and women of the highest moral and intellectual qualities. Most of them were sons and daughters of aristocratic or at least noble families, who offered their lives for the sake of the people. One of the central figures in their conspiracy was the daughter of the Tsar's Governor General of St Petersburg".[29]

In 1881 they celebrated an apparent triumph when they assassinated Tsar Alexander II. Yet all this did was enable the state to persecute and further isolate them, reducing their movement to a few isolated groups. They had expected the regime to crumble under their blow. They managed to assassinate an autocrat but not the autocracy.

Alexander III, whose tyranny proved even harsher, succeeded Alexander II. Individual terrorism proved useless. What was needed was the overthrow of a system, based not on the action of one or even a handful of individuals, but mass action.

Yet the Narodniks had the moral courage and determination to face danger and suffering. They were sent to solitary confinement, to Siberia and to the gallows by the hundreds. Women as well as men were involved, "truly remarkable women, strong determined and dedicated... In the person of Vera Zasulich there was a link between the terrorist and Marxist strands of the movement".[30] It was the growth of the revolutionary movement, which, according to Zasulich, made her feel the equal of any man. Trotsky acknowledged her importance for the early Russian Marxist movement. "It was not only her heroic past that placed her in the front rank. It was through Zasulich that the group in its day became connected with the old Engels".[31]

Two years in jail convinced her that Russia was one huge prison from which the only escape was the overthrow of Tsarism. In 1878 she tried to assassinate General Trepov, the governor of St Petersburg. After escaping to Geneva Zasulich turned to Marxism and became a leading light with Plekhanov in the émigré Emancipation of Labour Group, the forerunner of Russian Social Democratic Labour Party (RSDLP).

Maria Spiridonova, another terrorist, assassinated the Tsar's general appointed to lead a punitive expedition against the peasantry in Tambov. In revenge she was brutally beaten and sexually abused by soldiers before being imprisoned and then exiled to Siberia. A Socialist Revolutionary, she rejected Marx's materialism. She was finally freed in 1917 by the February Revolution. Her rejection of Marx did not stop her from allying with the Bolsheviks in support of the October insurrection. As a representative of the Left SRs she was a member of the first Soviet government until she broke with it over the peace with Germany in 1918.

The Russian Marxists

In 1883 the first Russian Marxist organisation, the League for the Emancipation of Labour, was launched. Its founder Georgi Plekhanov had been a supporter of Narodnism but broke with it completely, arguing against terrorism and insisting that socialism presupposed a development of the productive forces that only capitalism could achieve. Plekhanov rejected the Narodnik view that individual heroism could substitute for the struggle of the masses. He brought authentic Marxism into Russia by arguing for the new working class as the bearer of the future Russian Revolution. His constant theme was: "Political freedom will only be won by the working class or not at all".[32]

According to Lenin, "Plekhanov's first Marxian treatise had significance for Russia comparable to that which the *Communist Manifesto* had for the West".[33] Trotsky wrote, "the Marxist generation of the 1890s stood on the foundations laid down by Plekhanov. Next to Marx and Engels, Vladimir Ilyich owed the most to Plekhanov".[34] Plekhanov showed the old communal organisation of the peasants was actually in decline. He argued capitalism in Russia was inevitable and with it would come the growth of the working class, the future agency of socialism. He showed why the expansion of the world market and the consequent disintegration of the peasant communes, were necessary preconditions of socialist revolution.

For many years this argument was conducted abstractly in small, clandestine discussion circles. Then in the mid-1890s a massive strike wave proved the point about the working class and gave the Marxists a real opportunity to relate to the workers' struggle and engage in practical activity. It was then Lenin came to the fore as an agitator. Lenin was the pen name of Vladimir Ilyich Ulyanov. His father was a teacher, then a regional school inspector. The family lived in reasonable comfort and Vladimir studied law at Kazan University, where he was won to Marxism. He was subsequently expelled for his involvement in revolutionary activities and student politics.

Earlier in 1887, to the complete shock of Lenin and the rest of his family, his older brother Sacha was executed for complicity in a populist plot to assassinate Tsar Alexander III. Lenin, only 17 at the time, had not suspected for a minute his brother was interested in revolutionary politics. Lenin's was a close-knit family and to spare them anxiety, Sacha had kept his political affiliations to himself. Lenin loved and admired his older brother and was devastated by his execution. But to suppose, as the official Kremlin biography of Lenin claims, that the resultant trauma propelled the 17 year old Lenin immediately on the road to Marxism is another Stalinist legend. Lenin himself confirmed that it took him years of studying and thinking things through before he felt he could commit to Marxism.

As a youngster he had admired the daring and self-sacrifice of the Narodniks and it was not until the mid 1890s that he considered himself a Marxist. What is clear is that after reading *Capital* and joining a Marxist discussion group in Kazan, Lenin became an uncompromising opponent of individual terrorism for the rest of his life. Later he became a victim of it when he was badly wounded in a failed assassination attempt against him during the civil war.

Although he was as critical of the Narodniks as Plekhanov, Lenin's attitude to them was different. Plekhanov studied Russia from the standpoint of its productive forces, to prove to his populist opponents that the country was too backward to achieve socialism until such time as capitalism and a bourgeois revolution had created the conditions for it. Lenin formally agreed Russia was only ripe for bourgeois revolution but he used his own analysis of class in Russia to show the bourgeoisie was too cowardly and too dependent on foreign capital to ever lead it. Plekhanov overlooked or ignored the contradictory, dehumanising aspects of capitalist development in Russia and wrote and spoke like an apologist for industrialisation.

When Lenin challenged another of the early Russian Marxist pioneers Peter Struve, who like Plekhanov would become a Menshevik and move smartly to the right, he was attacking a crude, mechanical view of history known as objectivism. Unlike Struve and Plekhanov, Lenin insisted Marxism had nothing in common with "faith in the necessity of each country passing through a phase of capitalism or any other such mistaken ideas. When demonstrating the necessity for a given series of facts, the objectivist always runs the risk of becoming an apologist for them".[35]

Lenin's rebuke of Struve applied equally to Plekhanov. While Plekhanov was dismissive of the peasantry, pursuing instead an alliance with the liberal bourgeoisie, Lenin understood the smallholding peasantry and the agricultural workers, the bulk of the Russian population, could play a big part in the overthrow of Tsarism; but only under the leadership of an insurgent urban class. Lenin saw the need to destroy every vestige of serfdom and landlord power in Russian society as a key task of the revolution.

Where Plekhanov saw the aim of the revolution as establishing political reforms, Lenin was committed to fighting for a revolution that would destroy the social basis of every surviving aspect of feudalism.

So Lenin looked to a different and more realistic alliance of forces than Plekhanov's alliance of the workers and the bourgeoisie. Instead of the noble Narodnik "going to the people", Lenin saw the working class could lead the countryside. Like the peasantry it was a producing class that suffered exploitation and oppression and although only a small minority of the population, it was the only class with the interests and cohesion to assume the revolutionary leadership spurned by Russia's bourgeoisie.

From discussion circles to agitation

In 1895 Lenin went abroad to establish contact with members of the Marxist Emancipation of Labour Group. In Switzerland he first met Plekhanov and arranged for the publication of a series of important articles. On his return to Russia Lenin set up a branch of The League of

Struggle for the Emancipation of Labour in St Petersburg. He also contacted groups in other Russian towns, with the aim of breaking out of the closed circles and theoretical discussion groups to make contact with industrial workers. For the first time he began to relate his ideas to workers and to learn from them. To get the information for their factory leaflets, Lenin and the other League members distributed questionnaires to individual workers. Later Lenin wrote self-deprecatingly about this:

> I vividly recall my 'first experiment', which I would never like to repeat. I spent many weeks 'examining' a worker, who would often visit me, regarding every aspect of the conditions prevailing in the enormous factory where he was employed. True, after great effort I managed to obtain the material but at the end of the interview the worker would wipe the sweat from his brow, and say to me smilingly: 'I find it easier to work overtime than to answer your questions.'[36]

The years 1894-96 were crucial in Lenin's development as a workers' leader. Nadezhda Krupskaya, the young woman he met in 1894 and married a few years later and who as a schoolteacher had joined a Marxist circle in Brunev in 1890, wrote:

> This period of Vladimir Ilyich's work was of extreme importance. We were not concerned with heroic moves but with how to establish contact with the masses, to become intimate with them, to learn to be the expression of their best aspirations, to learn how to make them understand us and follow our lead. But it was precisely during this period in St Petersburg that he was shaped as a leader of the working masses.[37]

An extraordinary, competent woman

Krupskaya is often portrayed as an appendage, as Lenin's wife. Robert McNeal's biography of her, *Bride of the Revolution*, gives the impression she came to her politics under the influence of her husband but this is not so. In *Bolshevik Women*, Barbara Evans Clements describes her as "Lenin's administrative assistant" though she acknowledges, "no one was more important to the Bolsheviks...no one made a greater contribution to the creation and maintenance of the Bolshevik faction".[38]

Krupskaya saw herself as a revolutionary, a pioneer of Russian Social Democracy. She had become a Marxist and joined the movement before Lenin, and before she met him. In the early 1890s she taught workers at the socialist Sunday schools and at special evening classes. Arrested during the strike wave of 1896 she was imprisoned for six months then exiled for three years. From 1901 she lived abroad, playing the key role in developing Bolshevik organisation, serving as party secretary and contributing to its publications. During the 1905 Revolution she returned to Russia again to do crucial underground work for the Bolsheviks. She went abroad in 1908 to escape arrest. In April 1917 she returned to Petrograd with Lenin and concentrated her efforts on organising women workers and youth, while Lenin had to spend months away from the capital hiding from those that wanted to jail or assassinate him.

What is clear, according to Jane McDermid and Anna Hillyar in their book on women Bolsheviks and women workers in 1917, "is that her contribution to building and maintaining the organisation was considerable".[39]

Trotsky described how much the Social Democratic group in exile depended on her: "Secretary of the editorial board of *Iskra*, the group's journal, she was at the very centre of all the work. In her room there was always the smell of burned paper from the secret letters she heated over the fire to read. She often complained in her gently insistent way, that people did not write enough, or that they got the codes wrong. An extraordinary competent woman, she could write 300 coded letters a week, keep track of the addresses and aliases of people constantly on the run within Russia and maintain the financial accounts".[40]

Imprisonment and exile

In 1895 in addition to the factory leaflets that Lenin's Emancipation of Labour group were issuing, preparation was being made for the production of an illegal newspaper. Alas Lenin and five other members of the League were arrested in December and the material for the newspaper seized. Several more members, including Martov, future Menshevik leader, were arrested early in the New Year. But Lenin's factory leafleting was not in vain. A few months later the first real mass strike in Russia took place under the banner of social democracy.

Throughout 1896 and until his exile to Siberia in 1897 Lenin was under interrogation in the St Petersburg jail. Yet he found time there to write an obituary of Engels and prepare material for his groundbreaking work, *The Development of Capitalism in Russia*. During his exile in Siberia he thought through his ideas about party organisation. They centred on the creation of a party newspaper to be published abroad and smuggled into Russia. He discussed these plans with Krupskaya, who had joined him in Siberia, and with two other exiled Social Democrats, Potresov and Martov. On their release from Siberia in early 1900 they went to Geneva to meet their hero Plekhanov and seek his collaboration.

A popular weekly named *Iskra* (the Spark) and a theoretical journal *Zarya* (the Dawn) were to be published under the editorship of a board of six: Plekhanov, Axelrod and Zasulich representing the Liberation of Labour Group, together with Lenin, Potresov and Martov. Plekhanov's prestige as the doyen of Russian Marxism meant he was acknowledged as the guiding light of the project. But Lenin began to emerge head and shoulders above his fellow editors through his energy and the clarity of his ideas. According to EH Carr:

> he alone knew exactly what he wanted: to establish an accepted body of revolutionary doctrine and an organised revolutionary party. The first of these aims required, in addition to *Iskra*, the promulgation of a party programme; the second, the summoning of a party congress to take up the work begun and abandoned in 1898. *Iskra* was designed to give organisation to the scattered Russian movement.[41]

Lenin's programme for the party put the working class centre stage. In Russia the late arrival of capitalism meant it was grafted onto Tsarist absolutism. Alongside the most modern large-scale industrial enterprises, the administration remained autocratic, feudal and inefficient. The employers hid behind the autocracy, operating through corrupt officials beholden to the Tsar. Russian workers were subjected to the barbarism of capitalism without even the crumbs of bourgeois political democracy. In these circumstances the struggle for better conditions necessarily became a political struggle. According to Lenin, workers needed open struggle against the capitalist class so that,

> the intrigues and aspirations of the bourgeoisie may not be hidden in the anterooms of the Grand Dukes, in the salons of senators and ministers. So down with everything that hides the influence of the capitalist class! Workers need the abolition of the government's absolute rule only in order to wage an open, extensive struggle against the capitalist class.[42]

The aim was to allow the working class room to develop its independent activity as a class and to build the working class base and content of Social Democracy. Lenin's article *On Strikes* argued:

> A strike teaches workers to understand what the strength of the employers and what the strength of the workers consists in; it teaches them not to think of their own employer alone and not to think of their own immediate workmates alone but of all the employers, the whole class of capitalists, of the government and the laws as well.[43]

While Lenin had been in exile, a trend in Russian social democracy known as economism began to develop. The successful shift to agitation and the favourable response from workers led some social democrats to think they should restrict themselves to raising factory issues only and leave the politics to the liberal politicians. It was this separation between economics and politics that earned them the derogatory name, the economists. Lenin was at pains to stress the insult was not aimed at those socialists who campaigned for better wages and working conditions and supported strikes. His critical remarks were directed at those who subordinated the political struggle to the economic struggle by arguing the workers' movement should concentrate on bread and butter issues to the exclusion or the downplaying of socialist ideas.

In 1898 a document called the *Credo* appeared in Russia. It cited approvingly Bernstein's revision of Marx and argued Russian Marxism should limit itself to assisting the economic struggle of the workers and participation in the liberal opposition. The *Credo* sought to surrender the political terrain to the intelligentsia, abandoning the building of a revolutionary workers' party. For Lenin the fight against economism was part of the fight for an organisation of revolutionaries.

By the middle of 1902 *Iskra* was able to lay before its readers a draft party programme representing a careful blend of the views of the more cautious Plekhanov and the bolder more uncompromising Lenin.

What Is to Be Done?

About the same time Lenin published his work on revolutionary organisation, *What Is to Be Done?* Early in 1903 preparations were far enough advanced to summon a party congress in July of that year. Few political tracts have caused as much controversy.

At one level it is an attack on economism but it is essentially about turning a fledgling scattered organisation of individuals into an effective revolutionary workers party in the challenging conditions of Tsarist Russia in 1902.

Lenin knew that without mass struggle there could be no successful revolution but that mass struggle could not succeed without organisation and politics. There were already the beginnings of a rising class struggle in Russia and signs that the state would move to crush it. Without an organised network of socialists rooted inside the working class, revolts and rebellions would be isolated and defeated. Because the state is centralised, workers must have their own centralised organisation to combat it.

There was an obvious gap between Lenin's stated aim of overturning Tsarist Russia and the reality of what was going on on the ground. His solution to bridge the gap would prove effective: the party would be built through the distribution and selling of a regular national newspaper and the network of members and supporters grouped around it. More than half of *What Is to Be Done?* is about making the case for such a newspaper.

From 1901 to 1903 Lenin and Krupskaya carried the main burden of work on *Iskra*. Producing and distributing a socialist paper that combines agitation and ideas with working class appeal requires talent, commitment and hard work. Producing it in exile and organising its illegal distribution into and throughout Russia multiplied these difficulties. Lenin argued *Iskra* would provide communication and co-ordination between the localities, the militants building the party and the leadership in exile. The best ideas could be shared, errors and mistakes corrected and activities coordinated. In this way the newspaper would act as the scaffolding around the building of the party. But for Lenin it was not party building for the sake of it:

> The organisation that will form around this newspaper—the organisation of those working for it and supporting it—will be ready for everything, from upholding the honour, the prestige and the continuity of the party in a period of acute depression to preparing for, appointing the time for, and carrying out the nationwide armed uprising.[44]

The newspaper of such an ambitious organisation had to do more than simply expose the terrible conditions workers faced at work. It had to provide "an all round exposure" of society as a whole. To overthrow the state socialist organisation would need its own communication network that could operate under illegal conditions. The newspaper's agents could become the nucleus of such an organisation. But despite what his detractors say, in 1902 Lenin wasn't intent on a small tight-knit group, but on laying the basis for an organisation that, in more favourable conditions, the working class could flood into.

What Is to Be Done? shows Lenin aiming for the newspaper having 200,000 agents, capable of relating not only to workers' struggles but to every movement and minority campaign and every form of injustice in the Tsarist state. At the start of the 20th century this process was begun with a small vanguard of revolutionaries. This was out of neces-sity and Lenin never tried to make it a virtue. The aim was to grow into a mass party because it was the working class that would make the revo-lution, not some self-appointed vanguard. As Canadian Marxist Lars Lih explains in his book *Lenin Rediscovered*:

> The keynote about Lenin's outlook was not worry about workers but exhilaration about workers. In each of the various clashes over the issues within Russian Social Democracy, Lenin can easily be located. He is always on the side making the most confident assumptions about the possibility of a mass, underground, Social-Democratic movement.
>
> Lenin's urgency and polemical zeal have led most readers to sup-pose he was reacting to a crisis. His argument is put in a strikingly different light when we realise he was reacting to an opportunity... Worker militancy is not the problem because it is increasing in leaps and bounds on its own. The problem, the weak link—is effective party leadership of all this militancy—Social-Democratic deficiencies, not worker deficiencies.[45]

The sense of urgency that pervades Lenin's writing reflects his belief that in 1902 the growing working class struggle presented a huge politi-cal opportunity that the RSDLP could not afford to miss. This is why he insisted its members take themselves seriously, be accountable to the living workers' movement, and learn to co-operate under the collective discipline of the party. This is what marks him out from those leaders who ended up moving to the right at the 1903 Party Congress.

At the 1903 Congress, conceived as a unifying congress, those who would become the Mensheviks, the minority who split along with

Martov, attacked Lenin over organisation and spontaneity. They included Trotsky, a genuine revolutionary who sided with the Mensheviks at the Congress but, like Alexandra Kollontai, would break with them in 1904 over their tactic of working with liberals in the government. The prominent Polish-German revolutionary Rosa Luxemburg, not a member of the RSDLP so not present at the 1903 Congress, put in writing her disagreements with the kind of party she thought Lenin was trying to build, just before the Second Congress and immediately after it.[46]

The Mensheviks claimed to be for a looser, more spontaneous form of organisation. In reality this meant freedom for rightward moving reformists to ignore party policy whenever it suited them. In both the 1905 and 1917 revolutions the leaders of Menshevism were to show real contempt for working class spontaneity. In 1905 they would claim the working class went too far, scaring off its allies: the bourgeoisie and liberal politicians. In 1917 the Mensheviks showed complete disregard for working class spontaneity by seeking to take power away from the soviets and hand it to the bourgeoisie.

This charge cannot be levelled at either Trotsky or Rosa Luxemburg; but the weakness of their criticisms would become apparent during the course of the 1905 and 1917 revolutions. Both predicted Lenin's party concept would divorce the revolutionary party from the Russian working class: according to Trotsky it would fail to campaign; for Luxemburg ultra centralism would lead it to miss the coming revolution. These predictions were shown to be groundless: the Bolshevik Party more than punched its weight and grew in size and influence.

In 1902 the key for Lenin was establishing an organisation of committed revolutionaries throughout Russia, big enough to take advantage of the struggles he knew were on the horizon. During and after 1905, a period of mass strikes and the first ever workers' soviet, he was arguing to "open the gates of the party" because "the very essence of class struggle face to face with the bosses turns workers into socialists".[47] Some critics claim this change of tack makes Lenin a cynical opportunist. Lenin forestalled them as early as 1907, when he wrote: "the basic mistake made by people who polemicise with *What Is to Be Done?* is that they tear this production completely out of a specific historical context, out of a now long-past period in the development of our party".[48]

The perspective for a revolutionary organisation in a period of mass struggle is not the same as when workers are passive or on the defensive. Workers learn and gain self-confidence though struggle. Trotsky would later acknowledge that his disagreement with Lenin about what kind of party was required at the 1903 Congress was the biggest mistake of his life. Tragically in 1919 Rosa Luxemburg would pay for the same mistake with her life.

It was Lenin's optimism about building a revolutionary movement from below that drew the most militant youth towards the Bolshevik tendency after 1903. Valentinov, a young Bolshevik, later wrote: "Daring and determination were common to all of us. For this reason *What Is to Be Done?* struck just the right chord with us and we were only too eager to put its message into practice. In this sense we were one hundred percent Leninists at the time".[49] Lenin's focus in *What Is to Be Done?* on the role played by socialists is not a symptom of his general distrust of workers. On the contrary, he was more worried about the shortcomings of Russian Social Democracy. *What Is to Be Done?* voices a real concern that the Russian socialists needed to up their game if they were to avoid failing the working class.

Lenin is blamed for the historic split between Bolsheviks and Mensheviks at the 1903 Congress of Russian Social Democracy. That was not his original intention. The split was unexpected and hinged on what seemed like two relatively minor issues. First, whether the party should admit into membership anyone who supported it in any practical way, or whether membership should be restricted to those ready to "act under the party's direction". And second, whether three veteran intellectuals who were contributing precious little to the party publication *Iskra*, should remain on its editorial board.

Lenin and his supporters were for a disciplined party in which both members and its newspaper's editorial board were accountable to the party Congress. He argued the attitude of Martov and his group, the Mensheviks, reflected the undisciplined habits of the old discussion circles and the intellectuals that dominated them. He was defeated on the membership question but won on the issue of the editorial board. It is from this victory that the terms Bolshevik (majority) and Menshevik (minority) derive. Though focused on party organisation, the split was consolidated by a more profound argument over two very different assessments of the coming revolution and the role that the various classes would play in it. Martov looked to a coalition between workers and capitalists to overthrow Tsarism; Lenin insisted that a worker-peasant alliance would be needed to achieve a genuinely democratic revolution in Russia.

Back to 1896: the rising class struggle in Russia

The first big strike of Russian workers in 1896 coincided with Lenin's turn to agitation in Petrograd. When the strike erupted it came as a shock, especially to the Tsarist regime. Less than a year before the Tsar's finance minister Count Witte had made a rash, ill-informed statement denying that Russia's workers were like other workers in Europe and dismissing strikes and class struggle as an irrelevance in Russia:

> In our industry there prevail patriarchal relations between the employer and the worker. This patriarchy is in many cases expressed in the concern of the factory owner for the needs of the workers and employees in his factory. In Russia, fortunately, there is no working class in the same sense and same significance as in the West; consequently we have no labour problem; nor will either of these find in Russia a soil to produce them.[50]

This statement came on the eve of mass strikes of tens of thousands of textile workers in 1896-7, and only ten years before workers' councils in St Petersburg and other towns and cities, and armed workers' insurrection in Moscow. It shows how complacent Russia's autocracy was and how quickly times can change.

The Count must have felt sick when the predominantly women textile workforce in St Petersburg struck in May 1896 to mark the new Tsar and Tsarina's coronation. Rosa Luxemburg's lively description says it all:

> The St Petersburg general strike of 1896 appears as a purely economic wage struggle. Its causes were the intolerable working conditions of the spinners and weavers in St Petersburg: a working day of thirteen, fourteen and fifteen hours; miserable piece work rates; and a whole series of contemptible chicaneries on the part of the employers.
>
> The workers patiently endured the conditions for a long time, till an apparently trivial circumstance filled their cup to overflowing. The coronation of the Tsar, Nicholas II, was celebrated in May 1896 and on

that occasion the St Petersburg employers displayed their patriotic zeal by giving their workers three days compulsory holidays, for which curious to relate, they did not desire to pay their employees.

The workers angered at this began to move. A strike was decided upon and the following demands were formulated: first, payment of wages for the coronation holidays; second, a working day of ten hours; third, increased rates for piecework. Within a week every weaving and spinning plant was at a standstill and 40,000 workers were on general strike. Today this event, measured against the gigantic mass strike of the revolution, may appear small. In Russia at the time a general strike was something unheard of; it was a complete revolution in miniature. There began of course, the most brutal persecution. One thousand workers were arrested and the general strike was suppressed.[51]

Despite the repression the number of strikes doubled in the two years that followed but an economic slump brought them to a temporary halt. Even then thousands of workers joined a wave of student demonstrations to fight the Tsar's police and army. May Day became the symbol of resistance with a general strike in Kharkov in 1900 followed by the siege of the strike bound Obukhov munitions plant in St Petersburg in 1901, in which six workers were killed and 800 arrested.

A new generation

"Within the last three or four years", wrote the chief of the political police, "the easy going Russian lad has been transformed into a type of semi-literate intellectual who regards it as his duty to spurn religion and family, to disregard the law and to defy and scoff at the authorities. Fortunately, such young men are not yet numerous in the factories but this insignificant handful terrorises the inert majority of workers into following it".[52]

It was not just the "lads" who were being radicalised and attracted by socialist ideas. Women who went on strike in the mid 1890s, including tobacco and textile workers in the mills, were encouraged by revolutionaries to join study circles once their strikes were over. These circles were attracting a new generation of young women who would play an important role in drawing ever more women as well as men into the labour movement and towards the Bolsheviks. The economic slump gave workers all sorts of common grievances, laying the basis for a class wide response. Between 1902 and 1903 the heart of Russia's ultra-modern iron and steel industry was wracked by a series of general strikes. Again Luxemburg describes how big industrial centres like these were transformed into bastions of free speech and agitation against the forces of law and order:

> In Rostov every industrial plant was at a standstill. Every day there were monster meetings of 15-20,000 held in the open air, sometimes surrounded by cordons of Cossacks, at which for the first time Social Democratic speakers appeared publicly. Inflammatory speeches on socialism and political freedom were delivered and received with enormous enthusiasm. It goes without saying there were massacres here.[53]

By the spring of 1903 the whole of south Russia was aflame. Baku, Tiflis, Batumi, Odessa, Kiev, Nikolayev and Ekaterinoslav were on general strike. During July 1904 a strike began in the railway workshops at Kiev.

> The immediate cause was miserable conditions and rotten wages. During the night two delegates of the railway workers were arrested. The strikers immediately demanded their release and decided not to allow trains to leave the town. At the station all the strikers with their wives and families sat down on the railway track, a sea of human beings. They were threatened with rifle salvoes. The workers bared their breasts and cried, "Shoot!" A salvo was fired into the seated crowd, and 30 to 40 corpses, amongst them women and children, remained on the ground. The whole of Kiev went on strike the same day.[54]

The Zubatov unions

Tsarism reacted in its usual way with brutal repression and the murder of strikers and their families. But the repression, fierce though it was, wasn't having the desired effect. The regime had to try other methods to head off or defuse its industrial troubles. The head of the secret police, General Trepov wrote a report that argued:

> If the demands of the workers are exploited by the revolutionaries for such profound anti-government aims, then is it not up to the government to seize this weapon, that is so rewarding the revolutionaries, from their hands? The police are obliged to be interested in the same thing as the revolutionary.[55]

Not only were workers organising and striking, numbers of them were joining the revolutionary groups and the regime was worried. It was to outflank the revolutionaries that the secret police initiated a new form of police trade unionism: Zubatovism, named after the head of the Moscow Security Police Colonel Zubatov, who was made the head of police unions. It was intended that workers' societies be formed with police approval, to provide opportunities for self-help and protection against the influence of revolutionaries. Groups were organised in Moscow, Odessa, Nikolayev and Kharkov, the aim being to steer workers' activities into safe channels.

But the police strategy did not work out as planned. The workers used these unions to organise and raise their demands. Police plans went awry in 1904 when a strike led by Zubatov union members in Odessa was literally abandoned by the union. Marxists in the Emancipation of Labour Group stepped in to take over the leadership and proceeded to spread it to all the major workplaces in Odessa. Then they called mass political strikes in 1903 that spread throughout the whole of south Russia.

This turned the Tsarist regime against Zubatovism. All the societies with the exception of those in Moscow and St Petersburg were disbanded and Zubatov was sacked and exiled. But Tsarism continued to vacillate and police trade unions were re-introduced.

The Russo-Japanese War

On the night of 8-9 February 1904 a Japanese fleet attacked and sank Russian battleships anchored off Port Arthur on the Chinese coast, signalling the start of the Russo-Japanese War. Russia was a mighty imperial power; Japan was regarded as an inferior upstart. The Japanese began the conflict but it was Russian arrogance and chauvinism that provoked it.

The Tsar and his military advisers were obsessed by the prospect of grabbing a vast east Asian empire. Russia had steadily pushed into northern China and Korea, encroaching on what Japan regarded as her patch. Tsar Nicholas II, a nasty racist and anti-semite, hated the Japanese, who he referred to as "monkeys".

The mighty Trans-Siberian Railway was built to open up China to Russian exploitation and to earn vast amounts of foreign currency as the main transport artery between Europe and the Far East. The Russians used the Boxer Rebellion of 1898-1901, itself in part a consequence of Russian incursion into China, as a pretext for sending 180,000 troops to Manchuria, supposedly to protect its railways.

After the Boxer Rebellion subsided Russia simply ignored the demands from the other major imperial powers for the withdrawal of her troops. By the end of 1903 it was clear the Tsar intended to occupy Manchuria indefinitely. He rebuffed repeated requests from Japan for a formal demarcation of Russian and Japanese spheres of influence in Manchuria and Korea. But strengthened by their recently concluded alliance with Britain, the Japanese were confident enough to act.

The war that followed saw Japan humiliate Russia in a way no one had foreseen. Two of the three Russian battle fleets were destroyed. The third was only saved because it was in the Black Sea and its sailors threatened mutiny. Russian forces were overwhelmed and defeated in Manchuria. The Japanese besieged Port Arthur and the Russian army sent to relieve it was forced to retreat. In January 1905 Port Arthur surrendered.

As these disasters mounted mass strikes, political protests and uprisings swept across the Russian Empire, exposing the internal weaknesses of the Tsarist autocracy. At one stage a Russian army of 300,000, bigger than the force facing the Japanese in Manchuria, had to be stationed in Poland to restore order there.

As a decade later, war was the midwife of revolution, though it didn't seem like that at the start. At the outbreak of the Russo-Japanese war strikes fell to their lowest level in a decade. Initially a mood of war euphoria and patriotism swept the country. Lenin, still in exile, and now leading the Bolsheviks, was forced to admit, "our party has lost a good half of its influence during the past year".[56]

In February 1904 when the Tsar declared war on Japan, he had the full backing of a gung-ho bourgeoisie, including the liberal capitalists. But by late summer 1904 the war was going badly and sections of the middle class were jumping ship. The series of catastrophic defeats and the military blunders of the Tsar and his generals soon punctured the patriotic mood. Landlords, industrialists, members of the intelligentsia and sections of the professional classes began to question the war and to speak openly of the need for a constitution. These forces would later form themselves into a party called the Constitutional Democrats (Kadets as they became known) and refer to themselves as the liberals.

The weak and frightened Russian intelligentsia and liberal capitalists were angling for constitutional limits to the Tsar's dictatorship. Some of his court advocated such a compromise, seeing this as Tsarism's route to salvation. Lavish "reform" banquets sponsored by the liberal intelligentsia and pro-capitalist politicians were the toast of the European press, heralded as the force for change in autocratic Russia and praised for their "moderation and reasonableness".

But more importantly the growing anti-war sentiment began to fuse with and fuel workers' grievances about their worsening conditions and falling wages. Even the best-paid workers saw their wages falling by around 25 percent.[57]

The police trade union in St Petersburg was called the Assembly of Russian Factory and Workshop Workers. Led by Father Gapon, a prison chaplain and a protégé of the disgraced Zubatov, this legal union had police backing and was intended to be a moderating influence on the workers of Russia's biggest city. But as the union grew, its membership demanded more action from its holy leader.

At the beginning of December 1904 there was unrest in the giant Putilov factory where 12,000 workers were employed and where Father Gapon's union led its first strikes. Alarmed, the employers victimised and sacked four members of his union, provoking a wider stoppage that quickly spread across the city. Here was the spark that would ignite Russia's 1905 revolution.

1905: Russia's great dress rehearsal and the years of reaction

Mass strikes in a revolutionary period scatter millions of sparks in all directions—and all around there is the inflammable material of extreme bitterness, unprecedented starvation, endless tyranny and cynical, shameless mockery of the poor, the peasant and the rank and file soldier.[58]
—*Lenin*

The dramatic events that shook Tsarist Russia from 1904 right through to the end of 1905 were entirely unexpected. The drama began with a naval battle between Russia and Japan and ended with Russia, the defeated power, in the grip of a revolution that spread right across its Empire.

Only six years earlier Europe's social democratic parties, grouped together in the Second International, had been obsessed with the arguments for and against Eduard Bernstein's call to abandon revolution. The Second International was founded in 1898, the same year as the Russian SDLP, which affiliated to it. As the socialist movement expanded at the end of the 19th century a section led by German reform socialist Bernstein moved to reject Marxism.

They argued society would be changed not by revolution, as Marx had insisted, but through winning parliamentary representation and using the existing state to bring about reform. Bernstein's revisionism was rejected in the end, but it never went away. The whole affair had a distinct air of unreality. At the turn of the century no one really believed revolution was in the air. So the 1905 Revolution came as a big shock; and it was an even bigger shock that it came in Russia.

For Marx Russia was the bastion of counter-revolution. As the Great Power least affected by capitalist development, Tsarism had intervened time and again, sending troops to crush the rise of democracy in Europe's capitals. The view of Russia as Europe's policeman dominated the Second International. Common sense told the leaders of European social democracy that backward Russia would be the rearguard of the revolution. But 1905 transformed Russia overnight from the bulwark of reaction into a citadel of revolution.

Never had the crowned and uncrowned heads of Europe been so scared of the mob. Tsarism was teetering before their eyes. Sailors mutinied. Women denied the vote broke up election meetings and fought the soldiers sent to restore order. School pupils in oppressed Poland fought for the right to be educated in their own language and drove Russian teachers out of the classrooms. Peasants were up in arms against their oppressors, the rich landowners. But what really worried the rich and powerful was Russia's workers on the march, women as well as men. From economic strikes they moved to political strikes, to general strikes and finally to soviets and armed insurrection.

As the historian of German Social Democracy Carl Schorske wrote:

> 1905 was a turning point in European history...the relationship of Russia to western European political life was altered by her defeat at the hands of Japan. Almost overnight the significance of Russia for Europe was transformed. The bastion of 19th century reaction became the vanguard of twentieth century revolution. Repercussions of the Russian Revolution were felt throughout the European labour movement, but above all in Germany, where local sources of class antagonism were strengthened by the Russian example.[59]

For the first time ever mass strikes were central to a revolution. In 1905, and with a much smaller working class than the US, Germany, France or Britain, Russia experienced a mass strike movement unparalleled in Russia or any other developed capitalist state. The first democratic institution in Russian history, the St Petersburg Soviet of Workers' Deputies, was formed. The revolution involved an insurrection and tested the revolutionary socialists, who though few in number at the start of the revolution, played an important role and grew in size and influence as the great mass movement spread. The dramatic events gave rise to two of the most creative and significant developments of 20th century Marxism, Rosa Luxemburg's analysis of the mass strike and Leon Trotsky's theory of permanent revolution, and all this in a backward country, a dictatorship that had not previously experienced a bourgeois revolution.

The 1905 Revolution made a big splash in America as well as Europe. In Chicago, in June 1905 Big Bill Haywood opened the founding convention of the Wobblies (the Industrial Workers of the World or IWW), "the first Continental Congress of the workers of the world". In the most eloquent speech of the convention Lucy Parsons, an ex-slave, urged the delegates to cast their eyes "to far-off Russia and take courage from those who are fighting the battle there, and from the further fact that carries the greatest terror to the capitalist class throughout the whole world—that the red flag has been raised".[60]

Over the next year solidarity with the unfolding revolution would become one of the IWW's priorities. According to US labour historian Philip Foner, the IWW's passionate solidarity with the revolt in Russia won them enthusiastic support among immigrant workers in the eastern seaboard mill towns, opening the way for the IWW's key role in an epic strike wave that lasted until 1913. Hundreds of exiled Russian, Polish, Finnish and Jewish revolutionaries soon swelled its ranks.

The revolution starts here

Three big strike waves swept across the Russian Empire in 1905: in January, October and November. At the end of 1904 a series of strikes in St Petersburg involved some 150,000 workers. This was prior to the sacking of four workers in the Putilov plant, an engineering factory employing over 12,000. Within a week what looked like a minor trade union skirmish turned into a mass movement and a revolution. Within three days their strike had spread to the Neva shipyards, the textile factories and the city's bakeries.

Activists Vera Karelina and Anna Boldyreva had been instrumental in recruiting large numbers of women workers to the Factory and Mill Operatives Union. Led by their section leader Karelina, thousands of women textile workers joined this solidarity strike. Along with Alexandra Kollontai, who also worked around the strike and had only recently broken from the Mensheviks to join the Bolsheviks, Anna Boldyreva would be elected onto the Petrograd Soviet when it was formed later in October.

Following this strike all union branches in St Petersburg held meetings across the city. This made the dispute a focus for the many grievances and complaints associated with other strikes and a list of all the various issues was drawn up. More general demands: the eight-hour day, increased wages, proper sanitary facilities and free medical aid, were added. Father Gapon suggested it would be a good idea for the workers to march in peaceful procession to the Tsar's Winter Palace to beg for a constitution and plead for his assistance in their dispute. The police encouraged Gapon's move, to divert the movement from further strikes and more extreme forms of action. So the idea of a mass petition and a solemn procession was born.

Workers were encouraged to "humbly beg" their Tsar to redress their legitimate grievances. Meanwhile the Social Democrats, slow to get off the mark in Lenin's view, finally intervened and succeeded in amending the original list of demands. This resulted in a very different petition from the one Gapon had intended: now its demands included freedom of assembly for the workers, land for the peasants, free speech and a free press, an end to the Russo-Japanese war, and for a Constituent Assembly.

Bloody Sunday

On Sunday 9 January over 200,000 workers assembled and moved off in silence in an enormous peaceful procession to Tsar Nicholas's Winter Palace. Dressed in their Sunday best and accompanied by elderly relatives and small children, they carried portraits of the Tsar, religious banners and holy icons. A tiny group of Bolsheviks and Mensheviks were on the procession with their red banners.

According to Alexandra Kollontai's eyewitness account,[61] when the procession arrived at the Winter Palace they stood in the snow for two hours waiting for the Tsar to appear. A shot was fired, then another and suddenly blood was pouring and women and children were lying dead in the snow. People standing next to Kollontai kept telling her it must be a mistake, that the Tsar wouldn't shoot his unarmed subjects, but by then the gendarmes were galloping into the crowd with sabres drawn, wounding and killing at will. Instead of receiving his petitioners the "Little Father" had closed his palace gates on his subjects and ordered his police to slaughter them. Children who climbed trees to act as lookouts were fired on. Many of them fell like stones and were left lying in the snow.

Other workers were killed in the city that day, their blood spilt on the Troitsky Bridge, the Nevsky Prospekt and in Alexandrovsky Park.

By the evening barricades had gone up and some of the bolder elements raided the Schaff arms factory for guns. But few were able to defend themselves. In a deliberate massacre that came to be known as Bloody Sunday, over one thousand men, women and children were murdered and two thousand wounded. Alexandra Kollontai and all the other socialists who had marched with the workers knew what was at stake. Recalling the dead, the wounded and the children shot that day, she wrote that the Tsar,

> had killed something else—he had killed superstition. From then on everything was different. 9 January was the start of a great mass movement against old bourgeois, landowning Russia. However tragically this first show of workers' strength ended, it was an inevitable first lesson for them on the road to revolution.[62]

Lukerya Bogdanova, a textile worker in St Petersburg recorded that Bloody Sunday was the day she stopped believing in god and the Tsar. The events shattered the beliefs of huge numbers of workers who learned the hard way that icons and portraits of the Tsar are less effective than guns. The terrible shock of Bloody Sunday had blown open the door to revolution. Writing a month after the event Lenin said:

> 9 January fully revealed the vast reservoir of revolutionary energy possessed by the proletariat as well as the inadequacy of social democratic organisation. No wonder the European bourgeois press say that the Russia of 10 January is no longer the Russia of 8 January. A priest found himself at the head of the movement: one day he appealed for a march with a peaceful petition to the Tsar and the next day he issued this call for revolution: 'we no longer have a Tsar. Today a river of blood divides him from the Russian people. It is time for the Russian workers to begin the struggle for the people's freedom without him'.[63]

St Petersburg was immediately in the grip of a city-wide strike. Within two weeks the revolution had spread across the Tsar's vast Empire, from the Ukraine to the Baltic States to Poland. Huge and repeated strike waves were followed by mutinies in the army and navy, revolts of oppressed national minorities and peasant uprisings, invariably led by the women villagers. Large chunks of Poland were part of the Russian Empire and the Polish workers had an even higher level of strike activity than the native Russian workers: 93 percent of Polish workers went on strike during 1905. Describing the armed uprising in the Polish town of Lodz, Lenin stressed the impact of national oppression and the resistance to it:

> Where national oppression is added to the economic and general political yolk, the Tsarist police and troops are going out of their way to incense and provoke the workers. The proletariat of Lodz is setting a new example, not only of revolutionary enthusiasm and heroism, but of superior forms of struggle. Though still poorly armed and isolated from the general movement, they are throwing up barricades with amazing speed and inflicting serious losses on the Tsar's troops. Their armed uprising is gaining breadth and intensity. All these separate armed outbreaks form the picture of an all-Russian conflagration.[64]

In February the Tsar's response to the mounting crisis was to conscript more peasants and workers into the army and throw half a million troops into the Battle of Mukden in the war against Japan. 90,000 Russian troops were killed in three weeks of savage fighting.

Tsarist propaganda blamed the Jews for Russia's military defeats and the fascist, anti-semitic Black Hundreds rounded up and slaughtered thousands of Jews in pogroms backed by the Tsar in Odessa, Kiev and Yalta. Jewish workers and the socialist parties responded by forming self-defence squads. Cossacks were sent to the countryside to slaughter peasants rioting in Orlov and Kursk. Hundreds of protestors were killed in Baku and students were shot dead in Kazan after the police broke up their university occupation. But the arrests, the killings and the pogroms could not stifle people's rage. Workers continued to strike for better pay, better conditions and a shorter working day.

Kollontai was able to report that month after month women in the factories were joining the strike movement and significant numbers were joining the Bolsheviks. Before 1905 the small number of women in the party were responsible for the vital but unsung work of underground communication. "By 1905 however, women were joining the party on their own terms, taking underground names and joining the strikes and demonstrations as organisers, street-fighters and agitators".[65]

1905 was a turning point with wages increasing by over ten percent on average, having been held down in the previous five years. Workers' economic demands lead to political demands, economic struggle to political struggle and vice versa. June saw one of the largest strikes in Russia's history when over 11, 000 women textile workers downed tools in Ivano-Voznesensk near Moscow. As the demonstrators filled the streets they were attacked by gangs of *Black Hundreds*, who killed women and children and hacked to death a young Bolshevik named Olga Galinka.

More and more women began joining the Bolshevik street-fighting defence groups and the countryside exploded in new acts of violence against the landowners' estates with peasant women organising to fight the Cossacks sent in to crush them.

Faced with the irresistible power of the masses the Tsarist tyranny was forced to retreat as its support began to crumble.

Later in June the Black Sea port of Odessa saw clashes with troops turn the strike wave into a minor civil war and spark the first real mutiny on the battleship Potemkin. Sailors also mutinied at the Kronstadt naval fortress near St Petersburg, at the Baltic port of Riga and at Sevastopol on the Black Sea. Dissent and protest increased in the army and the peasants continued to burn down thousands of estates and distribute the liberated food stocks.

With most of the Russian fleet sunk, the Tsar was forced to settle what had been a disastrous war on Japanese terms. In early August, facing more strikes and riots at home, he offered a concession to the strike movement. But instead of conceding the long promised National Assembly, a parliament, all that was offered was a consultative body, the Duma. The workers knew it would be at the mercy of the Tsar, with no power to legislate. This only inflamed the popular mood and led to the second great wave of strikes in October, in which the demands were overwhelmingly political. This strike wave saw the birth of a new power, when the first ever soviet was created in St Petersburg. It began life as a strike committee but quickly developed into a democratic body representing all the workers of the city. The soviets multiplied as workers all over the country piled in behind St Petersburg.

It is worth explaining the origins of the soviets. In October printers in Moscow struck for better wages. Thanks to the rail networks their strike spread quickly throughout the Russian Empire and became a focus for militancy. When the strike reached St Petersburg, the Menshevik organisation there initiated a meeting of some 30 delegates. It was from this modest beginning that the first soviet emerged. The tiny meeting called for a political general strike and it caught the mood of the masses. Within a week it became the St Petersburg Council of Workers' Deputies and support mushroomed: soon the number of delegates reached 562, covering 147 factories, 34 workshops and 16 trade unions.

The October strike movement and the birth of the soviets again forced the brutal Tsarist state onto the defensive. This time Nicholas II was forced to concede a manifesto promising a constitution and a legislative assembly.

The Bolsheviks and the soviets

Lenin worried about the dismissive attitude of the local Petrograd Bolsheviks towards Gapon's trade union and their tardiness in responding to the strikes that led to Bloody Sunday.

Even more worrying for Lenin was the sectarian attitude of some leading Bolsheviks towards the newly established St Petersburg Soviet. Lenin quickly grasped the soviet was not just a strike committee; rather the embryonic form of future workers' power. It needed his intervention to break the local leadership from their dismissive attitude towards working class creativity. When the St Petersburg Soviet formed, one of the Bolshevik organisers, Krasnov, warned against "this intrigue by the Mensheviks" and the Bolshevik central committee even argued it would boycott the soviet unless it agreed to accept the party's programme. Lenin's response was:

> The Soviet of Workers' Deputies or the Party? I think it is wrong to put the question this way. The decision must certainly be: both the soviet and the Party. The Soviet of Workers' Deputies should be regarded as the embryo of a provisional revolutionary government of the whole of Russia as early as possible.
>
> It should broaden its base and enlist the participation of new deputies, not only from the workers, but first from the sailors and soldiers who are everywhere seeking freedom, second from the revolutionary peasantry and thirdly from the revolutionary intelligentsia. We are not afraid of so broad and mixed a composition—indeed we want it—for unless the proletariat and peasantry unite and unless the Social Democrats and revolutionary democrats form a fighting alliance, the revolution cannot be successful.[66]

At first 1905 was a fight to reorganise the party by opening it up to newly radicalised workers. In contrast to the necessarily clandestine method of *What Is to Be Done?*, Lenin now argued, "the working class is instinctively, spontaneously revolutionary".[67]

How could Bolsheviks like Krasnov be so negative in their response to trade unions organising strikes? Why would they want to boycott an organisation like the new soviet that wanted to coordinate the various struggles and challenge the hated regime? The problem was too many party members were stuck in the past, a period of factional struggle with the Mensheviks; a period when party routine and discipline were paramount because of the need to act cautiously and sometimes clandestinely; a period when only tiny handfuls of workers were attracted to revolutionary ideas and when most ordinary workers seemed apathetic—in other words, a period of small discussion group politics.

But during 1905 things were moving at a bewildering pace, so fast that many ordinary workers had become more revolutionary, more enthusiastic, than many existing party members. Far from being apathetic and backward many workers had moved far ahead of individuals who had been party members for years. Too often the old guard had a tendency to write off strikes over economic issues as non-political, failing to see how the dynamic of the new situation was breaking down the wall between the economic and the political.

Now the party needed not just a small group of revolutionaries but all the most militant activists in the working class. In contrast the Bolshevik Committee in Odessa were all for stressing the narrowness of trade unions and for urging "an energetic struggle" against the Mensheviks. Lenin's response was: "We must not stand aloof but endeavor to take part, to influence and create a tradition of Social-Democratic leadership".[68] It was time to leave behind many of the old methods:

> We must not forget that so far we have had to deal too often only with revolutionaries coming from a particular social stratum; now we shall have to deal with typical representatives of the masses. This calls for a change not only in the methods of propaganda and agitation but also in organisation.[69]

In a letter written as early as February 1905 Lenin had urged the Bolsheviks to "recruit young people more widely and more boldly. We need young forces. This is a time of war. The youth, the students and even more so the young workers, will decide the issue of the struggle... Enlarge the committee threefold by accepting young people onto it. Set up a dozen sub-committees, co-opt any and every honest and energetic person. Allow every sub-committee to write and publish leaflets without any red tape... (If the new people are active, there is no harm if they do make a mistake—they will learn)".[70]

In this way the sterile routinism of the old guard was overcome by the activity, enthusiasm and the impatience of youth and those new to the movement. As the Bolsheviks rose to the challenge the party expanded and renewed its membership. The Bolsheviks were able to learn from the workers who set the pace in the struggle, while the Mensheviks retreated from them.

Both factions were formally agreed the revolution would be a bourgeois revolution. But while the Mensheviks equivocated and in practice looked to an alliance with the bourgeoisie, the Bolsheviks were unequivocally for leadership by the independent workers' movement. On this point the former Menshevik Trotsky agreed with the Bolsheviks, but he pointed to a problem. During the course of 1905 Trotsky came to see that with the workers leading the revolution it was inconceivable that they would limit themselves to demands leaving the bourgeois order intact.

Trotsky's perspective seemed equidistant from the Bolsheviks and the Mensheviks but it wasn't at all. In early 1917 Lenin won the Bolsheviks round to Trotsky's approach, although Lenin himself would not put it quite like that, while the Mensheviks shifted even further to the right. In the years between 1903 and 1917 the Bolsheviks built their party on the working class. That was the key factor.

The new soviet soon had to concern itself with both the economic and political struggles. Rising to that challenge was what won it the mass support of the St Petersburg workers. It began to ensure food distribution and to see that power supplies were maintained. It overturned press censorship and intervened in disputes between landlords and tenants.

When the Kronstadt naval mutineers came under threat of execution the soviet organised a general strike in their defence. When the racist Black Hundred gangs launched pogroms against Jews, strikers or other socialists, the soviet formed workers' militias to protect local neighbourhoods. The soviet started its own newspaper, *Isvestia*. Very little moved in the capital without its say so. Trotsky, aged 26, was elected president of the Petrograd Soviet in November 1905.

Even the smallest issues affecting working people were taken up by the soviet. Its premises were always crowded with petitioners and plaintiffs of all kinds, mostly workers, domestic servants, shop assistants, peasants, soldiers and sailors. A small anecdote shows its grass roots nature and the breadth of its popularity:

An old Cossack from Poltava province complained of unjust treatment by the Princess Repnin who had exploited him as a clerk for 28 years then dismissed him without good cause. The old man wanted the soviet to negotiate with the Princess on his behalf. The envelope containing his petition was addressed simply to The Workers' Government, Petersburg, yet it was promptly delivered by the revolutionary postal system.[71]

In 1905 the mass of the St Petersburg working class saw it as *their* soviet; the vehicle for solving all the immediate problems of the working people as well as the body that could deal with the great political issues of the day. Unlike the trade unions, it represented the general interests of all workers. But the co-existence of two hostile powers inside the state could not last long. Throughout October and November as mass unrest continued, it became obvious that the power of the Tsar or the power of the soviets must conquer the other.

By mid-October the numbers on strike throughout Russia exceeded one million. Nearly all rail transport was halted, the post service was stopped, the schools were shut, and water and gas supplies closed down. Poland and Finland were at a complete standstill. On 17 October the Tsar retreated once again and signed a proclamation giving a constitution to the Russian people. It pledged civil liberties, freedom of speech and the right of free association. It promised facilities for spreading electoral rights, leaving the details to the new parliamentary Duma, and it agreed no law could be enforced without state approval.

But the workers were not satisfied and the proclamation only whetted their appetite for more substantial reforms. They demanded the dismissal of General Trepov, head of the Secret Police and Cossack troops in St Petersburg; the removal of troops beyond a twenty-mile perimeter outside the city; a general amnesty; and the formation of a citizens' militia. Instead of freedom of the press, censorship remained;

while there was freedom of assembly, meetings were still surrounded by troops; while there was freedom of learning, troops still occupied the universities; the jails were still filled with political prisoners; and though a constitution was forthcoming, the autocracy still retained total control.

So a third wave of strikes followed in November. The unifying demand of the eight-hour day dominated this movement. In St Petersburg the strike was total and the whole city shut down. But in the provinces the strike call was not supported and in St Petersburg itself the employers reacted by mass lockouts affecting tens of thousands of workers.

By the beginning of December the Tsarist regime felt strong enough to go on the offensive and launch repression. The Tsar had enough loyal troops to cow the workers and on 2 December police raided the offices of both the Bolsheviks and the Mensheviks and closed them down. Next day all the delegates of the Petrograd Soviet and the entire central committee of the Bolshevik Party were arrested.

The Moscow insurrection

Moscow was a different matter. Here the garrison was smaller and less reliable. The leaders of the newly formed Moscow Soviet, led by Bolsheviks, hoped a victory in Moscow would shift the balance in St Petersburg and spark a general rising. On 7 December a strike broke out in Moscow in protest at the repressive state measures. It spread to St Petersburg where 125,000 people came out on strike. This was the springboard for an armed insurrection in Moscow but after a week of bitter fighting it was crushed. Although the Bolsheviks organised the Moscow strike well enough, the call to armed insurrection was not properly carried through. Many thought the rising was taking place at some future date.

It was the logic of the strike and the initiative of the masses that had pushed things forward to an insurrection in Moscow. On 7 and 8 December there were peaceful strikes. Next day troops attacked the unarmed crowds. Workers built barricades and the government forces responded with artillery fire. It was only at this point that the armed workers' organisations were drawn into battle. For the next week there was an increasingly bitter struggle for control of Moscow. The total armed strength on the workers' side in Moscow was less than 2,000, yet led by the Bolsheviks they were able to pin down a garrison ten times larger. It was only with the arrival of state reinforcements that the tide turned in favour of the Tsar's army. The long resistance was only possible because the revolutionaries had the support of the mass of workers, and the bulk of the soldiers had no real heart for a fight. But the Moscow rising was drowned in blood: 1,000 were killed and about the same number wounded.

There were those like Plekhanov of the Mensheviks who concluded that since the rising was defeated it had been wrong to take up arms. Lenin's conclusion was different: "We should have taken to arms more resolutely, energetically and aggressively. We should have explained to the masses it was impossible to confine things to a peaceful strike and that a fearless, relentless armed fight was necessary".[72] In 1917 that lesson was put to good use.

1905 shows the strength and power of the mass strike. In western Europe it was Rosa Luxemburg who grasped the importance of 1905, having experienced it first hand in Warsaw when large parts of Poland were still under the Tsar's Empire. In *The Mass Strike, the Political Party and the Trade Union*, written in 1906, she shows how strike movements can raise political demands and open up an extra-parliamentary strategy.

1905 had a profound impact on the German socialist movement. A Russian police report of the time recorded that "in Berlin and other big German cities there was hardly a day on which there was not a meeting at which the situation in Russia was discussed; all end with collections for arms for the Russian people".[73] *Vorwärts*, paper of the German Social Democratic Party (SPD), carried a prominent daily column giving updates on the revolution. The dramatic events in Russia sharpened the debate between reform and revolution inside the German movement: 1905 was a year of intense struggle there too. With over half a million workers involved in strikes or lockouts and over 7 million strike days, it was the zenith of German militancy between 1848 and 1917.

In a situation of heightened struggle the left inside the SPD fought to make the party adopt a revolutionary stance. It was Rosa Luxemburg who best argued the case. But the leaders of the SPD and the union bosses rounded on her. They even told her to "go back to Russia". Their idea of a general strike was a peaceful one-day affair, summoned from above to pressurise governments; a passive token firmly under their control. Referring to those keen to keep a lid on German labour, she wrote:

> While the guardians of the German trade unions for the most part fear their organisations will fall to pieces in a revolutionary whirlwind like rare porcelain, the Russian revolution shows us the exactly opposite picture; from the whirlwind and the storm, out of the fire and glow of the mass strike and the street fighting, rise again—like Venus from the foam—fresh, young, powerful, buoyant trade unions.[74]

The Russian mass strikes inspired workers everywhere. In 1907 on the Belfast waterfront, unskilled and previously unorganised catholic and protestant dock labourers fought side by side to improve their conditions and build a union. It was the signal for a union drive throughout Ireland that culminated in the six month long Dublin Lockout. In Britain the Great Unrest saw huge strikes in the railways, ports and coalfields. Four years of mass struggle doubled trade union membership. Italy experienced mass strikes that led to battles with the police and the army, running right up to the First World War.

There was a rash of strikes, big and bitter, throughout North America, including battles that involved poorly paid immigrant workers from a dozen different national backgrounds, many of them women. They followed the lead of the IWW agitators in the struggle for better wages and conditions and for a militant, multi-cultural trade unionism.

The limitations of the mass strike

The key lesson of 1905 concerns the limitations of the mass strike. Despite the dramatic victory of the October strike wave in 1905, the old state structure remained intact and in December Tsarism crushed the revolution. Mass strikes in and of themselves, even if organised by soviets, cannot topple capitalism. They can win concessions and force it to retreat but they cannot make the capitalists give up their economic and political power. In the final analysis the ruling class has to be overthrown. As Marx put it: "Violence is the midwife of any new society." Trotsky's account of 1905 shows both the strengths and limitations of the mass strike:

> In the struggle it is extremely important to weaken the enemy. That is what a strike does. At the same time a strike brings the army of the

revolution to its feet. But neither the one nor the other, in itself, creates a state revolution. The power still has to be snatched from the hands of the old rulers and handed over to the revolution.[75]

A general strike only poses the problem of revolution but does not solve it. Revolution is first and foremost a struggle of state power. But a strike is a revolutionary means of exerting pressure on the existing power.[76]

This clearly implies the need for independent revolutionary organisation rooted inside the working class in advance of a revolutionary situation. In the USA the Wobblies of the IWW were founded in 1905 and drew inspiration from the events in Russia, but the conclusion they drew was that mass strikes, not political organisation, was the answer—part of the reason for their subsequent decline.

In Russia the 1905 revolt forced the Tsar to concede democratic reforms, including an elected parliament. But although 1905 saw mutinies in the imperial navy, the bulk of the army remained loyal. By the end of the year the state was able to use its overwhelming monopoly of violence to crush the revolt and claw back the reforms. The military isolated St Petersburg, arrested and jailed the Soviet and crushed the workers' uprising in Moscow. But it took two more years for counter-revolution of the utmost savagery to defeat this immensely powerful revolutionary movement. And even then it was unable to eradicate all traces of the revolution, as 1917 would prove.

One of the political casualties of 1905 was the founder of Russian Marxism, Plekhanov. It pushed him to the extreme right wing of Russian social democracy, isolated him from those who once revered him and finally separated him from the living workers' movement.

In 1905 he drew the wrong conclusion: that the working class had gone too far and had frightened its liberal allies by attempting to overthrow the Tsar. Forever afterwards his argument was that the socialists had to avoid alienating Russia's liberal bourgeoisie. As Trotsky later put it: "Plekhanov shut his eyes to the fundamental object lesson of the 19th century; that wherever the proletariat appeared as an independent force, the bourgeoisie shifted to the camp of counter-revolution".[77]

1905 was the dress rehearsal for 1917. As Trotsky put it, "the revolutionary leaders did not have to invent it. The experience of the soviets of 1905 was forever chiselled into the consciousness of the workers".[78]

1905 was less significant for what the workers learned from the revolutionaries, than for what the revolutionaries, or at least some of them, had learned from the workers. And although the workers had not won the 1905 Revolution, revolution had certainly won them. It also radically altered the party as thousands of young people in the factories and universities were caught up in the strikes and protests. Schoolchildren rebelled against their teachers and formed Bolshevik cells in their schools.

Trotsky was tried, jailed then exiled to Siberia for the second time in his young life, for his leading role in the 1905 Revolution. At one point it was feared he and others might be executed for treason. But while Tsarism wanted him behind bars, the last thing it needed at that point was to create a prominent martyr for a workers' movement it still dreaded. Trotsky used his time in prison to write one of his most influential books, *Results and Prospects*, his most complete statement of the theory of permanent revolution until he came back to the subject after 1917.

The impact of the 1905 defeat would last many years, but not forever. Lenin was clear on that: "Just wait. 1905 will come again. That is how the workers look at things".[79]

Trotsky, banished to remote Siberia, was equally upbeat: "the sacred crown of the Tsar's absolutism bears forever the trace of the proletarian's boot".[80] Looking back at the 1905 Revolution from the vantage point of 1922 he wrote:

> The events of 1905 formed a majestic prologue to the revolutionary drama of 1917. For a number of years when reaction was triumphant, the year 1905 appeared to us as a completed whole, as the Russian Revolution. Today it has lost that independent nature, without forfeiting any of its historical significance. The Red October, as we used to call it even then, grew after twelve years into another, more powerful and truly victorious October.[81]

The years of reaction: 1906-11

Meantime the exhilarating 1905 days of freedom were ending. It would take Tsarism another two years to finally crush the powerful movement from below. Peasants united against their landlords and there was violence in the countryside. Armed forces were deployed against these disturbances but the campaign of pacification continued into the following year. Mutinies broke out in the armed forces returning along the Trans-Siberian railroad from the disastrous war against Japan.

For a time struggle continued and the Bolsheviks fought on, the last to leave the battlefield. But by 1907 the dark days of reaction saw the revolutionaries persecuted and forced underground or into exile once again.

The Tsar had been forced to concede the Duma assembly, but the electoral qualifications and political composition he announced were so grossly undemocratic and discriminatory against the working class that the Bolsheviks declared a boycott—unlike the Mensheviks, who voted for limited collaboration with it. Lenin was in no mood to work "with a bunch of Kadets" and rounded on the Mensheviks as "liquidators, who wanted to destroy the underground party".[82] Throughout 1906 many Mensheviks, defeated and demoralised by a new onslaught of state repression, dropped out of revolutionary activity to work within the framework of the system. The differences between Bolsheviks and Mensheviks sharpened once again.

Despite the repression and persecution the Bolsheviks grew rapidly at first in the wake of the revolution, as younger and more class-conscious elements of the working class drew courage from the experience of the struggle and learned the lessons of its defeat. As a result the social composition of the Bolsheviks changed quite radically. On the basis of reports presented to the second Congress, membership of the RSDLP in 1903 (Menshevik and Bolshevik) was only a few thousand. By 1907 the RSDLP total membership had increased dramatically and the Bolsheviks with 46,000 members were now bigger than the Mensheviks.[83] They became a party of mainly young and increasingly proletarian people, which helped overcome inertia and the conservative resistance to change.

Lenin was proud that it was a party of youth: "We are a party that is waging a self-sacrificing struggle against the old rottenness, and youth is always the first to undertake a self-sacrificing struggle".[84] Although Lenin at first rejected participation in the Duma in December 1905, by May 1906 he changed his mind. He argued for an active boycott at the end of 1905 based on the assumption that the revolution would continue to gather momentum. After the defeat of the Moscow uprising in December, he continued to argue in favour of the boycott on the grounds that the revolution had been temporarily halted but that a further uprising was not far off. By the spring of 1906 he could see that wasn't going to happen anytime soon and he began to argue it was now time to end the boycott. At the 1907 RSDLP Congress he argued:

> Bear in mind we have always presented the question concretely. Now the time has come to cease the boycott. We should go into the second Duma when or if it is convened—we should not exaggerate its modest importance; on the contrary we shall subordinate the struggle we wage in the Duma to other forms of struggle—namely strikes and uprisings.[85]

Not one Bolshevik delegate at Congress supported Lenin; instead they accused him of "betraying Bolshevism". Lenin found himself in conflict with a group of ultra left Bolsheviks led by Alexander Bogdanov. They also denigrated trade union work and the fight for reforms, counter posing instead "the armed struggle". Lenin fought the issue and won by demanding from the Bolsheviks a readiness to look reality in the face: "since the counter-revolution has driven us into this accursed pigsty, we shall work there too for the benefit of the revolution—without whining but without boasting".[86] Later he said, "this was a compromise forced on us for the balance of forces made it impossible for the time being to conduct mass, revolutionary struggle. In order to prepare this struggle over a long period we had to work even from inside such a pigsty".[87]

Involvement in the Duma on the basis Lenin advocated gave the Bolsheviks a useful platform and a vehicle for legal agitation that enabled them to get their message of struggle out to a wider audience. The Bolshevik party was compelled by the situation it found itself in to be a disciplined organisation, for example the party leadership vetted all their Duma Deputies' speeches. But it is important to realise that discipline did not, as was often claimed, rule out independent initiative from below. The same repressive conditions that made unity in action such a necessity also compelled local branches and sections of the party to think and act for themselves. As Piatnitsky, an old Bolshevik, recalled:

> Were the Bolsheviks of Odessa, Moscow, Baku or Tiflis, always to have waited on directives from the centre, the provisional committee etc, which during the years of the reaction and of the war frequently did not exist at all due to arrests, what would have been the result? The Bolsheviks would not have won the working masses.[88]

1912-1914 upturn in the struggle

In the spring of 1912 the revolutionary workers' movement rose again in a massive response to yet another brutal Tsarist atrocity: the Lena goldfield massacre, a horrific re-run of Bloody Sunday 1905.

The Lena goldfields were in a region of the great Taiga forest, almost 2,000 kilometres from the Siberian railway. When 6,000 miners went on strike for better food and living conditions, their unarmed demonstration was repeatedly fired on by the police. This time 500 workers were killed or badly wounded. When the Social Democratic Duma group challenged the government on the mass murder of workers they got an arrogant, couldn't care less response from the Tsar's minister of the interior Makharov: "So it was, and so it will be!"[89]

Just three months before the massacre, the Bolshevik conference in January had noted: "the onset of a political revival is to be noted among broad democratic circles, chiefly among the proletariat. The workers' strikes in 1910-11, the beginning of demonstrations and proletarian meetings, the students' strikes and so on are all indications of the growing revolutionary feelings of the masses against the regime".[90] The demonstrations and strikes following the massacre raised the slogan of the "Democratic Republic", reflecting a much higher level of mass consciousness than at the start of the 1905 revolution, which began with a humble petition to the Tsar.

In April 1912 the Russian workers started where they had left off at the height of the revolution seven years earlier. News of the massacre aroused working class anger, with street demonstrations, meetings and protests throughout Russia; 300,000 workers taking part in protest strikes and a 400,000 strong May Day strike. Other political strikes soon followed.

Lenin encouraged many methods to adapt the Bolshevik party to this rising tide of struggle, including elections to the Duma. But central to everything was the launching of the Bolshevik daily paper, *Pravda*. Its first issue appeared on 22 April, 18 days after the Lena massacre.

Pravda was very different to many other socialist newspapers written by (sometimes) talented journalists. Lenin questioned whether one such paper was "a journal *for* workers as there is not a trace of workers' initiative or any connection with working class organisation".[91] In comparison *Pravda* included 11,000 letters and articles from workers in one year, about 35 items a day. Thousands of workers read it, wrote for it and sold it, and it encouraged the formation of workers' groups to collect money for it and distribute it. Lenin wrote in 1914: "5,674 workers' groups united by *Pravda* in less than two years is a large number given the harsh conditions prevailing in Russia. But this is only the beginning. We need not thousands, but tens of thousands of workers' groups. We must intensify our activities tenfold".[92]

War broke out only a few weeks later and *Pravda* didn't immediately hit the high target Lenin had set. However, the paper had been absolutely central in shaping the Bolshevik party of 1914, turning it into a sizeable organisation with tens of thousands of members and supporters organised in the factories. All these elements combined to make the Bolsheviks on the eve of the First World War, in Trotsky's words, "the most revolutionary—indeed the only revolutionary—section of the Second International".[93]

Since 1910 the Bolsheviks smuggled their newspapers and the writings of Lenin and their other exiled leaders into Sweden, and from there across the icy wastes of northern Scandinavia to Finland and finally to Petrograd. The organiser for this vast chain of communications, known as the Northern Underground, was an incredible Mr Reliable, Alexander Shlyapnikov, a skilled factory worker who spoke French, English and German. For years he led a hectic and dangerous existence. In 1914 he had been living in exile in Europe for six years, working as a skilled turner and travelling illegally under false passports, smuggling and distributing literature and tirelessly preparing for revolution.

Born to a poor Russian peasant family and one of four children of a widowed mother, Shlyapnikov had worked since the age of eleven, though he was unsure of his exact age because his family belonged to the Old Believers sect who did not register their births. The Old Believers were radical Christian dissenters, hounded by Tsarism and its Orthodox Church. The religious persecution he suffered as a child drew him to socialism.

When he moved to St Petersburg as a teenager to find factory work he joined the Bolsheviks and served his time as a lathe operator. He led several strikes for which he was arrested and imprisoned before finally escaping abroad. In the Tsarist reaction after the 1905 Revolution Shlyapnikov was drafted into the army as punishment for his part in the revolt. Refusing to take the oath of service to the Tsar he was sentenced to two years in a prison fortress. After being freed on bail he went underground rather than risk further imprisonment.

Barbara Allen in her biography, *Shlyapnikov: Life of an Old Bolshevik*, writes, "along with Shlyapnikov's charisma—his intelligence, organisational skills and leadership ability explain why at the age of twenty two he became a member of the Petersburg Committee RSDLP(B)—the leading Bolshevik organisation in Russia".[94] His *Reminiscences from the Revolutionary Underground* inform us that,

> in April 1914, after six years of wandering around the workshops of France, Germany and England, I safely crossed the frontier carrying the passport of a French citizen and reached Petersburg, my native city, now red and already a seething cauldron of revolutionary energy. It had just seen a political strike on the anniversary of the Lena shootings and was preparing to celebrate May Day.[95]

The purpose of Shlyapnikov's clandestine return was to rebuild the Russian Bureau of the Bolshevik central committee, renew the Russian end of the Northern Underground and check the state of revolutionary organisation there. His knowledge of German allowed him to find work as soon as he arrived in the German-owned Lessner engineering plant in the Vyborg district. He was immediately struck by the enormous changes in the attitude of workers since he had last worked there illegally in 1907: "the absence of timidity hits you in the eye...Bolshevik workers would get up at workshop meetings and a little strategy was practised: workers capable of speaking on political subjects were spread around the district, so that the same worker did not always get up in any one factory, preserving the vital secret of the agitator's name from the Okhrana".[96]

Cautiously he began to piece the organisation together again, establishing new local committees and contacts. In mid-December 1916 he went to Moscow to help co-ordinate a demonstration on 9 January, the 12th anniversary of Bloody Sunday, and was able to renew direct contact with Bolshevik organisers in Moscow, Nizhny-Novgorod and Vladimir. He also set up communication with Bolshevik organisations in Kiev, Tula, Voronezh, the Donbas, the Urals and Siberia. Because of this trip to the provinces, Shlyapnikov was not in Petrograd to see the prelude to the February Revolution.

In his memoirs he wrote of how the downturn in struggle after 1905 had left its mark on the organisation: "Typical of the pre-war period of party work was its lack of intellectuals. The exodus of intellectuals that had begun in 1906 meant party workers and full time staff were, in the main, ordinary workers".[97] He tells how, in an earlier clandestine trip back to Petrograd in the spring of 1914, the atmosphere in the factory districts was tense. How every conflict at work, small or large, provoked a protest strike or a walkout; how skirmishes between workers and the police were everyday occurrences. Significantly he noticed how the workers were making contacts among the soldiers at the nearby barracks:

> Revolutionary propaganda was taken to the soldiers at the barracks and the army camps. Women workers—the weavers and mill girls—took a lead in this. Some of the soldiers were from the same villages as the women workers. For the most part the young people came together on the basis of 'interests of the heart', and kinship relations were established between barracks and factory. It was impossible to turn such troops against the workers.[98]

The resurgence of class struggle and the myriad of student protests that followed the Lena massacre of 1912 would culminate in the raising of barricades in St Petersburg in the summer of 1914, on the very eve of the First World War. Shlyapnikov contrasted the enthusiasm for war among the middle and upper classes with the more sullen, subdued mood in the factory districts of Petrograd. "The Petersburg[99] press did much to kindle popular chauvinism... But even this hostile atmosphere did not drive workers to an excess of nationalism...one could not conclude that the Russian workers hated the Germans, as the newspapers claimed".[100] Shlyapnikov's reading of the situation was confirmed by events: on the day the Russian army was mobilised, twenty factories in St Petersburg struck in opposition to the war.

With the war came further repression. *Pravda*, which had been published since 1912, was suppressed. In December 1914 when the Bolshevik central committee gathered for a secret meeting, the secret police were waiting and arrested everyone, including Kamenev and the other five Bolshevik Duma members present. They were jailed and despatched to Siberia. Led by the Bolsheviks, the left faction in the Duma was almost the only parliamentary group in Europe to oppose war credits from the start; the other was the socialist group in Serbia.

The arrests continued as the war ground on. Bolshevik rank and file members were forced to develop ideas and initiatives of their own. They couldn't rely on Lenin, Kamenev, Krupskaya or Zinoviev who were in jail or exile. The organisation of the Vyborg district with over 500 members was particularly good at this; invariably they were in advance of the formal leadership.

Lenin believed the war could be the midwife of a new international and that the Bolsheviks had to fight for that position. In a letter to Shlyapnikov he wrote: "Our task is now an absolute and open struggle with opportunism. This is an international task. It rests upon us, for there is no one else. We cannot put it aside".[101]

In September 1915 delegates from 11 countries gathered at a conference of anti-war socialists at Zimmerwald, Switzerland. The conference rejected Lenin's draft resolution, which argued to turn imperialist war into civil war. In spite of this Lenin saw the conference as a first step. The hard left, including the Bolsheviks, voted for the majority position as well as publishing their own rejected resolution.

The follow up to Zimmerwald was held at Kienthal in Switzerland in April 1916. This second conference marked another step along the road towards Lenin's position: the necessity of mass struggle to end the violence of imperialism. Lenin could now look to groups in Germany, France, Britain, the Netherlands, Sweden, Bulgaria and Italy who agreed on the need to break from the Second International. Trotsky wrote: "In every significant national movement a left radical faction aligned with Lenin's position had come into being. The Zimmerwald left tendency was well on the way to becoming a movement".[102]

As secretary of the central committee in Petrograd, Shlyapnikov kept Russian workers in touch with developments abroad, and as messages filtered out from Petrograd to the rest of Europe, exiled revolutionaries began to look forward to the day they might return.

Lenin could not know for sure how Bolshevism was faring in Russia, relying on Shlyapnikov and Alexandra Kollontai, another crucial figure in the Northern Underground operation. But the notion, popular in bourgeois historiography, that Lenin and Krupskaya had lost touch with the reality of wartime life in Russia for the working class and the peasantry is nonsense.

Lenin was well informed but he was an inveterate worrier. His frustration came not from ignorance, but from his sense of impotence in exile. The picture was not quite as bad as he feared. Although the Okhrana, the Tsar's secret police, had hacked away at the Russian underground for years, most commentators on the ground thought the Bolsheviks were the best organised and most serious of the surviving socialist factions.

The Okhrana thought so too. They saw the Petersburg Committee of the Bolsheviks as a serious threat. Rooted in the trade unions and workplaces, with a young and energetic membership, Bolshevik networks of activists had survived the crackdown of 1906 and continued to recruit members in wartime, Tsarist Russia. In 1913 the Director of the Tsar's Police Department paid the Bolsheviks this backhanded compliment in his secret report:

> Lenin's faction is always better organised than the others, more resourceful in propagating its ideas among the workers... Over the last two years his followers came closer to the workers than the others— the first to proclaim purely revolutionary slogans. The Bolshevik nuclei and organisations are now scattered throughout all the cities. Permanent correspondence and contacts have been established with all the factory centres.
>
> There is nothing surprising in the fact that at the present time the assembling of the entire underground Party is proceeding around the Bolshevik organisations and that the latter really are the Russian Social-Democratic Labour Party.[103]

The party had retained its committed supporters in the factories and among the sailors at Kronstadt. Petrograd was still its stronghold and by the end of 1916, according to Shlyapnikov, there were 3,000 Bolshevik workers there.[104] More importantly, the party had passed the test its Menshevik competitors and most other socialist organisations across Europe had failed: the acid test of the First World War.

The outbreak of war and the collapse of official socialism

> If war is declared, the working classes as well as their parliamentary representatives, have the duty to mobilise to prevent hostilities breaking out. If war should break out, their duty is to struggle actively for a speedy end to the fighting and make every effort to use the crisis to rouse the people and hasten the abolition of the rule of the capitalist class.
> —*Resolution of the Stuttgart Congress of the Second International 1907: re-affirmed at its Basel Congress in 1912*[105]

In August 1914 the long predicted war between the great powers finally arrived. It was a war for colonies, for markets and spheres of influence, a war for profits and a war for oil. It shattered the fake unity of what everyone had assumed was a powerful socialist movement. The leaders of the Second International—the parties of European social democracy—forgot about Marxism and internationalism. Abandoning the resolutions and the brave words of Stuttgart and Basel, they capitulated to their own national governments.

In the decade before 1914 everyone in the socialist movement was clear that competition between the rival economic and political empires was creating major crises and that war was likely. Germany had overtaken Britain to become the world's second industrial power behind the USA. It had the fastest industrial growth of all the European powers, allowing it to make enough concessions to a well-organised working class to ensure decades of social peace. But German capital's success destabilised the international environment.

Britain and France were weaker economically but each had greater global presences. Britain had an empire on which "the sun never set" and the French empire was considerable too. Germany was without an empire to speak of and German capital was demanding one. So Germany built battleships to challenge Britain's naval supremacy and Britain retaliated by building Dreadnought battleships. Germany planned the Berlin-Baghdad railway, to run through southeast Europe and Turkey to the Persian Gulf. Britain and France formed a military alliance with Russia against Germany and its allies, Austro-Hungary and Turkey. France increased its conscript army to match Germany's military might and Russia designed its railway system with a future war against Germany, Austro-Hungary and Turkey in mind.

The Balkan Wars and Serbian nationalism

That imperialism meant wars between colonial powers as well as the enslavement of colonial peoples had been shown as early as 1904, when Russia's drive to the Pacific collided with Japan's drive west. Russia's unexpected military defeat sparked the 1905 Revolution. War between the great powers threatened again in 1906 and 1911, with a clash of French and German interests in Morocco. Rival imperialisms pushed and collided throughout Africa, the Middle East and Asia and China. But the truly dangerous area was southeast Europe: the Balkans, where the Great Powers regarded particular local states as clients.

There had been wars between these states in 1912 and 1913. First Serbia, Greece, Montenegro and Bulgaria fell upon the remaining Turkish territories of Thrace and Macedonia, leaving Turkey with only a narrow strip of Eastern Thrace. Then Greece, Serbia and Romania, egged on by the Great Powers, fell upon Bulgaria. Trotsky was a war correspondent in the Balkans in 1912-13. On the eve of the First World War he reported on the terrible legacy left by Russia, France, Germany and Britain as they meddled in Balkan affairs and competed for access to important trade routes:

> The states that today occupy the Balkan Peninsula were manufactured by European diplomacy around the table at the Congress of Berlin in 1879. There it was that all the measures were taken to convert the national diversity of the region into a regular mêlée of petty states. None of them was to develop beyond a certain limit, each separately was entangled in diplomatic bonds, and counterposed to all the rest, and finally the whole lot were condemned to helplessness in relation to the Great Powers and their continual intrigues and machinations.[106]

The first Balkan War of 1912 ended in the treaty of London; the second Balkan War of 1913 ended in the treaty of Bucharest. But Trotsky warned treaties could not remove the drive to war: "The new boundary lines have been drawn across the living bodies of nations that have been lacerated bled white and exhausted. Every one of the Balkan states now includes within its borders a compact minority that is hostile to it. Such are the results of the work carried out by the capitalist governments".[107]

The whole region was an explosive powder keg. In June 1914 heir to the Hapsburg dynasty, Archduke Franz Ferdinand visited the Austrian-run province of Bosnia. Serbian nationalists who wanted to drive the Austrians out of the province and incorporate it into neighbouring Serbia, assassinated him in Sarajevo.

What happened next is a matter of diplomatic record; Austria declared war on Serbia, Russia's client state; Russia declared war on Austria; Germany told Russia to stay out of the crisis; France backed Russia, her ally; Britain supported France and went to war against Germany, using the pretext of German troops moving through Belgium as the excuse. Within weeks, 44 years of peace in western Europe gave way to war involving all its major states. Some historians have argued the First World War was an avoidable accident; it was an accident waiting to happen. The shooting of the Austrian Archduke by Gavrilo Princip was the spark but not the cause of the First World War.

The rivalries and conflicts of the great robber powers exploded into the greatest organised slaughter the world had yet seen. Tens of millions went out to fight for their masters and 20 million would die, half of them civilians. What Lenin dubbed "an epoch of wars and revolutions" had begun for real. It shattered the international socialist movement. Although it was an imperialist war—a war for colonies, markets and profit—the vast majority of the leaders of the Second International parties in nearly all the warring states abandoned internationalism; instead they chose national unity and backed their own governments.

There were a few brave exceptions. The Russian socialists, particularly the Bolsheviks, refused to support the Tsar's war machine. The Serbian party and the Bulgarian majority party stood their ground too, in the face of murderous persecution. The Italian and American socialist parties were not forced to choose immediately as their ruling classes remained neutral at the start, while the Spanish, Scandinavian and Dutch were in this position throughout the war. Everywhere else the socialists who openly opposed the war were at first a small minority: Rosa Luxemburg, Clara Zetkin, Franz Mehring and Karl Liebknecht in Germany; John Maclean and Sylvia Pankhurst in Britain; Alfred Rosmer in France; and James Connolly in Ireland.

From opposition to capitulation

The German Social Democratic Party (SPD) was the biggest and most influential socialist party in the Second International and claimed the heritage of Marx and Engels. With 111 elected deputies in the Reichstag in 1914, it set the example for all the other parties in the Second International and socialists everywhere looked to it for a lead.

On 20 February 1914 Rosa Luxemburg, leader of the SPD left wing and, with Lenin, joint author and mover of the anti-war resolution at the 1907 International Congress in Stuttgart, was arrested for inciting soldiers to mutiny. The basis of the charge was a public speech in which she argued; "If they expect us to murder our French or other foreign brothers, then let us tell them, 'No, under no circumstances'".[108] In court she turned defence into attack and her speech, later published under the title *Militarism, War and the Working Class*, is one of the sharpest condemnations of imperialism. She was sentenced to a year in jail but not detained on the spot. On leaving the court she went straight to a demonstration and repeated almost word for word the same anti-war message.

On 25 July an emergency edition of the SPD newspaper carried the leadership's appeal for mass demonstrations to stop the war:

> The class conscious German proletariat raises a fiery protest in the name of humanity and civilisation, against the criminal activities of the war-mongers. Not a drop of a German soldier's blood must be sacrificed to the Austrian despots' lust for power. Comrades, we call on you to express in mass meetings the unshakeable will for peace.[109]

On Tuesday 28 July workers went onto the streets all over Germany. The next day the newspapers reported that big anti-war demonstrations had taken place in all the cities and larger towns, especially in the industrial areas. The same night thousands packed into Brussels' biggest meeting hall for an anti-war rally. They cheered as French socialist leader Jean Jaurès put his arm around Hugo Hasse, the SPD parliamentary deputy.

Two days earlier in Paris the CGT union newspaper ran the headline, "Workers must answer any declaration of war by a revolutionary general strike" and the following day there was a massive anti-war march in Paris.[110] On 30 July the SPD paper *Vorwärts* declared: "The socialist proletariat refuses all responsibility for the events being conjured up by a ruling class blinded to the point of madness".[111] On 31 July the International Socialist Bureau of the Second International issued its call for a struggle against war. But the following day the German government declared war on Russia and proclaimed a state of emergency. That afternoon Jaures was assassinated on his return to Paris by right-wing army officers.

Two days later on 3 August, the parliamentary group of the SPD dropped a bombshell by deciding it would vote in favour of war credits to finance the Kaiser's armies. Of their 111 deputies only 15 were prepared to vote against war but when their request to be allowed to do so was voted down, they submitted to party discipline. On 4 August the SPD parliamentary group of deputies trooped into the Reichstag and voted en-bloc to fund the war aims of the German government. The party then issued the following statement, a complete about turn from its anti-war stance issued days earlier:

> For our people and its peace, much, if not everything, is at stake in the event of the victory of Russian despotism. Our task is to ward off the danger, to safeguard the culture and independence of our own country. We do not leave the fatherland in the lurch in the hour of danger.[112]

The shock of betrayal

For Lenin, exiled from Russia, the outbreak of war was not unexpected. What shook him was the betrayal of the German Social Democrats.

When he read the report of the Reichstag vote he assumed the newspaper was a forgery published by the German High Command to demoralise opponents of the war. He was not the only stunned socialist. For Rosa Luxemburg it was a terrible blow but she overcame her immediate feeling of despair. On the same day the SPD deputies capitulated, a small group of socialists met in her Berlin apartment to organise against the war and mount a fight within their own party. It was not until November that Karl Liebknecht, one of the 15 SPD deputies opposed to war, defied party discipline to vote with his conscience in the Reichstag against further war credits. He joined the group around Rosa that would form the Spartakus League.

Trotsky remembered how "the telegram telling of the capitulation of German Social Democracy shocked me even more than the declaration of war in spite of the fact that I was far from a naïve idealising of German socialism".[113] Bolshevik economist Bukharin wrote that the vote on 4 August "was the greatest tragedy of our lives".[114]

Lenin was quick to come to terms with the truth. In July, weeks before the outbreak of war, he had written an article which argued for revolutionary opposition to war. It was no surprise the Bolsheviks were the first to take a clear position on the 4 August debacle. On 24 August Lenin drafted *The Tasks of Revolutionary Social Democracy in the European War*, which laid out a clear path for revolutionaries in the tough years that lay ahead. He was in no doubt about the "imperialist and dynastic" character of the war, or that the SPD vote was:

> a betrayal of socialism. The leaders of the International committed treachery by voting for war credits, by justifying and defending the war and by joining the bourgeois governments of the belligerent countries.[115]

The task of the working class was to fight the imperialist war by using the weapon of class struggle, culminating in civil war. In this Lenin was unequivocal. Revolutionary defeatism means welcoming the defeat of your own country: "The socialists of all belligerent countries should express their wish that all their 'own' governments should be defeated".[116] Though Lenin was for the defeat of his own ruling class, it did not imply that he considered the German ruling class any less imperialist. For him the war was not produced by the crimes of one country but by the general crisis of monopoly capitalism that could only be ended by revolution.

Class or nation?

By contrast, when it came to the crunch the leaders of German socialism were terrified of betraying Germany. The Kaiser had taunted them as, "fellows without a country". On 4 August they responded by declaring "we will not leave the fatherland in the lurch in its hour of danger",[117] and betrayed the international working class instead. The majority of the Social Democrat leaders followed the SPD and backed the war. The Belgian Emile Vandervelde, executive secretary of the Second International, entered his country's war cabinet. How could the leaders of the working class movement justify such a betrayal to their own followers? The excuse was that the enemy abroad was worse than the enemy at home!

To hide their betrayal, the SPD leaders argued Germany was a more progressive society than backward Russia. They told German workers that the Kaiser's army was defending the prospects of socialism and its future victory in Europe when it fought reactionary Tsarism and British colonialism. In the name of socialism they sent millions of young men to their deaths.

The Russian socialists who supported the war claimed they were fighting despotic Prussian militarism. In France the leaders of the Socialist Party and the syndicalist leaders of the CGT, the main union federation, swung behind their country's war effort using the capitulation of the German socialists as their excuse. Because the SPD had voted for the Kaiser's war budget, the French claimed they had no choice but to enter a "sacred union" to defend their own country. They argued German imperialism had to be destroyed if the possibility of socialism was to be assured.

The response of the leaders of the British labour movement

In Britain, the Labour Party and the union leaders backed the war as "a war for democracy" despite the fact that they were fighting alongside autocratic Tsarist Russia. Labour leader Ramsay MacDonald was a pacifist and when he voiced doubts about the conflict he was deposed by the patriotic trade union bureaucracy and replaced by Arthur Henderson.

In 1915 Henderson would be rewarded with a cabinet post in the National Government. He was the man who arranged the 1915 agreement by which the unions abandoned their members' defence, including the right to strike. Speaking for the union leaders who now controlled the Labour Party, Ben Tillett championed patriotism and spoke at army recruitment rallies. His war cry was: "In a strike I am for my class, right or wrong; in a war I am for my country, right or wrong".[118]

The supposedly Marxist leader of the British Socialist Party (BSP), H M Hyndman, argued that a defensive war against Germany in support of Belgium's freedom was justified. His decision to throw the weight of the BSP into the government's recruiting drive produced a storm of protest from local BSP branches. "One after another branches at Stepney, West Ham, Bow and Bromley, Central Hackney, Pollokshaws and elsewhere expressed their opposition. Fifteen of the 18 London branches assembled at an all-London conference and demanded that the statement be withdrawn".[119] In Glasgow John Maclean opposed the BSP leadership's line and won the local branches to an anti-war position:

> It is our business as socialists to develop 'class patriotism', refusing to murder one another for a sordid world capitalism. The absurdity of the present situation is surely apparent when we see British socialists going out to murder German socialists with the object of crushing Kaiserism and Prussian militarism. The only real enemy to Prussian militarism was and is German Social Democracy.[120]

Lenin was quick to expose the hypocrisy of all the European ruling classes: "The bourgeoisie of each country is asserting that it is out to defeat the enemy—not for plunder and the seizure of territory but for the liberation of all other peoples except its own".[121] He castigated the official leaders of the working class movement for tailing behind their own ruling class and for lying to themselves and their followers about the nature of the war.

Paying the price for illusions in the 'peaceful road' to socialism

The Second International died on 4 August 1914 but its death was not quite as sudden as it then seemed. With hindsight it is easy to see that the vote for war by the SPD in the German Reichstag did not come out of the blue but was the culmination of years of adapting to imperialism and parliamentary politics.

While the leaders of the Second International talked class struggle and Marxism at May Day rallies, their day-to-day practice was strictly reformist. The prospect of a peaceful road to socialism had seemed to open up; instead it led to the slaughter of 1914. How had this betrayal come about?

Symbolically, the Second International had been founded at a special congress in Paris on 14 July 1889, the centenary of the storming of the Bastille and the start of the French Revolution. It proclaimed itself heir to the First International in which Karl Marx played a leading role. The International became the focus for some flourishing workers' parties that commonly called themselves social democratic—a term Marx disliked, preferring communist. They were not the only workers' parties but they grew to dominate the movement in the years up to 1914.

The rapid expansion of industry and the growth of the working class created a new, mass audience for these socialist organisations in the late 19th century.

But, following the defeat of Chartism, the failure of the European revolutions of 1848 and the crushing of the Paris Commune in 1870, their leaders did not feel up for a direct challenge to the state. Instead they followed a strategy developed by the German SPD, which took advantage of limited electoral reforms to win seats in local councils and national parliaments. Alongside this electoral approach and subordinate to it, they focussed on building trade unions and other forms of working class organisation like co-ops, sports and cultural clubs.

The German party, founded in 1875, became the model for the others. In France the United Socialist Party (SFIO) was founded in 1905 and won over 100 seats in the 1914 election. The year before the Italian Socialist Party (PSI) won a quarter of the total vote cast and 78 deputies. The Austro-Hungarian party had won over a million votes and 82 deputies. In the USA the American Socialist Party, founded in 1901, by 1912 gained 125,000 members and polled 800,000 votes. Parties on similar lines were built in Poland, Sweden, Belgium and the Netherlands. In Britain success was more modest but real. In the 1906 general election the newly formed Labour Party returned 29 MPs.

From Scandinavia to the Balkans, Marxist social democratic parties gained members, votes and deputies. Weaker but nonetheless significant movements developed in Chile, Spain, Switzerland and Uruguay, all affiliated to the Second International and apparently committed to the socialist reconstruction of society and an uncompromising opposition to nationalism and war. It was an illusion. There were differences between the various parties but basically they were pseudo revolutionary, combining an uncompromising verbal hostility to capitalism with a practical activity that was confined to winning members and votes. The British and Australian Labour Parties were exceptional in lacking Marxist rhetoric and revolutionary pretensions.

Karl Kautsky, leading theoretician of both the German party and the International, had long argued the downfall of capitalism was inevitable. Socialists could sit back and wait for it. This mechanical, do nothing Marxism was the negation of Marx's insistence on the centrality of class struggle and working class self-activity.

The apparatus had become an end in itself. Confrontation with the state or even the employers was avoided where possible. The politics of the SPD and most of the other social democratic and labour parties that took their lead from it, were in theory orthodox Marxist; but really the SPD was a reformist, not a revolutionary party. It was geared to the patient work of convincing workers to vote socialist in elections. Though the German trade unions were strong, they were seen as having an auxiliary and subsidiary role in the economic struggle. By 1913 the SPD and its trade unions owned property worth 90 million marks. The party had a layer of parliamentarians, trade union bureaucrats and full time staff. They certainly had a lot more to lose than their chains.

August 1914 shattered the illusion. The shadow boxing was over and the party leaders had to choose: stick to their internationalism, oppose the war, face imprisonment and the seizure of their assets; or support their own state and back the slaughter.

Opposition to the war
There were groups of workers ready to resist the jingoism and war fever. Socialists and trade union militants were used to lies in the press and their principles coming under attack. In Britain, the last few years before the war had seen enormous industrial upheaval that continued right through from 1910 until the summer of 1914. The Great Unrest, as this four-year period came to be known, saw a doubling of trade union membership and the emergence of a range of socialist groups who rejected parliamentarianism and stressed direct action. During the build up to the war these groups campaigned against it.

The leaders could hardly claim no one would support an anti-war stance. In the days before hostilities broke out there were mass demonstrations of workers against war throughout Europe. Thousands flocked to rallies in London, Paris, Brussels, Berlin and St Petersburg. The huge rallies organised by the SPD had so scared the Kaiser that he considered proclaiming martial law to have the SPD leadership arrested.

As late as August 1914 the official leadership of the British Labour Party was involved in anti-war agitation and participated in the monster Stop the War rally in Trafalgar Square, where Keir Hardie and Arthur Henderson put their names to the leaflet that argued: "Workers stand together for peace! Combine and conquer the militarist enemy and the self-seeking imperialists today, once and for all. Down with class rule! Down with the rule of brute force! Down with the war!"[122]

The moment war was declared, those same leaders rushed to support it. The German and Austrian Social Democratic Parties, the British Labour Party, the TUC and the leaders of the British Socialist Party, French socialist and trade union leaders, the veteran Russian Marxist Plekhanov and the anarchist Kropotkin, all backed their own rulers. Those who had doubts: Hugo Hasse and Karl Kautsky in Germany, Keir Hardie, Philip Snowden and Ramsay MacDonald in Britain, fudged or kept quiet in order to preserve party unity and avoid being accused of betraying the nation. Keir Hardie opposed the war on pacifist grounds and had even suggested that the threat of a European general strike could prevent it. Yet only a few days after it started he wrote: "A nation at war must be united. With the boom of the enemy's guns within earshot, the boys who have gone forth to fight their country's battles must not be disheartened by any discordant note at home." At the end of 1915 he wrote, "I have never said or written anything to dissuade young men from enlisting".[123]

The lack of a movement was not the explanation or excuse for the cowardice of the socialist and trade union leaders; rather it was the cowardice of these leaders which demobilised the movement as it faced its greatest test. Of course there is no denying the growing pro-war mood after war was declared, but the existence of a widespread anti-war movement before the war, and the mounting opposition as it went on, showed the basis for resistance always existed. In the week war began, James Connolly expressed his anger and frustration in the Glasgow-based socialist newspaper, *Forward*:

> What then becomes of all our resolutions, all our protests of fraternisation, all our threats of general strike, all our hopes for the future? Were they all as sound and fury, signifying nothing? Even an unsuccessful attempt at social revolution by force of arms would be less disastrous to the socialist cause than the act of socialists allowing themselves to be used in the slaughter of their brothers in the cause. A great continental uprising of the working class would stop the war: a universal protest at public meetings will not save a single life from being wantonly slaughtered.[124]

Having voted for war the German SPD leaders were admitted to the inner sanctum around the Kaiser's government, where they stayed for four years, increasingly isolated from the German workers and losing any feel for the mood among them and the soldiers at the front. If instead the leaders of the SPD and the other European parties had stood by their principles, like the Russians and Serbians, they could have shortened or even stopped the bloodbath to come.

Few really grasped what the war would be like, how long it would last or where it would lead. One who did was Karl Marx's friend and collaborator, Friedrich Engels. As far back as 1887 he envisaged:

A world war of an extent and violence hitherto undreamt of. Eight to ten million soldiers will slaughter each other and devour the whole of Europe until they have stripped it barer than any swarm of locusts has ever done. The devastation of the Thirty Years War compressed into three or four years and spread over the whole continent; famine, pestilence, demoralisation both of armies and of the mass of the people, produced by acute distress; chaos in our trade, industry, commerce and credit, ending in general bankruptcy; collapse of the old states to such an extent that crowns will roll on the pavements and there will be nobody to pick them up.

The absolute impossibility of foreseeing how this will all end and who will be the victors; only one result is absolutely certain: general exhaustion and the creation of the conditions for the final victory of the working class. This is the prospect when the system of mutual outbidding in armaments, taken to its final extreme, at last bears its inevitable fruits.[125]

Yet almost everyone involved in the war thought it would be short. "The German crown prince spoke of a 'bright, jolly war'. He expected a repetition of the Franco-Prussian war of 1870, when the French army was defeated within weeks. French soldiers wrote 'à Berlin' on the railway carriages taking them to the front. 'It will be all over by Christmas' was the common British refrain".[126]

The early predictions on both sides of a short war and a quick victory proved utterly misplaced. In the first few months the German army raced through Belgium and northern France to within 50 miles of Paris, while on the Eastern front the initial Russian advance against German lines drove west into East Prussia. But both advances were checked and forced back. On the Western front, after the battle of the Marne and the first battle of Ypres, the Germans retreated to form a defensive line of trenches stretching from the North Sea to the Swiss border, while on the Eastern front the Russians suffered terrible losses at the battles of Tannenberg and the Massurian Lakes and were driven back east out of German territory.

The pre-war military mind-set was the cavalry charge, but the war that was supposed to be over by Christmas became a battle of attrition with armies bogged down in unrelenting artillery bombardments and trench warfare that lasted four years. It spread from the Eastern and Western fronts to the Italian-Austrian border, Greece and the Balkans, Turkey, Mesopotamia and Egypt. There was fighting in Togoland, South West Africa, East Africa, New Guinea and Samoa, China and the Pacific Islands. There was naval warfare too—in the Pacific and Indian Oceans, the Falklands, the Baltic, the North Sea and the North Atlantic. The allies imposed a naval blockade of Germany and Germany retaliated by launching a submarine war against their merchant fleets. This drew the USA into the war in 1917.

It is now estimated the war killed 20 million: at least ten million military dead and the same number of civilians. The French lost almost 20 percent of their men of fighting age (1.4 million), the Russians 15 percent (2 million) and the Germans 13 percent (2 million).

Britain lost an entire generation: 750,000 men under the age of 30 killed and another 1.5 million permanently wounded (British figures include Ireland). Two hundred and thirty thousand troops from the rest of Britain's Empire were killed. Of these India lost the greatest number, something that is ignored or forgotten.

It was the first war involving all Europe since 1815. It involved the mass of the populations of the countries that fought it, including the USA from 1917. In France and Germany 80 percent of males of military age were conscripted. Austro Hungary mobilised 75 percent of its adult male population, while Britain, Serbia and Turkey called up between 50 and 60 percent. In Russia sixteen million served in the war.[127]

The international labour movement was now split into three main tendencies: the reformist right wing, outright supporters of the war; the centre, led by Karl Kautsky, who sought to achieve peace within the framework of capitalism; and the revolutionary left: Lenin and the Bolsheviks, the group around Rosa Luxemburg and Karl Liebknecht and various other socialists for all of whom only socialist revolution could put an end to war.

Rosa Luxemburg stuck to her principles and as a result spent over three years of the war in a German prison. There she wrote what remains one of the best denunciations of war and those socialists who supported it, the *Junius Pamphlet*. On her release from jail at the end of the war, she plunged into intense activity to prevent a repetition of the slaughter. Because of that political stand and her editorship of the newly founded German Communist Party's newspaper *Die Rote Fahne* (the Red Flag) she was brutally murdered in January 1919 by a paramilitary Freikorp unit under the explicit orders of the right-wing SPD leadership.

Lenin's revolutionary defeatism

In Russia the consistent record of resistance and opposition to the war by Lenin and the Bolsheviks was crucial. From his Swiss exile Lenin issued a stream of statements and pamphlets, from *The Tasks of Revolutionary Social Democracy in the European War*, written in August 1914, through to *Socialism and War*, written jointly with Zinoviev in July 1915. This argued: "The so-called Centre of the German and other social democratic parties has in actual fact faint-heartedly capitulated to the opportunists. A new, Third International must be built on the basis of uncompromising internationalism".[128]

Lenin insisted that the key task for the Bolsheviks was to agitate for the working class to end the war through revolution and the overthrow of Tsarism, to "turn the present imperialist war into civil war".[129] Lenin's "revolutionary defeatism" urged workers in every country to fight their own governments and see their own ruling class as the enemy, whatever the military consequences. Revolutionary defeatism flowed from Lenin's distinctive application of Marxism that directly linked monopoly capitalism to imperialism and war. From this analysis came his insistence that "politics is concentrated economics", that workers' struggles could only deal with the power of the capitalist class if they ignored the false division between economics and politics and made their target the capitalist state.

Of course Lenin's position was highly controversial and provocative. Many Bolsheviks rejected it at first, finding it too extreme. However, after initial confusion and a period of argument and debate, it proved to be clear, sharp and productive. Because more and more Bolshevik groups began to adopt this principled stand against the war, the party was able to conduct widespread propaganda and agitation, among the workers and peasants and also inside Russia's armed forces, with the specific aim of encouraging mutinies.

The Bolshevik soldier agitators were instrumental in splitting the Tsarist army on class lines and were thus able to instil a confidence among the rank and file to challenge their officers and generals. And because it was largely a peasant army, the spirit of rebellion, already present in the villages, was increased there too by soldiers returning from the front on leave—or by those deserting the front.

This was one of the key differences between 1905 and 1917. In 1905 the Tsar's peasant army remained largely intact and was able to smash the workers' uprising in Moscow and crush the soviets. In 1917, because of their agitation inside the army and navy between 1915 and 1917, the Bolshevik soldiers and sailors were able to recruit and influence thousands of their comrades in arms, undermining both the officer corps and Kerensky's pro-war Provisional government.

What Ralph Darlington calls, "the initial political stupor inside the Russian labour movement" gave way from mid-1915 onwards to a revival of militant strike activity.

This meant the Bolsheviks were increasingly able to give a voice to the mounting political and industrial opposition to the war and the Tsar, which eventually exploded in February 1917.

Working class women

In Russia like everywhere else, the First World War resulted in such a huge increase in the numbers of women workers and their significance for the war effort, that their active involvement was essential for any generalised protest of the working class to be effective.

In Russia government, employers, liberals, feminists and some revolutionaries considered women workers to be the most backward section of their class; they were in for a shock. From the second year of the war there were growing numbers of strikes, scattered throughout the country, involving women industrial workers striking not only over pay and deteriorating working conditions, but also the lack of respect shown them by their employers and foremen. The strikes and demonstrations initiated by women in Petrograd in February 1917, which triggered the overthrow of Tsarism and the Russian Revolution, need to be seen in the context of this growing popular unrest.

Despite the repression and an initial pro-war euphoria stoked up by the ruling class, women from the Bolshevik Party in Petrograd made efforts from the outbreak of the war to organise women workers and soldiers' wives, the *soldatki*. As popular dissatisfaction at deteriorating living conditions and anger at the enormous military casualties spread, this grassroots agitation found an increasingly receptive female working class audience.

At the beginning of the February Revolution two Bolsheviks, Nina Agadzhanova and Mariia Vydrina, organised mass meetings of workers and soldiers' wives, workplace strikes and mass demonstrations, searches for weapons to arm the crowds as well as securing the release of political prisoners and setting up first aid units.[130]

Russian women were not unique in this respect. Women in Turin, Glasgow, Paris, Berlin, Leipzig and countless other centres were also initiating struggles against the war and its impact on their lives. The Bolsheviks spearheaded the international opposition to the war among the growing socialist forces.

February 1917: Soviets and the Provisional government

The February revolution was begun from below, overcoming the resistance of its own revolutionary organisations, the initiative being taken of their own accord by the most oppressed and downtrodden part of the proletariat—the women textile workers.[131]
— *Trotsky*

Revolutions always seem to come like a bolt from the blue. No one forecasts them. The Russian Revolution began like this but it was no isolated thunderbolt. Like the Dublin Rising in 1916, it was part of the growing international storm brewing against the horrors and hardships of the First World War. By the start of 1917 the world was trapped in the third year of a terrible bloodbath with no end in sight. Slaughter on this scale had never been seen before. Strikes, food riots and disaffection at home combined with desertions and mutinies at the front to push a number of countries close to breaking point.

Russia's backward peasant economy and its archaic state structure made it the first to crack. Military incompetence at the top led to a series of calamitous defeats. The pattern was set from the start at the battle of Tannenburg in 1914, where 300,000 Russian soldiers were slaughtered and 90,000 taken prisoner by a far smaller German force. General Samsonov committed suicide when he realised the scale of the defeat but the Tsar's commander-in-chief said: "We are happy to have made such a sacrifice for our allies".[132]

By 1917 over 2 million Russians had been slaughtered in battles no less bloody than the Somme or Verdun. There was famine in the countryside and desperate food shortages in the cities. Rampant inflation and the collapse of the transport system fuelled the chaos. Three years of total war brought prolonged hardship and suffering for the vast majority of Russians. For the rich, profits were sky high:

> Speculation of all kinds and gambling on the market went to the point of paroxysm. Enormous fortunes arose out of the bloody foam. The lack of bread in the capital did not stop the court jeweller Faberge from boasting that he had never done such a flourishing business. Lady-in-waiting Vyrubova says that in no other season were such gowns to be seen as in the winter of 1915-16, and never were so many diamonds purchased.
>
> The nightclubs were brimful of the heroes of the rear. Nobody had any fear of spending too much. A continual shower of gold fell from above. 'Society' held out its hands and pockets. Aristocratic ladies spread their skirts high. All came running to grab and gobble, in fear lest the blessed rain should stop. And all rejected with indignation the shameful idea of a premature peace.[133]

The war unleashed rampant inflation. The rich didn't notice it but it hammered Russia's workers and peasants. If the index of prices in 1913 was equal to 100, then it reached 220 at the end of 1916, and 512 by the end of 1917.[134] Real wages fell, slowly during 1914 and 1915, then rapidly as 1916 wore on. A very sharp rise in prices in the winter of 1916 brought massive food shortages and led to a sharp fall in the wages of the metalworkers—an important cause of the February Revolution.

There were two revolutions in Russia in 1917. The first was completely spontaneous, not called by anyone: certainly not by the revolutionaries who were taken aback. In January 1917 Lenin was living in Switzerland and had already spent ten years abroad in his second period of state imposed exile. Addressing a meeting of young workers in Zurich three weeks before the February revolution, he said: "The coming years in Europe, precisely because of the predatory war, will lead to popular uprisings under the leadership of the proletariat." But he went on to say: "We of the older generation may not live to see the decisive battles of the coming revolution".[135]

The revolution starts here

To everyone's surprise the revolution was begun on 23 February in Petrograd[136] by angry women textile workers celebrating International Working Women's Day. With only ten days' supply of flour and the bread shops empty, the military chief of Petrograd had cut the already meagre food ration. Vasilii Kayurov, factory worker and leading member of the Vyborg District Committee of the Bolshevik Party, was prominent in the February events. Later he confirmed that on 23 February, "no one thought of such an imminent possibility of revolution".[137]

The night before a group of women textile workers had met to plan how they might organise a strike on the following day: to celebrate International Women's Day itself, to express their anger at the lack of food and to show solidarity with male workers at the nearby Putilov works, locked out for striking over wages and demanding the reinstatement of their sacked workmates. These women were part of a group established by Bolsheviks in Petrograd, in recognition of the growing importance of women workers to the wartime labour movement. They had been working around the factories where large numbers of women were employed, carrying out anti-war agitation and drawing the *soldatki*, the soldiers' wives, into their movement.

Kayurov was invited to their planning meeting and strongly advised them against striking at this time. The local leadership saw May Day as a more appropriate time for action. The bitterness at bread shortages among the textile workers, many with husbands fighting at the front, was such that they went ahead and organised a strike on the following morning anyway. Later Kayurov wrote:

> To my surprise, on 23 February at an emergency meeting in the corridor of the Erikson works, we learned of a strike in the textile factories and of the arrival of delegates from the women workers who announced they were supporting the metal workers. They had blatantly ignored the decision of the District Committee of the Party and gone on strike after I'd appealed to them only the night before to stay cool and disciplined. With reluctance we agreed to spread the strike and other workers followed. Once there is a mass strike, you have to call everybody out and take the lead.[138]

The women at the textile plants in the Vyborg district held morning workplace meetings, downed tools, walked out together and moved swiftly in large groups from one factory to another. They demanded workers in other industries, notably metalworkers seen as the vanguard of the local labour movement, join the strike to show the bosses and the government that the Petrograd workers were not prepared to take it any more. The slogans they were chanting as they marched through the streets made it clear their strike was about more than the lack of wages and food: "Down with the War! Down with high prices. Down with hunger!"[139]

At the engineering factories they made their point by throwing whatever they could get their hands on—snowballs, stones, sticks—at the factory windows and doors, and by invading the premises. They managed to convince the mass of workers to join them. The main priority was to persuade the men, soldiers as well as workers, to join them. The fact that so many did showed that the women were expressing what most workers felt: enough was enough! They were joined by thousands of other women who for weeks had been forced to queue morning noon and night in the cold winter streets for fuel and food.

According to an eyewitness, "the women, driven to desperation by starvation and war, came along like a hurricane that destroys everything in its path with the violence of an elemental force. This revolutionary march of working women, full of hatred of centuries of oppression, was the spark that set light to the flame of the February revolution".[140] Police blocked the bridges into the city centre, so the women, their numbers now swollen, simply slid down the embankments and walked across the ice on the frozen river Neva. They looted the food shops of the rich. They stopped the tramcars as tram workers, many of them women, came out on strike to join the protest. Demonstrators were overturning the captured trams to serve as barricades and hinder the movement of police and troops sent to quell them. By noon over 50,000 had joined their protest on the Sampsonievsky Prospekt, one of the city's main thoroughfares.

The government brought out its most reliable troops, the feared Cossack cavalry. Rather than run away the women stood their ground and simply encircled them, making their case to the Cossacks in simple terms and expressing their anger at being exploited by war profiteers, while their men were being slaughtered at the front. Seamstress Zhenia Egorova, secretary of the Vyborg district Bolsheviks, appealed to the Cossacks to disobey their orders and not shoot down the protestors.[141] The women were amazed when the soldiers lowered their rifles and sabres, leading their horses away from the crowds. They did not mutiny but they did not do what they were ordered to do either. The women cheered them.

Trotsky described another incident involving Cossack cavalry:

The Cossacks, without openly breaking discipline, failed to force the crowd to disperse, but flowed through it in streams. This was repeated three or four times and brought the two sides even closer together. Individual Cossacks began to reply to the workers' questions and even to enter into momentary conversation with them.

The officers hastened to separate the Cossack patrol from the workers and abandoning the idea of dispersing them, lined the Cossacks out across the street in a barrier to prevent the demonstrators getting to the city centre. But even this did not help; standing stock still in perfect discipline, the Cossacks did not hinder the workers from 'diving' under their horses.

The revolution does not choose its paths; it made its first steps towards victory under the belly of a Cossack's horse. A remarkable incident![142]

The following day the movement doubled in size. Historian Orlando Figes, a leading proponent of the "Bolshevik coup" interpretation, tells us "the masses were barely involved and motivated purely by economic need". In his 1990 publication, *The Russian Revolution 1899-1919*, Richard Pipes also ignores what actually happened: "The Russian Revolution was made neither by the forces of nature nor by anonymous masses but by identifiable men pursuing their own advantages".[143]

The British Consul General in Russia, Bruce Lockhart, depressed at the collapse of military authority, understood much better than Figes and Pipes both the mass involvement and the highly charged political nature of the revolt: "For the first time in the capital since 1905 there were cries of 'Down with the autocracy'".[144] By the time the Bolsheviks finally got round to issuing a leaflet on the third day of the revolution calling for a general strike, the Petrograd mass strike was already developing into an armed uprising!

Although the Okhrana already knew the February events were not Bolshevik inspired, it didn't stop them arresting Elena Stasova and Lenin's older sister Anna Elizarova, both leading Bolsheviks in the city. Stasova was held with 17 other women in an overcrowded cell.

Later in the evening the women heard gunfire from outside the prison and a man appeared and opened the cell door, telling them to leave. The younger women hesitated, fearing they would be shot trying to escape.

Stasova, the oldest among them, decided to chance it and led them out into the courtyard. To their great delight they saw crowds of firemen shouting "liberty!" They had come to free all political prisoners.

The demonstrations grew bigger over the next few days. The Tsar's armed police attacked them and the government tried to use the thousands of troops garrisoned in the city to crush them. The Military Governor of Petrograd issued the order to fire on any demonstrators refusing to disperse and in one incident alone 40 were killed and many more wounded as police machine-gunned the unarmed crowds from the rooftops. But some of the army regiments refused to fire on the strikers and on the third day mutiny spread among the troops. The first to rebel was the Volinsky regiment, deployed against the crowds the previous day. Sickened by what their comrades had been forced to do, a group of young lads turned against their officers and marched out of the barracks to side with the workers. Other regiments followed.

The key moment came when the crack Preobrazhensky regiment sided with the revolt. There was no turning back now, for when its officers and commanders tried to physically stop them, this regiment shot their officers. By day four virtually the entire city workforce was on strike and mutinies swept through the remaining barracks.

There were organised raids on the government armouries. Rifles and ammunition were seized to arm the anti-government revolt. Mutinous soldiers and sailors turned up at all the other jails to release the prisoners. Russian commanders on the Eastern front were ordered to send trainloads of troops to restore order in the Tsar's imperial city but on arrival the troops went over to the side of the revolution and joined the huge workers' demonstrations. Similar movements swept Moscow and other Russian cities.

On the 26 February the Tsar ordered the Duma to disperse. 27 February saw the whole city on strike. 70,000 troops joined 400,000 strikers on a mass demonstration; ominously for the authorities, the slogans chanted were, "Down with the autocracy! Down with the war!"

Right up until February 27, with Tsarism teetering on the brink, the bourgeoisie still tried to avoid the revolution and to compromise with the monarchy. As the Menshevik Sukhanov wrote: "Attempts were being made at deals with Tsarism. This was not only independent of the popular movement but at its expense and obviously aimed at its destruction. The position of the bourgeoisie was clear: it was a position on the one hand of keeping their distance from the revolution and betraying it to Tsarism, and on the other of exploiting it for their own manoeuvres".[145] But this position became untenable as it became clear revolution would triumph.

The return of the soviets

On 27 February the Petrograd Soviet of Workers' Deputies re-emerged, twelve years after the Tsar had crushed its predecessor during the failed 1905 revolution. While this was happening the remaining Duma deputies decided they had better meet and form some kind of Provisional Committee to ride with a revolution they had not supported.

On 28 February the Tsar's ministers were arrested. On 1 March the soldiers' section of the Petrograd Soviet formed, there was a general strike in Moscow, and the Moscow Soviet held its first session. The last remaining troops still loyal to the Tsar surrendered. On 2 March Nicholas II, who days before seemed all-powerful, was forced to abdicate in favour of his brother, Grand Duke Mikhail.

The Provisional Committee of the Duma, with the full agreement of the Menshevik/SR block that dominated the executive of the Petrograd Soviet, declared itself the Provisional government. The next day it was Grand Duke Mikhail's turn to abdicate. The newly formed Provisional government announced the revolution to the world by radio broadcast. The Romanov dynasty, rulers of Great Russia since 1613, had been toppled in a week. But who or what would replace it?

In the weeks following the Tsar's abdication, soviets popped up everywhere to represent not just workers but also conscript soldiers in revolt against Russia's involvement in the war, and the growing numbers of poor peasants seizing the land and burning the estates of the wealthy landowners.

The Provisional government

In the days before the new soviets could really take root, and with the Tsar only just overthrown, the new government was announced at a mass meeting in the Tauride Palace, the same building where, bizarrely, the new soviet also met. With hundreds of workers and soldiers crowded into the room, Miliukov, leader of the pro-capitalist Constitutional Democrats and a key member of the new self-appointed regime, responded to a heckler who asked: "Who elected you?" He blurted out the lie, "we were chosen by the Russian Revolution".[146]

Tired of war and corruption, people were demanding a new society, but what kind of society? No way could the women textile workers who ignited the revolution identify with their predatory bosses. No way could the peasantry share the aims of a rich, landowning aristocracy who had been bleeding their class for centuries. It seemed the whole world was being turned upside down, yet despite getting rid of the Tsar, the workers were still exploited while the peasants toiled for the landlords or were dragooned off to war to be slaughtered for the benefit of the rich. John Reed highlighted the source of the problem:

> The propertied classes wanted merely a political revolution, which would take the power from the Tsar and give it to them. They wanted Russia to be a constitutional republic, like France or the USA, or a constitutional monarchy like England. On the other hand the masses of people wanted real industrial and agrarian democracy.[147]

The former autocratic state came alive with politics because politics mattered. The radicalisation promised more than an occasional vote for a distant government run by a rich elite. It meant power to the people, opening up the possibility of real, democratic control of society from below. This was evident right from the start of the revolution in 1917. People would often go in their best clothes to be photographed on demonstrations. Even the waitresses and waiters of Petrograd went on strike. A photograph shows them beneath their banner, which reads: "We demand the human being in the waiter be recognised". Behind them are other union banners saying "Down with Tipping".[148]

As never before there was political discussion and argument on the streets. John Reed described the excitement and the mass engagement of ordinary folk:

> Lectures, debates, speeches—in theatres, clubs, circuses, school-houses, soviet meeting rooms, union headquarters, barracks; meetings in trenches at the front, in village squares and in the factories. What a marvellous sight to see the Putilov armament factory pour out its 40,000 to listen to Social Democrats, Socialist Revolutionaries, anarchists, any body, whatever they had to say as long as they could talk!

For months in Petrograd and all over Russia, every street corner was a public tribune—in railway trains, streetcars, always the spurting of impromptu debate, everywhere. It was against this background of a whole nation in ferment that the pageant of the rising of the Russian masses enrolled.[149]

The second revolution that began to develop after February was the product of two social movements that took place side by side. In the countryside, where the vast majority still lived, the class struggle was between the landlords and the poor peasants who had risen in revolt before. But never had their masters' rule looked so fragile as in the spring of 1917. The peasants began to seize the estates of the landowners and looked to their own peasant party, the Social Revolutionaries (SRs), to represent their interests.

In the towns and cities the revolution bore a different stamp. Here the struggle was between the new classes thrown up by the rapid development of industry as Tsarist Russia tried to drag itself into the 20th century, a struggle sharpened by the war economy. On one side the employers and the financiers making fabulous wartime fortunes out of the modern manufacturing plants. Ranged against them was the enemy industrialisation had created: a powerful working class, marshalled in huge factories. Numbering less than 5 million in a country of 150 million, its real social weight was greater than the arithmetic suggested. The workers had already shown an ardent desire for real democracy in the revolutionary dress rehearsal that terrified Tsarism 12 years before. Learning the lessons the Bolsheviks had built their membership and a wider following inside the industrial working class.

The spontaneous February revolution had again shown the capacity of the Russian working class to act on its own initiative. But its spontaneity was also its weakness. The leaders of the new Soviet had put people in charge of Russia that believed getting rid of the Tsar was more than enough, a Provisional government of capitalists, lawyers and parliamentarians whose sole aim was a liberal republic. Overwhelmingly on the side of the landowners, the businessmen and the generals, the new regime was immediately recognised by the allied powers of France, Britain, the USA and Italy—all desperate to keep Russia in the war and halt the revolution.

How is this to be explained?

We need to examine the three main political forces at work. First, the most powerful remnants of the old regime: the officer corps of the Tsarist army, supported by the Constitutional Democrats (Kadets), the main capitalist party in the state Duma. The Kadets favoured a constitutional monarchy and had been collaborating with Tsarism since the outbreak of war in August 1914, working with it to organise the war industries and profiting handsomely. They sought reform of the Tsarist system but certainly not its overthrow; indeed they were still negotiating to reform the monarchy right up until the very moment of the Tsar's abdication.

The second political force was the Social Revolutionaries (SRs), a petit bourgeois party of peasant socialism formed at the beginning of the century from the remnants of the Narodniks. It had a base in the largely peasant army but was led by intellectuals, lawyers and sections of the urban middle class. Its leaders backed the war, supported the Provisional government and had abandoned their own programme of land reform.

Finally, the two working class parties that emerged from the earlier split in the Marxist Russian Social Democratic Labour Party (RSDLP): the Bolsheviks and the more moderate Mensheviks. By the summer of 1914 the Bolsheviks were the larger of the two parties among Petrograd's working class, producing a daily newspaper *Pravda* and winning most of the votes for the very limited number of workers' deputies in the State Duma or parliament. The war made the differences between them clearer.

The Bolsheviks opposed the war, although some of its leaders had baulked at Lenin's revolutionary defeatism. As a result of the party's anti-war stance, its Duma deputies had been arrested and banished to Siberia for treason. The Mensheviks supported the war, though a minority, the Menshevik Internationalists grouped around Martov, opposed it but made sure they maintained their links with the pro-war Mensheviks.

Both parties agreed Russia needed a revolution and although they disagreed over what class would lead and consolidate it, both accepted it could only be a bourgeois revolution. This meant that the first leading Bolsheviks returning to revolutionary Petrograd from foreign exile, Kamenev and Stalin, agreed to critically back the Provisional government, even though it was dominated by capitalists. The only well-known revolutionary to insist the revolution would be socialist was Trotsky. But in February he was still in exile with no party of his own. He was associated with a small Marxist grouping inside the RSDLP that sought to unite its two big factions.

The workers of Petrograd and the soldiers of the city garrison had formed a soviet right away, soon to be followed by similar bodies across Russia. In those first days effective power was in their hands. The old state machine was in tatters. Lenin called this contradictory state of affairs, "dual power":

> Dual power is evident in the existence of two governments: the one is the real, the actual government of the bourgeoisie, the 'Provisional Government' of Prince Lvov and Co, which holds in its hands all the organs of power; the other is a supplementary, parallel government, a 'controlling' government in the shape of the Petrograd Soviet of Workers' and Soldiers' Deputies, which holds no organs of state power but directly rests on the support of an obvious and indisputable majority of the people, on the armed workers and soldiers.[150]

For Plekhanov and the Mensheviks the new government was the best hope for the bourgeois regime they felt Russia was ready for and the Soviet's role should be merely that of a legal opposition. This was despite the fact that the government existed only insofar as its decisions were authorised by the Soviet. But dual power by its nature could only be a temporary, unstable equilibrium. An armed test of strength between the two forces was inevitable. The revolution had begun spontaneously but it could not end spontaneously. Lenin, still exiled in Switzerland, expected the Bolsheviks to fight within the soviets with the aim of winning a majority for the seizure of power.

On 23 March a million turned out on the streets of Petrograd in a funeral march for those slaughtered by forces loyal to the Tsar during the February days. Men, women and children marched from every corner of the city to escort 183 of the martyrs' coffins to the Field of Mars where they were to be buried: a real show of mass support for the revolution.

So why did the Petrograd Soviet and the soviets forming elsewhere let the Provisional government assume control after the Tsar was deposed? Many workers' delegates to the soviets were unhappy with the composition of this new government. They distrusted Prince Lvov and the landowners and industrialists around him. But they did not have the confidence to tell their own political leaders, with their apparent knowledge of Marxism, they were wrong. The soldiers' delegates were even more easily won to support this government than the workers' delegates. Most had never taken political action before and even though bitter experience made them turn against the Tsar and the senior officers, they still deferred to those above who seemed on the same side as themselves; to the many junior regimental officers and to the Provisional government.

The inheritance of the past is always an obstacle to the success of any revolutionary struggle. It means, paradoxically, that time after time it is the reformist organisations and politicians who initially benefit from a revolutionary situation, by talking left. Workers, especially the so-called backward and unorganised masses who often take the initiative in situations when the vanguard holds back, are at first likely to place their confidence in established leaders whose cautious, conservative ideas offer a sense of security and familiarity to those who have made enormous, previously unimaginable leaps in a very brief space of time.

This, and the fact that many of the Bolshevik leaders and working class militants were either in jail because of their anti-war stance or not yet back from exile, explains why in March 1917 the SRs and Mensheviks were able to dominate the leadership of the new soviets. They argued capitalism still had a role to play in Russia and the task of the revolution was to get the most radical concessions, while still recognising the bourgeois nature of the revolution. This meant doing nothing to antagonise or frighten off the liberal capitalists, as the Mensheviks claimed had happened in 1905. To make matters worse the leading Bolsheviks inside Russia went along with this. But it was clear that significant parts of the Bolshevik rank and file did not.

With most of its leaders still abroad, Shlyapnikov and the few radicals on the Russian central committee were time and again outvoted by a majority too nervous to assert themselves against the Provisional government, or accept the message in Lenin's letters to *Pravda*: his appeal to soldiers at the front to refuse to fight; to turn the imperialist war into a revolutionary war by directing their guns against the enemy at home.

Through the Northern Underground Kollontai had been delivering Lenin's letters to the editors of *Pravda* in Petrograd, but only one of them was published and even then a third of it was deleted. Following the Tsar's demise, the first issue of the Bolshevik paper *Pravda* said "The fundamental problem is to establish a democratic republic".[151] The local Bolshevik leaders' fear to go beyond the democratic revolution meant a policy of waiting and accommodating to the Mensheviks. Local Bolshevik organisations felt confused. In Saratov they wrote: "Our party after taking a very active part in the insurrection has evidently lost its influence with the masses and has been caught up by the Mensheviks and Social Revolutionaries. Nobody knew what the slogans of the Bolsheviks were".[152]

Trotsky was not then a member but even from afar he could see what was going on inside the Bolsheviks at this crucial time:

> The left Bolsheviks, especially the workers, tried with all their force to break through this but they did not know how to refute the premise about the bourgeois character of the revolution and the danger of an isolated proletariat. They submitted, gritting their teeth, to the direction of the leaders.
>
> *Pravda* reflected this cloudy and unstable intellectual state of the party. The situation became still more complicated towards the end of March after the arrival from exile of Kamenev and Stalin, who abruptly turned the helm of official party policy to the right. Although a Bolshevik almost from the very birth of Bolshevism, Kamenev had always stood on the right flank of the party.[153]

The revolution was young and immature. Hating the old regime and craving unity against it, newly radicalised forces were naïve and prepared to trust politicians who spoke of liberty. For millions who hitherto supported the Tsar and the war, a move left did not mean straight away joining or voting with the Bolsheviks, who were seen as the hotheads.

At this stage the Mensheviks and the SRs seemed a more attractive proposition. Along with the Kadets they stood for reforms and looked to the liberal capitalists to introduce and preside over them. Menshevik leader Tsereteli, soon to become a minister in the Provisional government, tried to justify his party's compromise with Russian capitalism:

> There can be no other road for the revolution. It's true we have all the power and that the government would go if we lifted a finger but that would mean disaster for the revolution.[154]

For the Mensheviks years of mechanical adherence to the orthodox formula, that Russian socialism would have to wait until capitalism was fully developed and assumed complete political power, blinded them to the developing situation. Their attempt to halt the revolution despite the evidence of workers' power in the soviets, and make it conform to their preconceptions, led the Mensheviks into supporting the new capitalist government. Seven months later its leaders would find themselves in the same camp as would-be dictators like Admiral Kolchak, Baron Wrangel and the Generals Denikin and Krasnov.

The paradoxical character of the February Revolution, a bourgeois' revolution undertaken by workers and soldiers, brutally exposed the social weakness of the bourgeoisie, once the crutch of the Tsarist state had been knocked out from under it.

Dual power

The government, headed by a Tsarist nobleman and elected by no one, was desperate to end the revolution. Yet it was not strong enough to either suppress the soviets or ignore them. It had no basis of support except the soviet leaders, whose acquiescence gave it unwarranted credence in the eyes of the newly radicalised masses. It was a weak government and its frailty was evident. Minister of war Guchkov wrote to General Alekseev on 9 March admitting:

> The Provisional government has no real power at its disposal and its decrees are carried out only to the extent that this is permitted by the Soviet of Workers' and Soldiers' Deputies. The Soviet controls the most important elements of real power, such as the army, the railways, the posts and the telegraphs. It is possible to say flatly that the Provisional government exists only as long as the Soviet of Workers' and Soldiers' Deputies allow it to.[155]

Yet the masses swept into political activity for the first time at first put their trust in the moderate socialist parties, the Mensheviks and the Social Revolutionaries (SRs). They dominated the leadership of the newly emerging soviets, arguing the ordinary people were not yet mature enough to take power. Both Mensheviks and SRs regarded the soviets not as a vehicle for working class power but merely a stepping-stone to a government of the capitalist class. And for a short time it was possible for the politicians to maintain the fiction that they alone had the necessary intelligence and ability to govern: but not for long.

The Soviet, to use Lenin's words, "has surrendered and is surrendering its position to the bourgeoisie".[156] First from outside the government, then from May onwards when they entered into a coalition with the liberals, the Menshevik-dominated soviet majority sought to end the dual power by helping to rebuild a stable capitalist state.

It was true the soviets were powerful, but parallel to them was the bourgeois Provisional government. There were soldiers' councils, but still the Generals commanded the army. The soviets expressed the wish of millions for peace, but the imperialist war continued. Powerful workers' committees existed in the factories but the capitalists still owned them. Millions of peasants were organised in soviets but the landlords still owned the land.

The Kadets, the party of liberal capitalism, were out to restore order by re-establishing the power of the officers over the rank and file soldiers and by restoring the authority of the factory management over the workers. Everything was to be subordinated to the war effort.

Russian imperialism was as important to the liberal bourgeoisie as to any Tsar. The Kadet leaders hoped to revive Russia's Great Power status and extend the empire. They believed helping their allies win the war would realise long coveted gains such as strategic control of Constantinople (Istanbul): "Even many left-wing members of the Provisional government secretly agreed with the aims of carving out a new empire, including the Dardanelles and 'satellite states' in Eastern Europe".[157]

"The Russian Revolution is the most patriotic, the most national, the most popular of all time",[158] claimed a patriotic Russian intellectual. But the revolution already contained elements within it that would push the majority of the people in the opposite direction. Because the government's priority was war, the issues of land reform, the demands of the non-Russian peoples of the empire, the election of a popular assembly and the demands of the workers were all postponed indefinitely.

But the voice of the militant minority ready to oppose the government was growing. By 17 March workers in 49 towns and cities had set up their own soviets and by 22 March another 28 had joined them. The soldiers also established their own revolutionary committees. The idea of fighting a war for democracy and liberty fitted with the sentiment of overthrowing the Tsar. But the act of ridding Russia of its monarchy gave people a sense of how society can be changed, and when the Provisional government refused to stop the war, it failed to stop the momentum for revolutionary change.

Remembering the outcome of 1905, the soviets stubbornly refused to disband. Instead the February Revolution heralded a whole-scale dismantling of the repressive apparatus of the Tsarist state from below. Police stations and prisons were burnt to the ground; 40,000 rifles and 30,000 revolvers were seized. The hated Tsarist police force was replaced by a civil militia and a separate workers' militia formed by groups of factory workers. The workers at the Rosenkrantz Metal works, the Phoenix Arsenal and other large factories formed the first Vyborg workers' militia.[159]

The factory committees under the guidance of Shlyapnikov, currently the only Bolshevik delegate on the Petrograd Soviet's executive committee and a key leader in the metal workers union, established militias and appointed commissars to oversee the militiamen and women. They did not leave their jobs permanently to serve in the local workers' militia but served according to a rota drawn up by the factory militia committee. At the Metal works 470 served in the Vyborg workers' militia. At the Arsenal, Cartridge, Radiotelegraph, Siemens-Schuckert and Siemens-Halske works, factory committees lost no time in demanding that management pay workers serving in the militia at the average wage. Reluctantly, most employers were forced into doing so.[160]

In this fluid situation the Bolsheviks needed to agitate among the workers, soldiers and peasants looking for leadership, encourage their initiatives and convince them that their interests were irreconcilably opposed to those of the Provisional government. Yet between the end of February and mid-April the leading Bolsheviks inside Russia, Kamenev and Stalin, proved incapable of this. The general line of the party was, in the words of its leaders back in Russia from exile, "to support the Provisional government conditionally, insofar as it defends the gains of the revolution and insofar as it struggles against reaction or counter-revolution".[161]

It followed from this that no immediate call could be issued for an end to war and under the editorship of Stalin and Kamenev, the Bolshevik paper *Pravda* backed the Provisional government in all the essential questions.

In March at a week-long party conference in Petrograd, Kamenev and Stalin argued for co-operation with the Mensheviks. Kollontai and Shlyapnikov, the main speakers for the radical minority, argued against them. Kollontai angrily attacked Kerensky's claim that the most the Soviet could do was to persuade the government to propose a just peace to the warring countries.

Proceedings were then interrupted by another terse telegram from Lenin: "our only guarantee is to arm the workers—no alliance with the other parties." This encouraged the radicals to propose a motion describing the soviets as "the embryo of revolutionary workers' power" and the Russian Revolution as the "point of departure for the movement of the European proletariat". But they were hugely out-voted. Stalin's motion that the soviets should back the Provisional government and that, "there could be no thought of seizing power" won.[162]

Lenin and Trotsky on the nature of the revolution

The position the local Bolshevik leaders adopted in February 1917 derived from the perspective adopted by virtually all Marxists at the time. Lenin's earliest writings analyse the class forces in pre-revolutionary Russia at the turn of the century.

It is clear, even in his early writings like *The Development of Capitalism in Russia* and *The Agrarian Question and the Critics of Marx* that far from being the opportunist characterised by bourgeois historians, Lenin had a better grasp of Marx's *Capital* than any of his contemporaries, apart from Rosa Luxemburg and Nikolai Bukharin. For Lenin theoretical knowledge was never acquired for its own sake. In this case he applied it to identify the forces capable of overthrowing Tsarism in early 20th century Russia.

In 1905 Lenin envisaged a revolutionary government of workers and peasants, which would overthrow Tsarism and establish a parliamentary republic. But for that to happen, he insisted there had to be a revolutionary party rooted in the working class that would not compromise with the bourgeois democrats and their hangers-on inside the working class. His position is contained in *Two Tactics of Social Democracy in the Democratic Revolution*, written in the summer of 1905. Not only does it predate the First World War, it also predates the final outcome and the lessons of 1905 revolution.

In February 1917 the workers and peasants achieved part of the task Lenin ascribed to them in his 1905 writings, by overthrowing Tsarism. But in its place came dual power, workers', soldiers' and peasants' councils on the one hand and a capitalist government on the other. Moreover, Russia was embroiled in an imperialist war that had also provoked working class resistance in all the European states, yet the bourgeois Provisional government was committed to continuing it. Lenin had not anticipated these developments back in 1905. Trotsky alone had foreseen why the orthodox Marxist approach to Russia's coming revolution would come unstuck. During the 1905 revolution he developed a different perspective:

> The working class of Russia has developed into an organised fighting force without precedent. There is no stage of the bourgeois revolution at which this fighting force, driven forward by the steel logic of class interests, could be appeased. Uninterrupted revolution is becoming the law of self-preservation of the proletariat.[163]

Later in 1906 Trotsky wrote *Results and Prospects*, elaborating the lessons of 1905 and highlighting the significance of the workers' soviet. His argument was that if the Russian working class took the lead in a future revolution, it would not and could not limit itself to bourgeois democratic demands. It would go beyond them to demand the arming of the workers, the expropriation of the capitalists and to establish government by soviets. He pointed out Russian industry did not exist on the same scale as in Germany or Britain, but where it did exist, it had a very advanced and concentrated form. Putilov was one of the largest, most technically advanced factories of its kind anywhere in the world. Trotsky coined the phrase "combined and uneven development" to describe the processes at work in Russia at the start of the 20th century.

He was fully in agreement with Lenin that the Russian bourgeoisie was far too timid and too tied to Tsarism to lead a democratic revolution. But he differed by insisting the key lesson of 1905 was that the class that had grown inside Russia's new industries could make a revolution that would blow away both Tsarism and the bourgeoisie at the same time.

Trotsky was well aware Russian backwardness was an obstacle but he completed his analysis by explaining how socialist revolution in Russia could sustain itself. Its salvation would lie in internationalisation. Although Russia by itself was not ripe for socialism, the world economy as a whole, and the economy of western Europe, certainly was. The spread of revolution westwards would remove the threat of the military restoration of capitalism, relieve Russia from the pressure of international economic competition and make available resources to allow the rapid development of Russia's productive forces.

This was Trotsky's theory of permanent revolution.[164] Seen as a heretic by Mensheviks and Bolsheviks alike, he was isolated on this issue until February 1917. But with Russia's Provisional government enmeshed in war, with the workers and soldiers struggling against it for their own interests, and with a revolutionary mood developing Europe-wide, Lenin was forced to rethink his position.

For the Mensheviks, soviets were simply temporary instruments to help put power into the hands of the bourgeoisie and nothing more. They opposed soviets as a new form of political power. Lenin's 1905 formula was superior to Menshevism but it had a flaw. His "democratic dictatorship" showed how power might be wrested from Tsarism but it would only be temporary if the revolution were to be constrained within bourgeois limits. The democratic dictatorship would have to step aside in favour of bourgeois democracy in the shape of a Constituent Assembly.

It was this ambiguity about the primacy or otherwise of soviets and workers' power that sparked the conflict between the "old Bolsheviks" and Lenin in April. Stalin and Kamenev's position was indistinguishable from the Mensheviks. In seeking to understand the nature of the February 1917 revolution after it had taken him and everyone else by surprise, Lenin analysed the disparate elements that came together in February to produce what he called "an abrupt turn in history".[165] He identified "unexpected and specific combinations" including the impact of the First World War, Russia's weakness in relation to the other Great Powers, the conservative and liberal politicians who, with the encouragement of their allies, had concluded the Tsar's clique was an obstacle to winning the war; and crucially the rising discontent among the workers, the garrison of Petrograd and the poor peasants.

Before returning to Russia in April, Lenin had worked out that subordinating soviet power to bourgeois democracy would mean putting the revolution in jeopardy and backing a government waging imperialist war. So either the Bolsheviks stuck with Plekhanov's doctrine that the revolution could not go beyond capitalism and that workers' interests had to be subordinated to the war, or they mobilised the workers, peasants and soldiers against the government and the war. For Lenin it was a no-brainer—even though it meant breaking with the past. Real life and the class struggle were more important than formulae.

When preparing material for this book, I came across the *Observer Sunday Magazine* of 5 April 1970, a special edition to mark the centenary of Lenin's birth. Reading it again, it struck me how Lenin's stock was so much higher in 1970 than it is now. Written by journalist Neal Ascherson and titled "Lenin: the man who broke the system", it pays Lenin the respect he deserves. Ascherson's narrative concludes with the dramatic events of 1917:

> And now it was Lenin, with Trotsky back beside him, who threw away the book of Marxist orthodoxy and—as he had done in 1903—followed his nose. He saw that the workers could now seize power. If they didn't seize it, moreover, the Mensheviks and the Provisional government would lose it to the gathering counter-revolution. Once again, in the supreme hour of his life, Lenin's incomparable political instinct took over.
>
> As a young man, still under the shadow of his brother's execution, he had sensed that the fierce old man lying in Highgate cemetery had meant his books to be a guide to action, a weapon, rather than a dogma to excuse the revolutionary from making decisions.[166]

Lenin's "political instinct" brought a change of tack that would create shock and consternation among the Bolshevik leadership. He was breaking the mould of social democratic orthodoxy and, according to some, capitulating to "Trotskyism". But for Lenin the old scenario had been made obsolete by the actual course of events.

The danger lay in the soviets ceding power to the bourgeoisie. The new task was to reverse this process, by getting the masses to see "the soviets of workers' and soldiers' deputies were the only possible form of revolutionary government" and through "patient, systematic and persistent explanation", prepare the way not for a bourgeois parliamentary republic, "a retrograde step—but for a soviet one".[167]

April 1917: Re-arming the party

Before his return to Petrograd, Lenin knew Trotsky's critique of the "old Bolshevik" strategy of 1905 was now vindicated by events. In March he was still in Switzerland frantically trying to arrange his own return to Russia. He was livid when he learned the leadership in Petrograd was supporting the Provisional government.

Increasingly frustrated at the direction they were travelling, he denounced them in a series of *Letters from Afar*, insisting the war was still an imperialist war and that to support the government waging it was to support imperialism. Lenin's letters also pointed out that the workers had played the decisive role in toppling the Tsar and that the soviets they had created were far more democratic than any bourgeois parliament. He argued the workers could move to impose their own interests and those of the peasants, on condition that the soviets take power, replace the army with a workers' militia, nationalise the banks and give the land to the poorest peasants. His second letter from afar spelled out the need for a second revolution and a workers' government: "Only a proletarian republic, backed by the rural workers and the poorest section of the peasants and town dwellers can secure peace, bread, order and freedom".[168]

He couldn't wait to get back to Russia. "From the moment the news of the February revolution came", recalled Krupskaya, "Ilyich burned with eagerness to go to Russia".[169] It took him five weeks but nothing could stop him taking the only route into revolutionary Russia open to him. For obvious reasons, as Lenin had noted, "the British government was preventing emigrant revolutionary internationalists from returning to their native land to take part in the struggle against imperialism".[170]

On 27 March 32 exiled Bolsheviks risked the route from Zurich to Petrograd through Germany, Denmark, Sweden and Finland in a sealed train. Lenin was on board for the revolution. With him were

Krupskaya, Inessa Armand, Zinoviev and his wife Zina and their small son. The chief of the German High Command, Field Marshall Ludendorff, allowed Lenin's party travel visas, in return for the release of imprisoned German diplomats in Russia and on the calculation that his presence in Russia would subvert Germany's enemy. But as a German historian pointed out, Ludendorff was remarkably short sighted:

> One instinctively puts the question in this context, whether the German agencies responsible were not aware that working with Bolshevism in this way was playing with fire. Did the belief really hold sway that imperial Germany could come to terms with the Russian social revolution without itself one day being burned by it?[171]

There is no doubt who was the more farsighted or who gained the better advantage. Six months later the Bolsheviks led the seizure of power. A year after that the German workers and soldiers, under the influence of the Russian Revolution, overthrew their Kaiser.

In travelling on the sealed train at the risk of being called a German agent, a slander used against the Bolsheviks in the coming summer months, Lenin showed real foresight and political courage. Miliukov, the Kadet party's leading light in the Provisional government, had threatened to jail him on arrival.

In his *Farewell Letter to the Swiss Workers*, Lenin wrote, "the objective circumstances make it certain the revolution will not be limited to Russia. Transformation of the imperialist war into civil war is becoming a fact".[172]

Lenin at the Finland Station

Lenin embarked on an epic and history-making railway journey from Zurich on Easter Monday, 9 April (29 March in Russia). He bought issues of *Pravda* as soon as he arrived in Finland. In her recent account of that journey, *Lenin on the Train*, Catherine Merridale describes how Lenin started leafing through *Pravda* while in the customs house at Tornio on the Swedish-Finnish border:

> He looked for his own contribution, for he had sent two articles (his first *Letters from Afar*) to Russia in the care of Alexandra Kollontai. He could find only one of them. It had been printed at the bottom of the

inside pages but the section calling for a boycott of the bourgeois Provisional government had been removed. He noted more deletions from the piece; the cuts were systematic and deliberate. It was clear, as he read on, that there were leading Bolsheviks in Petrograd actively contemplating an alliance with the Mensheviks.[173]

Lenin had been prepared for a fight when he got back to Russia. His telegram of early March had been explicit: no support for the Provisional government. The *Letters from Afar* had called for a transfer of power from "the agents of British capital" to the soviets. The war, he had insisted, was "an imperialist adventure" and not what Kamenev was now calling in *Pravda*, a fight "for revolutionary self-defence". It was clear Lenin's letters had been doctored and kept from the party rank and file by those now in control of the party in Petrograd: Stalin and Kamenev.

Petrograd is very close to Finland. Shlyapnikov and a number of Bolsheviks went to meet Lenin off the sealed train on 3 April, to accompany him on the last leg of his journey into Petrograd. Among them were Kamenev and a young Bolshevik naval officer Fyodor Raskolnikov. "Hardly had Comrade Kamenev entered the train compartment and sat down," recalls Raskolnikov, "than Vladimir Ilyich turned to him; 'what's this you're writing in *Pravda*? We've seen several issues and when I read what you wrote I called you all sorts of names', we heard Ilyich say in a tone of fatherly reproof".[174]

On arrival at the terminus in the Vyborg district of Petrograd, Lenin was welcomed by a formal delegation of moderate socialists then leading the Petrograd Soviet. Although Lenin hated pomp and ceremony, Shlyapnikov, so glad to see him back, had also mobilised several thousand rank and file workers, soldiers and sailors to greet him there. The Soviet spokesperson welcomed Lenin on behalf of the revolution and expressed a hope Lenin would toe the line by supporting the Provisional government. He then gave Lenin a bunch of flowers. Laying them aside, Lenin turned to address those who'd come to see him: "Comrades, sailors, soldiers and workers, I greet you as the vanguard of the world-wide proletarian army. The hour is not far off when the people will turn their weapons against the capitalist exploiters".[175]

Lenin went on to deliver a fierce polemic against the Provisional government that shook not only the Mensheviks present, but also some loyal Bolsheviks. His *April Theses* called for a new workers' revolution and the end of the war. The Bolshevik Petrograd committee met to discuss it the next day and one of the delegates later described how, "Lenin's *Theses* produced the impression of an exploding bomb. Lenin could not even find sympathisers in our own ranks." Another said, "it seemed utopian and only to be explained by Lenin's prolonged lack of contact with Russian life".[176]

At first the *April Theses* got virtually no support among the other party leaders. Some accused Lenin of treachery and anarchism; others thought he'd gone mad. In the course of the next few days he defended the *April Theses* at all sorts of meetings.

At first there was no occasion when his proposals were accepted. At the subsequent central committee meeting only Kollontai voted for his position; 13 voted against and one abstained. But he found an echo among ordinary members in the industrial districts, for he articulated what some of them already felt. Chris Harman argues: "He did for the militant section of Russia's workers what Tom Paine did for people in the American colonies early in 1776, or what Marat had done for the Parisian sans culottes in 1792—providing a view of the world that made sense in a situation that contradicted all the old beliefs. He helped masses of people move from being angry victims of circumstance to active subjects of history".[177]

By the end of April Lenin had won the majority. His reputation and skills of persuasion were considerable but more powerful factors were at work. The Vyborg Bolsheviks had been calling for the transfer of power to the soviets since early March. An early convert to Lenin's view and a Bolshevik of long-standing, Ludmilla Stal, said, "all the comrades before Lenin's arrival were wandering in the dark. We knew only the formula of 1905. In accepting Lenin's slogans we are now doing what life suggests to us".[178] Lenin's *April Theses* prevailed at the All-Russian Party Congress because it gave his undoubted stamp of authority to what the most advanced section of the workers were sensing themselves, and because it pointed a clear though certainly not easy, way forward.

> The masses must be convinced that the soviets of workers' deputies are the only possible form of revolutionary government and that therefore our task is, so long as the soviets yield to the influence of the bourgeoisie,

to present a patient, systematic and persistent explanation of the errors of their tactics.

As long as we are in a minority we carry on the work of criticising errors. At the same time we preach the necessity of transferring state power to the soviets so that the people may overcome the mistakes by experience. Not a parliamentary republic but a republic of soviets of workers' and peasants' deputies throughout the country, from top to bottom![179]

Lenin had won the party to the idea of soviet power but it would take far longer to win the wider mass of workers, let alone the soldiers and peasants. A furious press campaign was launched against the Bolsheviks and their call for a second revolution, but they persisted. Lenin urged party members to "patiently explain" the need to overthrow the Provisional government and end the war. But he emphasised it was not an immediate call for insurrection; that was premature. The task was to win over a majority in the soviets. He insisted the Bolsheviks could not achieve these aims as a minority that had not yet won the majority of workers.

Party members threw themselves into every struggle to keep wages up with rising prices, to resist attacks on working conditions and to resist factory closures. Whereas the Mensheviks and their SR allies in the soviets sought to restore the authority of the employers, the Bolsheviks agitated for workers' control and workers' takeovers.

Organising the unorganised
Once again some of the most downtrodden women, the soldiers' wives (*soldatki*) were the first to raise a protest at the failure of the Provisional government. Their monthly allowance of seven roubles had been wiped out by inflation. They had more faith in the Petrograd Soviet than the government. On 24 April 15,000 of them marched along the Nevsky Prospekt to demonstrate outside the Tauride Palace, the Soviet's HQ.

The then chair of the Soviet, Menshevik F I Dan, who supported the war, had the gall to attack the women for demanding public money and tried to stop Kollontai, one of the few women delegates to the Soviet, from addressing the demonstration. She did so anyway, urging the women to hold meetings at which they would elect their own delegates to it. Bolshevik women had already been organising these hungry, desperate women, struggling to feed their families since the beginning of the war. Bolshevik Anastasia Deviatkina and a soldier's wife named Fyodorova had set up a union of soldiers' wives in Petrograd after the February revolution. Similar unions soon sprang up across Russia and in the Ukraine.

In the Vyborg District Krupskaya, just back from exile, took over the running of the local Committee for the Relief of Soldiers' Wives at the end of April. Krupskaya was struck by how political some of the poorest working women had become: "The first to carry on Bolshevik agitation among the soldiers were the sellers of sunflower seed, cider and so on—many were soldiers' wives".[180]

Maids and domestic servants in the capital were also demonstrating in their thousands for better pay and conditions. The newly formed restaurant workers' union appealed to *Pravda* for support in a letter "from all women workers and waiters in the tea-rooms of Petrograd". In June the waiters and waitresses went on strike against the indignity of tipping and demanded a proper wage. "We need a bigger hall!" one of them wrote in a letter to *Pravda* after a union meeting overflowed onto the street.

Women working in the tobacco factories demanded protection for pregnant workers, and those at the Mignon Chocolate Factory called on the Soviet to protest against their terrible working conditions. Workers at the Frolic Textile mill demanded a 100 percent increase for the men and a 125 percent increase for the women. The number of peasant women arriving to work in the cities had jumped dramatically after the outbreak of the First World War and they now represented 40 percent of the workforce. Soon after leaving their villages they were coming out on strike. Women who had lived in the most oppressed conditions flooded into the revolutionary movement, which made their true liberation its priority.

Alexandra Kollontai, just returned from exile, was only now beginning to meet these women. Her main contact with them was through Klavdia Nikolaeva, a young typesetter who had become a highly effective Bolshevik organiser in the city. It was from her Kollontai learned of the terrible conditions of Petrograd's 4,000 laundresses. Paid 30 kopeks a week to work a 14-hour day in steamy underground basements, they were plagued by rheumatism and other illnesses resulting from the foul conditions they had to endure at work. Their strike on 1

May was the first in Petrograd under the Provisional government, demanding shorter hours, better pay, the municipalisation and mechanisation of the city laundries and the arrest of their managers. The strike covered 400 different establishments across the city but the women displayed determination and a fantastic capacity to organise themselves. Despised and downtrodden like the *soldatki*, they defied the government's orders to return to work.

Bolshevik strike leader Sofia Goncharskaia, from a mining family, had joined the Bolsheviks during the 1905 Revolution. One of the first exiles to return to Petrograd after the February Revolution, she was given the task of organising the laundresses. She had gone from laundry to laundry persuading the women to join the strike. In one laundry the owner attacked Goncharskaia with a crowbar and she was only saved because the laundresses were able to disarm him. *Pravda* devoted a page every day to their battle, exposing the employers' intimidation and the use of hired scabs. It backed the women and included their appeals for strike funds. The strikers agreed to include in their demands the Bolshevik slogans against the war and the Provisional government. Kollontai was a regular speaker at their meetings.

At the Bolshevik Party conference in late April, Lenin asked Kollontai to present her ideas on how the party should step up its work. She argued that the Bolshevik support for the strike and the party's dramatic rise in popularity made it urgent to set up women's sections that could work with the strikers in a more organised fashion.

On 3 May the laundresses finally won their demands for shorter hours and better pay, and in Kollontai's *Pravda* article, "In the Front Line", she celebrated a victory for the entire working class: powerful evidence that it could take on the bosses and win. The strike raised the prestige of laundresses and it was an important turning point in the general struggle.

The Bolsheviks won many of these working class women to their organisation, which went to great lengths to ensure women were part of the struggle; out of concern for the women and because without women like them, socialist revolution could not succeed. The Bolsheviks had fought hard for equal pay, in the workplaces, the trade unions and the soviets. An article entitled, "A Serious Gap", in *Pravda* on 5 May 1917, criticised the agenda of a forthcoming trade union congress for not including any discussion on equal pay for women.

Revolution in general, and the Russian Revolution in particular, is often portrayed as a male dominated event. Not only did large numbers of working class women start the February revolution, they would remain a big cog in the revolutionary movement in both city and countryside throughout Russia's red year.

On 1 May a new coalition cabinet was announced following a crisis for the first Provisional government. Towards the end of April cabinet minister Miliukov had issued a diplomatic note to appease Russia's allies, Britain and France. The note was leaked and it confirmed "the general aspirations of the whole Russian people was to bring the war to a decisive victory" and that Russia "would fully observe its existing treaty obligations".[181] This meant Russian expansion in the Black Sea region and the Dardanelles, committing Russia to a war of annexations: a war of imperialism. It meant prolonging the war, contradicting everything the Mensheviks and the SRs had been saying about it being purely defensive and promising it would be ended soon.

Miliukov's note provoked an explosion. An impromptu angry demonstration against the war by 40,000 workers and soldiers terrified the government, forcing Miliukov to resign. To maintain power the Provisional government co-opted a few moderate socialists to shore up support for what it called a new coalition and a fresh start. Kerensky, the SR, was given greater prominence, taking responsibility for defence in an attempt to reassure what was left of the government's support.

Workers' control and the factory committees
Trotsky arrived back from his exile in the USA at the Finland station on 4 May—two months after the Tsar's abdication and a month later than Lenin. The Menshevik and SR leaders of the Petrograd Soviet put on their customary welcome ceremony, but this masked the fact that most of them detested Trotsky's revolutionary perspectives while some of the Bolshevik leadership were yet to be convinced he could be a dependable ally. But Trotsky had always been hostile to any deal with the liberals and continued to argue for a workers' government.

His insistence that a working class that toppled absolutism would not meekly hand over power to their capitalist exploiters was vindicated throughout the spring and summer of 1917. The confidence that had overthrown a brutal despotism now turned to how the factories were to be run. Steve Smith's study of Petrograd factory life in 1917 argues the struggles of workers in work and the activities of the factory committees and trade unions:

> were of central importance in promoting revolutionary consciousness in 1917. This is not to suggest it developed solely on that basis. Revolutionary feeling grew in response to the wide range of problems: war, government ineptitude and the crisis in the countryside. Nor is it to suggest that revolutionary consciousness grew in a purely 'spontaneous' fashion. But the Bolsheviks did not themselves create revolutionary feeling; it developed primarily out of attempts by workers to grapple with the problems of survival.[182]

Workers seized the opportunity to settle scores with their immediate enemies, clamouring to remove the owners, bosses and foremen who had behaved like tyrants, abused their authority, taken bribes, preyed on women workers or acted as police informers. Sometimes they were removed peacefully, sometimes forcibly. The Putilov workers killed the director and his deputy and flung their bodies in the canal; 40 managers were expelled in the first days of freedom. In the engine shop the chief of the factory's Black Hundreds (fascists) had red lead poured over his head before he was ceremoniously carted out of the factory in a wheelbarrow and dumped in the street.

Carting administrators out of a factory in wheelbarrows was a well-established form of protest in the Russian labour movement. Prior to 1917 the working class had precious few institutional means to defend its interests and devised other ways of defending themselves.

Anna Litveiko was a factory worker who joined the Bolsheviks in Moscow in 1917. She started work aged 12 and at the start of the revolution was a young worker employed in a Moscow factory making light bulbs. Initially impressed by Menshevik students, she soon came to see their moderation was useless in the situation she and her workmates faced. Litveiko was elected to her factory committee, where she came in touch with a Bolshevik, Natasha Bogecheva, a soldier's wife and mother in her thirties. Litveiko began noticing that all the Bolsheviks in her factory were workers, whereas the Mensheviks who came to address their meetings were usually intellectuals. She also noticed the Bolsheviks were uncompromising toward the employers. When a foreman at her work struck a woman and burned her shoulder with a hot rod, Bogecheva called a meeting to decide what to do. The outcome was that the women got together, stuck the foreman in a wheelbarrow and carted him out of the factory. He never returned. The women gained a sense of collective power.[183]

Later in October, straight after the overthrow of the Provisional government in Petrograd, Litveiko and some of her female workmates played a part in the bitter street-fighting in Moscow against the counter-revolutionaries, building barricades, transporting weapons and organising medical help for the injured and wounded.

The expulsion of the old administration and its bullying managers was the negative side of democratising factory life. The positive, and more important, side consisted in creating factory committees to represent the interests of the workforce and the creation of collective organisation and confidence.

The soviets were composed of elected workplace delegates rooted in the factories of Petrograd, Moscow and the other large industrial centres. It was in the workplace that the decisive struggle for influence was fought. During and after the February revolution factory committees spread rapidly across the country. They represented the interests and aspirations of rank and file workers within the process of production itself. Immediately after the Tsar's fall the factory committees led a stormy wave of strikes for higher wages, better working conditions and the eight-hour day. As class polarisation developed these committees were forced to take on the political task of imposing workers' control to combat economic sabotage by the employers.

Another historian points out the positive role played by the Bolsheviks: "The key Bolshevik intervention in the revolutionary process was at this level. The party convened regional then national conferences of what had until then been delegate committees isolated in the factories".[184]

It was these conferences, not the town soviets, which discussed essential practical questions of workers' control, demilitarisation of industry, fuel shortages, employer sabotage, the control of supervision, the formation of Red Guards and so on. The predominance of the Bolsheviks in these conferences was the basis for the party's predominance in the workers' sections of the soviets and eventually in the soviets as a whole. The conditions for the creation of factory committees and for Bolshevik hegemony within them had been created during the war and in the way the war had transformed the working class.

Many militant workers had been conscripted to the front, while the skilled men who remained found their position undermined by a massive influx of women and peasant labourers from the countryside into new mass production industries, created to serve an expanding war economy. Trotsky described the effect of this process: "During 1915 and 1916 this diluted working class had to go through an elementary school of struggle before the partial economic strikes and demonstrations of hungry women could in February 1917 fuse in a general strike and draw the army into an insurrection".[185]

Where factory committees existed they originally represented in the main the older, skilled workers who could exploit their scarcity in economic terms as pay differentials increased enormously. But the revolutionary element among them could also recruit and lead a new, younger, vibrant rank and file for what were more political ends. Dilution of labour meant the peasants, immigrants and women—the new rank and file—were being trained in seven weeks for work on adjacent rows of electric and pneumatic lathes. While this undermined the basis of the skilled turners' power, it gave the best of them a new army to organise.

The factory committees developed in the struggle against the government's War Industry Committees. An early form of "partnership", these bodies aimed at involving workers in boosting the war effort. The Bolsheviks led a highly effective campaign against them; factory committees emerged first in the munitions factories run by the Tsarist state departments responsible for the war effort. Here the soviet or workers' council experience after February was strongest.

The workers elected supervisors, foremen and floor managers. The former management had seen itself as agents of the Tsarist government and therefore kept its head down during and after the February revolution. And the highly skilled munitions workers thought they could manage production and run the shop floor better than the bosses. Under the influence of the Bolsheviks the struggle fused together the different layers of the Russian proletariat: the new, green labour created by the war economy and the traditional skilled craftsmen.

The soviets provided the framework for this because first, they united the class as a whole, rather than just the revolutionaries (as the party did) or just the skilled workers (as the unions did); secondly because of regular elections and the right of recall, they were based on, and uniquely responsive to, the shifts of mood in the workplace; and thirdly because the soviets embodied the direct power of the working class plus the rank and file of the army. The labour movement of western Europe was dominated by skilled artisans for most of the 19th century. Only at the end of the century did it expand beyond the elite artisans and skilled factory craftsmen. The evolution of the Petrograd labour movement was much more telescoped than its counterparts in the West.

Working class women, peasant women and the youth who poured into the factories had little prior experience of wage-work in modern industry, but they quickly adapted to the fevered tempo of work in the war industries.

The new workers were often more turbulent than the older skilled workers. They combined the discontent of the low-paid with the grievances of the poor peasants and the oppression of women and youth. Their militancy, however, was often an explosive and volatile kind that tended to threaten the attempts of the factory committee and the union leaders to build stable, sustained organisation.

> The leaders were sympathetic to the plight of the newer workers but they sought to direct their militancy and they had some success in this, for in 1917 women and peasant workers began to join trade unions. Young workers in particular displayed a remarkable propensity for self-organisation and working class unity became a reality after February, in spite of the profound divisions within the factory workforce.[186]

The push for action always came from below. Newer forces took the initiative in February, catching the Bolshevik leadership unawares. They would do so again during what came to be known as the "July Days". But in October, the Bolsheviks would harness the energies and aspirations of a united working class and lead it in a successful struggle for power. That second revolution would arise out of the radicalisation of the Russian working class within the process of production itself. Over the coming months the factory committees and soviets would expand and develop to give this radicalisation an organised expression.

After February the removal of the worst managers and foremen was followed by struggles against the capitalists, as workers fought for the eight-hour day, equal pay, higher wages, the right of women to represent their sections and against management sabotage and closures. The political awakening led to a massive wave of economic struggles, which boosted rank and file confidence to tackle political issues. It saw workers acting collectively through factory committees to take decisions about the day to day running of the workplace and challenging every aspect of management control. It became clear that in order to settle accounts with their own bosses they would have to deal with the capitalist class and the state machine.

In July the Provisional government planned to evacuate plant and equipment from Petrograd, dismissing most of the workers on two weeks' pay. They wanted to rationalise war production because they feared a collapse at the front and a German occupation of the city. But the workers saw it as a cynical attempt to break the soviets and the revolutionary movement, so they opposed it. A resolution from the Putilov workers denounced the plan as a counter-revolutionary plot, and went on: "We the workers and peasants will stay put since we believe that the people will have the opportunity to take power into their own hands."

Throughout the duration of the First World War Petrograd had been working flat out to meet orders, particularly in munitions, and making big profits. But in the spring and summer of 1917 economic crisis meant factory committees found themselves fighting to keep factories running against the logic of profitability and the various attempts at sabotage by the owners.

Changing the rank and file leadership

In was through these struggles that Petrograd's factory leaderships changed. In February and March the pro-war Mensheviks and SRs had strong representation in many factories. But as workers learned bitter lessons in the struggle for control, in the fight against closures and against the military conspiracies aimed at counter-revolution, then the locally-elected leaderships were overturned and replaced. Increasingly the factory committees came to be dominated by Bolsheviks because they were the ones putting forward consistent arguments and demands to meet the needs of the hour.

These changes were reflected in the composition of the soviets. The same process was underway in Moscow and in other major centres, but at a slower tempo than in Petrograd. Historical research has unearthed material that proves the popularity of Bolshevik demands and slogans was the result of the practical experience of ordinary workers. In a collection of essays entitled, *The Workers' Revolution in Russia: The View from Below*, Steve Smith writes:

> There is a notion the Bolsheviks won their following by 'manipulating' the base instincts of the masses by a fearsome combination of demagogy and lies. To be sure Bolshevik agitation and organisation played a crucial role in radicalising the masses. But the Bolsheviks themselves did not create popular discontent or revolutionary feeling...
>
> They won support because their analysis and proposed solutions seemed to make sense. A worker from the Orudiinyi works, formerly a bastion of the moderates where the Bolsheviks were not even allowed to speak, stated that "the Bolsheviks have always said, 'it is not we who will persuade you, but life itself'. And now the Bolsheviks have triumphed because life has proved their tactics right".[187]

In the same collection of essays, historian Diane Koenker makes a similar point: that the women textile workers, for example, did not become radicalised because they were dazzled by pie-in-the-sky promises as some historians would like to think, but because specific incidents and examples proved the Bolsheviks could be trusted:

> For example when a factory manager would announce the shutdown of a plant because there was no fuel left to fire the boilers, a workers' delegation would then investigate the warehouses and discover ample reserves. The Bolsheviks, almost alone of the socialist parties, claimed the bourgeoisie could not be trusted and here was proof.[188]

According to McDermid and Hillyar, "the Bolshevik Party fought to have women represented on factory committees in industries where they constituted a significant portion of the workforce—notably textiles—which involved persuading the men to vote for them".[189] This was important because fears of unemployment due to the collapsing economy led some male workers' representatives to deal with layoffs by protecting men's jobs at the expense of women's, arguing the men were the breadwinners while women's wages were supplementary.

This backward attitude annoyed most women and especially the *soldatki*, women breadwinners whose husbands were in the army. Many of them responded: "So where were you on International Women's Day when we were all fighting for bread?"

The Bolsheviks acted with the metal workers' union, a union led in Petrograd in 1917 by Alexander Shlyapnikov, to challenge attitudes and tactics that discriminated against women, arguing every job had to be defended. In one textile factory in March, five women Bolsheviks and two non-party women were elected to the factory committee. Women were also elected to the control commission to oversee working conditions. This example was repeated elsewhere.

Skilled men were also worried about being replaced by youth through the apprenticeship system and the Bolsheviks fought for youth rights on the same uncompromising basis they fought for women's rights. Lenin was proud that the Bolsheviks were a young organisation and put special effort into recruiting young people. Krupskaya and Vera Slutskaia were in charge of youth work and collaborated with three young Bolsheviks; one of them, Liza Pylaeva, quickly understood the importance of winning over young people and played a leading role in helping build a successful socialist youth movement. In June *Pravda* published an appeal directed at 18 and 19 year old workers, to set up such an organisation in Petrograd. It attracted 3,000 to its first meeting.

Peasants and soldiers

After April the Bolsheviks needed a clear strategy for the peasantry. Peasant land seizures mushroomed after the February revolution and Lenin saw the various local and regional insurgencies needed linking with the struggles of the workers in the towns and cities. The Menshevik-SR bloc used their majority in the soviets to call on the peasants to wait until a Constituent Assembly, whose election they constantly postponed, could settle the land question. Instead the Bolsheviks called for the immediate implementation of the original SR programme of land distribution, and encouraged peasant land seizures.

The Menshevik-SR soviet majority also demanded the oppressed nationalities within the former Tsarist Empire, well over 50 percent of its population, defer their national aspirations until the non-existent Constituent Assembly could discuss a limited measure of autonomy. The Bolsheviks called for immediate recognition of national rights, up to and including secession. In the first months of its existence many were fooled by the Provisional government's claim to be on the side of the popular revolution. By May it had shown its true colours in refusing to distribute land to the peasants, in offering nothing to the workers except greater sacrifice and, above all, by continuing the bloody and increasingly unpopular war.

The Bolsheviks set out to prove to the exploited and oppressed that they themselves had the power and the ability to run society through the soviets they had created. The Bolshevik's slogan "Peace, Land and Bread—All Power to the Soviets" became well known.

Two million Russian soldiers deserted between February and October 1917.[190] Sabotage at the front began with stories of senior officers being shot. On sections of the Eastern front during Easter 1917 there was fraternisation with enemy troops, similar to that in Flanders between Christmas 1914 and February 1915. After April the Bolsheviks called for the election of all army and naval officers, for fraternisation with the enemy and for an immediate peace.

Armed force is the central question in every revolution. Russia was no different. If the power of the officer corps over the rank and file was restored the counter-revolution would triumph. 1905 had shown that for revolution to succeed the disintegration of the old Tsarist army had to be completed. The process was beginning to happen and it was significant that alongside the spread of factory committees many workers had started forming groups of armed Red Guards to act as a workers' militia.

After the Miliukov crisis at the end of April, Prince Lvov's Provisional government was reorganised as a coalition with five moderate Mensheviks. Prominent SR member Kerensky as minster for war became its key figure, acting as a bridge between the government and the Soviet Executive, of which he was still a member.

In June Kerensky ordered a major offensive, using the best army units, in an attempt to turn the tide. For Lenin and Trotsky this was proof that the desire to annex territory had not faded with the resignation of Miliukov. A declaration prepared by Trotsky, denouncing Kerensky's military preparations, was read out by the Bolshevik caucus at the First All-Russian Congress of Soviets. The rapprochement between Trotsky and Lenin was strengthening by the day.

Kerensky's June offensive proved to be another deadly fiasco: 40,000 were killed and after an initial advance the collapse of the army intensified. Nikolai Golovin, a Tsarist General who later became a historian, reported that in the Eleventh Army, "authority and obedience no longer exist. For hundreds of miles one can see lines of deserters, armed and unarmed, in good health and in high spirits, certain they will not be punished".[191]

Elected committees started to appear in the armed forces. The most radical army units were on the Western and Northern fronts, where the Bolsheviks would later win over 50 percent of the vote in the elections for the Constituent Assembly. The 100,000 strong Baltic Fleet was even more radical. Based at Kronstadt, Tallinn and Helsinki, rank and file sailors challenged the military authority from February onwards. In April 1917 they elected the Tsentrobalt, the Central Committee of the Baltic Fleet, chaired by a Bolshevik sailor Pavel Dybenko.

Still the Provisional government remained committed to war and this drove more and more soldiers and sailors towards the Bolshevik slogan "Down with the War!" The total number of Bolsheviks in the army at the time of the February revolution was a couple of thousand. By April it had risen to 6,000 and in June it was 26,000. Thereafter soldiers in practically all corps, divisions and other units began to join the party. On 5 October, on the Northwest front alone there were 48,994 party members.[192]

Bolshevik influence in the army spread well beyond it. Like the population at large, the conscript army was overwhelmingly peasant. While soldiers' families toiled on barren plots of earth, the rich landlords kept the most fertile land. Through the influence of the Bolshevik soldier-agitators, the peasant villages were drawn into the revolution.

The government became increasingly paralysed. Workers, peasants and soldiers wanted to see change and were quite willing to sweep aside those who stood in their path. General Kornilov, the Tsar's commander-in-chief and an unreconstructed monarchist, was in charge of the army. In June the soviets combined to form their All-Russian Congress and remembering the lessons of 1905, they began to take seriously the creation of armed workers' militias: the Red Guards. Dual power was becoming increasingly unstable, and, as Trotsky points out, it was not only the left that could see it:

> By the beginning of July Petrograd was already completely on the side
> of the Bolsheviks. Acquainting the new French Ambassador with the
> new situation in the capital, journalist Claude Anet pointed across the
> river Neva to the Vyborg district, where the largest factories were

concentrated: "There Lenin and Trotsky reign as masters. The regiments of the garrison were either Bolshevik or wavering in the direction of the Bolsheviks. Should Lenin and Trotsky desire to seize Petrograd who will deter them from it?"

But as Trotsky noted, "taking power was not yet possible because the provinces lagged considerably behind the capital".[193]

In June Kerensky announced another offensive and the Bolsheviks predicted yet another catastrophe. They decided to counter Kerensky's militarism and test the strength of their support by calling a demonstration for 10 June. Their slogans were to be "Power to the Soviets" and "Down with the Ten Capitalist Ministers". But as Trotsky explains, "the compromisers (the Menshevik-SR majority) were alarmed and in the name of the Soviet Congress forbade the demonstration. The Bolsheviks submitted to this decision. But frightened by the bad impression of their interdict against the masses, the Soviet Congress had to call a demonstration for eight days later on 18 June."

The result was unexpected: a demonstration which had been called in support of the government turned into its opposite. All the factories and regiments came out with Bolshevik placards. This undermined the authority of the Menshevik-SR dominated executive of Soviet Congress. The workers and soldiers of the capital sensed their own power. Two weeks later they attempted to cash in on it. "This developed into the 'July Days'—the most important borderline between the two revolutions".[194]

The July Days
Suddenly the Bolshevik leadership was in an extremely difficult situation. A mass movement of a violently revolutionary character was developing, armed with Bolshevik slogans and led by many of their rank and file militants. The question was being put in an increasingly stark manner on the streets, in the factories and in the barracks: was it the moment for insurrection? Could revolutionary Petrograd carry the whole country?

On 3 July the 1st Machine Gun Regiment called for armed demonstrations against the government. This was supported by others who started touring the factory districts for support. The central committee meeting on the night of 3 July decided that although the time was not yet ripe for insurrection, if the mass of workers, sailors and soldiers were to appear on the streets next day, then the duty of the Bolsheviks was to be there with them.

Lenin faced opposition from his own ultra-left militants and in particular from the Machine Gun Regiment and the Kronstadt naval fortress. Raskolnikov, the sailors' leader, appeared the next morning outside the party HQ with 20,000 heavily armed sailors from Kronstadt. Raskolnikov was only the tip of an ultra-left iceberg. For some weeks the Bolshevik military organisation and its newspaper *Soldatskaya Pravda* had been at loggerheads with the central committee. While the main party paper *Pravda* was urging moderation and a campaign to win majority support in the Petrograd Soviet, *Soldatskaya Pravda* was demanding the seizure of power.

To add to Lenin's difficulties, what he had to rely on was not a smooth-running party machine with a large cadre of well-established local leaders, but a party undergoing a tremendous explosion of growth. How could there be stable leadership in Ivanovo-Voznesensk, where party membership grew from ten to 5,440 in five months; in Ekaterinburg where membership grew from 40 to 2,800 in the same period; or in Saratov where it grew from 60 to 3,000?[195] The authority of the central committee rested on a relatively small cadre of old Bolsheviks, and the influence that the most experienced section of the party could exercise over the new, enthusiastic, radicalised and rapidly growing membership. In many cases the old Bolsheviks bowed to the pressure of the new rank and file and from this came the crisis of the July Days.

On 3 June the second conference of workers' militias elected the Council of the Petrograd Popular Militia. This consisted of 11 members, including seven Bolsheviks and at least one Left SR. It was this Council, rather than the embryonic Red Guards, which played a key role in the events leading up to the July Days: the attempted uprising against the Kerensky government by workers and soldiers. In agitating for an armed demonstration against the government at the start of July, the Bolsheviks on the Council acted quite outside the control of the Bolshevik party central committee.[196] None of this activity was to Lenin's liking.

Without developing into an armed insurrection, largely thanks to Bolshevik restraint and Lenin's influence, the July Days went well beyond the bounds of mere demonstration, reflecting the anger and impatience of the Petrograd factory workers, soldiers and sailors who wanted to seize power. On 3 and 4 July the mass movement against the new military offensive culminated in huge demonstrations, the second of which had well over half a million workers and troops "armed to the teeth and with red banners and placards, demanding the transfer of power to the soviets," according to *Izvestia*.[197]

This huge march was dominated by banners and slogans demanding "Down with the Ten Capitalist Ministers", "Down with the Provisional Government" and "All Power to the Workers' and Soldiers' Councils". Lenin addressed the sailors from Kronstadt, urging moderation. His emphasis on a peaceful demonstration left them disappointed so they marched onto the Tauride Palace, then the headquarters of the Petrograd Soviet. Only the quick thinking of Trotsky, present at the time but not yet a member of the Bolsheviks, prevented them from lynching the executive leaders of the Soviet majority. There were provocative shots from windows and rooftops. There were armed clashes without a plan or a clear purpose but with many killed and wounded. There was the half-seizure of the Peter and Paul Fortress by the Kronstadt sailors and there was a siege of the Tauride Palace.

The party leadership held its nerve and maintained its course. Lenin was more cautious than the most militant workers, soldiers and sailors who wanted, there and then, to overthrow the Provisional government and establish soviet power. The pressure to do so was massive. The Bolshevik leaders knew technically they could have taken power in Petrograd with little difficulty; they could have overthrown the government because in the capital it had no reliable troops at all. But they also knew the rest of Russia lagged far behind: Moscow lagged behind Petrograd, and the provinces lagged behind Moscow. In her book, *Moscow Workers and the 1917 Revolution*, Diane Koenker highlights this:

> The July days, which provoked armed confrontations in Petrograd between revolutionary soldiers and workers and the defenders of the Provisional government, brought forth in Moscow a small procession of unarmed Bolsheviks, taunted by larger crowds of local citizens.[198]

Lenin insisted the key task remained the winning of a Bolshevik majority in the soviets, the workplaces and the army. He knew that would mean several more months of hard work and argument to expose the vacillations and betrayals of the Menshevik and SR leaders to the wider masses not yet convinced of the need for insurrection. Lenin argued bluntly that taking power at this juncture would mean a repeat of the Paris Commune in 1871, when an insurgent Parisian workers' movement, in advance of and isolated from the rest of the country, was drowned in blood. Such a defeat would set the Russian movement back for decades—a bigger and more serious setback than the defeat suffered in 1905.

Of course the Bolshevik party could not turn its back on the July demonstrations. Unable to stop them, as the leadership would have preferred, it sought to lead them, and lead them in the least dangerous direction. Just as Marx, who had opposed the Paris rising in 1871, sprang to the defence of the Commune once it occurred, so Lenin, who had opposed the whole orientation of the Bolshevik left on armed demonstrations at this time, wrote: "Had our party refused to support the 3-4 July mass movement, which burst out spontaneously despite our attempts to prevent it, we should actually and completely have betrayed the proletariat".[199]

By July the Bolsheviks had built such a decisive influence amongst industrial workers in Petrograd that they were able to restrain the demonstrations and hold back a premature insurrection. A combat party of long-standing, the Bolshevik leadership was used to exile and persecution. It had been through the havoc of the 1905 revolution and learned that the art of retreat is an essential survival skill, especially in the heat of a revolution when events seldom unfold at an even tempo, in a straight line or only on a rising curve. Lenin devoted his efforts to ensuring there would be no premature rising. Other revolutionaries in Europe, as the German revolution would later show, were to pay with their lives for not being able to make the right assessment in similar circumstances.

Repression
July was a necessary retreat, a most difficult and dangerous manoeuvre that had to be carried out against the opposition of some of the best and most militant party members, but a manoeuvre essential for a leadership that held to a Russian, as opposed to a local Petrograd, perspective. But the retreat still incurred very heavy costs.

The ebb of a mass movement always provides opportunities for the forces of reaction. Lenin's success in restraining the July demonstrations from insurrection, necessary though it was, opened up the opportunity for the Provisional government to strike at the Bolsheviks. The ruling class and their Menshevik-SR allies had been provoked and terrified, but their power had not been broken.

Pereverzev, minister for justice in the Provisional government, had already circulated a false story to the press claiming the Bolsheviks had deliberately provoked the July Days on the instruction of the German General Staff. It created a storm and repression inevitably followed.

The moderate leaders of the Soviet had no intention of breaking with the Provisional government. After the July Days, Prince Lvov resigned and Kerensky became its head. Two weeks later he formed a new coalition. In the meantime a vicious witch-hunt was launched on the Bolsheviks. Warrants were issued for the arrest of Lenin, Kamenev, Lunacharsky and Zinoviev. The charge was treason. The Bolshevik print shop was smashed by elite military detachments acting on Kerensky's orders.

With *Pravda* raided and closed, the party for a time depended on *Rabotnitsa*, the Bolshevik paper for women, re-launched as a weekly in May and a marked success. When police turned on *Rabotnitsa*, they found its editorial office empty. The women who wrote and produced it had taken all the copies to the factories during the night and avoided arrest. But not all women Bolsheviks were so fortunate. The police, searching for Lenin, arrested Krupskaya.

Alexandra Kollontai was arrested as she returned from an anti-war conference in Sweden. Her memoirs describe a series of interrogations by a colonel from the counter-espionage department, "a cocaine addict, prone to disconcerting bursts of violence". He told her that her friend Dybenko, the Bolshevik sailor's leader, was in jail along with Lenin, Trotsky and Lunacharsky and that unless she gave information about their role in the uprising, she would be charged with organising an armed insurrection, holding discussions with the German enemy and assisting Russia's defeat by encouraging mutiny in the ranks.

The Bolshevik party, now under severe attack from all sides, was branded "an agency of German Imperialism" and persecuted and driven underground. Lenin, slandered as a "German spy", had to flee from the Russian capital. Trotsky, not yet a member of the party, was about to be imprisoned too. Just before his arrest he came out bravely and defiantly to defend the persecuted Bolsheviks and publicly proclaim his solidarity with them. In a letter dated 10 July 1917, addressed to the Provisional government, Trotsky writes:

Citizen Ministers,

I learn in connection with the July Days, a warrant has been issued for the arrest of Lenin, Zinoviev and Kamenev but not for me. I therefore call your attention to the following.

I agree with the thesis of Lenin, Zinoviev and Kamenev and have advocated it in my writings and all my public speeches.

My attitude to the July events is the same as theirs. Kamenev, Zinoviev and I first learned of the plans of the Machine Gun and other regiments on 3 July. We took immediate steps to stop the soldiers from coming out.

When the demonstration did take place my comrade Bolsheviks and I made speeches in front of the Tauride Palace, in favour of the main slogan of the crowd 'All Power to the Soviets', but called on demonstrators, both soldiers and civilians, to return to their homes and barracks in a peaceful manner. At a meeting late on the night of 3-4 July between the Bolsheviks and the soviet organisations, I supported their motion that everything be done to prevent a recurrence of the demonstration on 4 July.

When it was learned the regiments and factory workers had already decided to come out it was impossible to hold back the crowd. All present agreed the best thing to do was to direct the demonstration along peaceful lines and to ask the masses to leave their guns at home. In the course of the day of 4 July, which I spent in the Tauride Palace, we urged this course on the crowds.

That I am not connected with *Pravda* and am not a member of the Bolsheviks is not due to political differences, but to certain circumstances in our party history, which have now lost all significance.

You cannot logically exclude me from the warrant of arrest made out for Lenin, Zinoviev and Kamenev. There can be no doubt I am just as uncompromising an opponent of the Provisional government as the above named comrades. Leaving me out merely emphasises the counter-revolutionary high-handedness that lies behind the attack on Lenin, Zinoviev and Kamenev.[200]

As the reaction gained confidence, arrests and intimidation were extended to broader sections of the movement. The Menshevik Woytinsky recalled how "the pendulum swung to the right. Reactionary forces tried to capitalise. 'Vigilantes' roamed the city, breaking into apartments in search of suspects. Public opinion demanded drastic measures".[201] Sukhanov, another prominent Menshevik, wrote: "Self-appointed groups of officers, military cadets and gilded youth, rushed to the 'help' of the new regime, trying to present itself as a 'strong' government." Mutinous regiments and Red Guards in working class districts were disarmed. Every suspected Bolshevik that could be found was seized and imprisoned. Kerensky and "his military friends were trying to wipe them off the face of the earth".[202]

It was a grim time for the Bolsheviks. They faced government harassment and the anger of workers who thought they bore some responsibility for the debacle at the front. Women, who constituted the majority of the lengthening bread queues, whose husbands were at the front, were more prone to rumours that Bolsheviks were spying for the Germans, undermining the war effort and taking German money. Female Bolsheviks were physically as well as verbally attacked. Elena Tarasova described her reception on 5 July at the factory in the Vyborg district where she worked. The moment she entered the plant she was pelted with nuts and bolts thrown by other women who screamed she was a German spy. When her face began to bleed, however, the women stopped hitting her, and some even helped clean and dress her cuts.

The women explained their hostility as they bandaged her, saying that while she had been hiding for the last two days, a Menshevik woman had been agitating against the Bolsheviks. This wavering among women workers seems to have been widespread. Konkordia Samoilova, who had organised the first ever International Working Womens' Day in Russia, was aghast when numbers of women workers who had recently joined renounced their Bolshevik membership.

On the other hand many Bolshevik women had been active in the July days. The youth organiser Liza Pylaeva, along with two other women comrades, had spent the night before the demonstrations at the party HQ. The Provisional government's efforts to suppress the Bolsheviks forced them into hiding on 5 July, and with Bolshevik soldiers and sailors the three young women hid out at the Peter and Paul fortress, armed and prepared to resist government troops. The women were carrying party documents, considerable party funds and a brief-case belonging to leading party member Sverdlov who, along with Elena Stasova, ran the party secretariat.

The young women comrades were determined these materials should not fall into the hands of the government forces. The fortress was under siege for a few hours before the women managed to escape, disguised as nurses. When stopped by government troops and challenged to identify what was in the baskets they were each carrying, Pylaeva replied, with a smile, "dynamite and revolvers". When the soldiers glanced into her basket and saw only bandages and medical equipment lying on the top, they did not pry any deeper, but instead chided her and let them go.[203]

The Machine Gun Regiment, which had been to the fore on the July demonstrations, was publicly disarmed and disgraced, as a warning to the rest of the armed forces. Krupskaya, who witnessed the scene, wrote: "so much hatred burned in their eyes, there was so much hatred in their slow march, that it was clear a more stupid method could not have been devised. And as a matter of fact, in October, the Machine Gun Regiment followed the Bolsheviks to a man, the machine gunners guarding Lenin at the Smolny".[204]

Lenin on the run

Lenin had to decide whether to appear in court to defend himself: "Now they will shoot us all", he told Trotsky. "For them it is the best moment".[205] He wanted to give himself up and argue against the accusations. Prevailed upon by Stalin and other leading Bolsheviks, Lenin agreed instead to go into hiding with Zinoviev. Trotsky and Kamenev gave themselves up, partly to take the heat off Lenin, and they were arrested and jailed. Then Kollontai and Lunacharsky were arrested. Hundreds of other Bolsheviks were jailed, some murdered without trial. The monarchist Kornilov was appointed supreme commander-in-chief of the Russian military and the death penalty was restored at the front. Trotsky described July as "the month of slanders":

> The opponents of Lenin's surrender were proved right by the story of the officer commanding the troops, General Polovtsev, who admitted, 'the officer going to Finland in hope of catching Lenin asked me if I wanted to receive that gentleman whole or in pieces. I replied with a smile that people under arrest very often try to escape.'[206]

This was clearly not a question of bringing a criminal suspect to justice but of seizing and killing Lenin, as the German Social Democrat leaders two years later killed Rosa Luxemburg and Karl Liebknecht. The repression following the July Days was vicious and for a period it disrupted the Bolsheviks, halting their momentum and puncturing the growing respect they had earned since March. But it was a temporary setback and the Bolsheviks would recover. Their real base was in the factories, particularly among the metal workers, and Kerensky's repression couldn't extend there.

Even in the immediate aftermath of the July Days, district soviets resisted the government's attempts to disarm workers and transfer the radicalised army units from the capital to the front.

The State and Revolution

But the situation remained enormously difficult for Lenin. He was now more than ever a marked man, forced into hiding from July until the October Revolution, a period of 111 days. At first he camped with Zinoviev in a forest on the outskirts of the city, then moved across the border to Finland.

At the end of September he returned to live clandestinely in Petrograd in a safe apartment. From July to October he was compelled to remain virtually isolated. But he took advantage of the relative peace and isolation to write his most important work, *The State and Revolution*.

He wrote it in a matter of weeks and it was published in the run up to the October revolution. It argues against a "parliamentary road to socialism" and against those who identify socialism with state ownership and control. Above all it explains why the capitalist state cannot be taken over and reformed by the working class: "Bourgeois democracy, although a great historical advance in comparison with medievalism, always remains, and under capitalism is bound to remain, restricted, truncated, false, hypocritical—a paradise for the rich and a snare and deception for the exploited".[207]

Reiterating the lessons Marx drew from the experience of the Paris Commune, *State and Revolution* was written to explain why there is no possibility of carrying through a socialist transformation of society without first destroying the old state apparatus with its standing army, police, judiciary, bureaucratic hierarchies and its corrupt, fake democracy. In 1848 Marx wrote: "The executive of the modern state is but a committee for managing the common affairs of the whole bourgeoisie".[208] The minority, who own the wealth and the means of production, also control the forms of government, its laws and the enforcement of those laws via the police, the armed forces, the various arts, science, academic and religious institutions and, above all, the press. They form themselves into a ruling class and use the powers at their command to ensure their continuing predominance.

Marx lumped all these various agencies of capitalism under one heading and called it "the state". Nikolai Bukharin, one of the most prolific and articulate of the Bolshevik theoreticians, pointed out in his book *Imperialism and the World Economy*, written in 1915, that the state was becoming more powerful and more concentrated; that the ruling class was forced to act more and more like "the executive committee of the bourgeoisie".

The various components of the state were not as they pretended, neutral between rich and poor. On the contrary, argued Bukharin, they were increasingly organising themselves into "one solid reactionary mass". Even the mother of parliaments had become "a decorative institution, passing on decisions prepared beforehand in the businessmen's organisations and gives only formal sanction to the collective will of the consolidated bourgeoisie as a whole".[209] Bukharin's points were expanded and developed by Lenin and applied to the concrete situation in Russia in the autumn of 1917: "The way out is not, of course, the abolition of representative institutions and the elective principle, but the conversion of the representative institutions from talking shops into working bodies".[210] In place of parliament, he argued, there has to be established the rule of directly elected and recallable workers' delegates. Only the working class organised as the ruling class can start the long transformation to a classless society.

It was Lenin's preparedness to think through the implications of working class power and self-activity that made him such a creative revolutionary, observing the real movement and measuring the basic principles against what actually happened on the ground. Bourgeois scholarship portrays Lenin as a scheming, Machiavellian opportunist, ignoring his real essence entirely. His obsession was not with power for its own sake but with greater freedom and real democracy. The sharp shifts and turns he was prepared to make were not the whim of a capricious mind but the result of his clear analysis of the working class, its revolutionary potential and the changing rhythm and tempo of class struggle.

State and Revolution gives concrete form to the theory of the workers' state, rescuing Marxism from its falsifiers who before the outbreak of the war were championing an evolutionary, gradualist socialism that failed the world so disastrously in August 1914. In 1917 the Mensheviks claimed that Provisional government and soviets could peacefully co-exist. But in August, as we shall see in the next chapter, an attempted military coup would prove otherwise and show the mass of workers that the choice was either "all power to the soviets" or the drowning of their movement in blood.

In *State and Revolution* Lenin anticipated such a threat and was adamant that the capitalist state could not be adapted to meet the needs of the revolution. For Lenin "the truth is concrete", and the best time for theoretical work on the state is when the question of state power is on the agenda. Writing *State and Revolution* helped him re-arm Bolshevism during the autumn of 1917. But he did not have time to complete it exactly as he had planned. Forced to deal with much more pressing matters at the end of September, Lenin's postscript to the pamphlet reads:

> I had already drawn up the plan for the next, the seventh chapter, 'The Experience of the Russian Revolutions of 1905 and 1917'. Apart from the title, however, I had no time to write a single line of the chapter. I was 'interrupted' by a political crisis—the eve of the October Revolution. Such an interruption can only be welcomed; but the writing of the 'Russian Revolutions of 1905 and 1917' will have to be put off for another time. It is more pleasant and useful to go through the 'experience of the revolution' than to write about it.[211]

The Kornilov coup and the road to workers' power

The period of intense repression after the July Days was not strong enough to inflict a decisive defeat on the working class. But it was strong enough to expose what Lenin called "the conciliators" squeezing the remaining working class support for the Mensheviks and accentuating the split in the SRs that had already begun. This pushed the Left SRs closer to the Bolsheviks.

Provocateurs and reactionaries had raised the cry that the Bolsheviks were German agents but the Provisional government was unable to substantiate its accusations; the documents "proving a pro-German conspiracy" were discovered to be forgeries, and one by one the Bolsheviks were released from prison without trial, on nominal bail or no bail, until only six remained incarcerated. Lenin, however, had to remain in hiding. He was still a marked man.

But by clamping down on the movement and targeting the Bolsheviks, the Provisional government had unleashed forces that wanted to destroy the soviets and every last vestige of the revolution, including the Provisional government itself. In an attempt to muster support, the Provisional government hurriedly convened a State conference in Moscow on 12-15 August. It was conceived as a consultative conference, where representatives of every class and profession could express their views. But it was a symptom of the post-July reaction that the propertied classes, the capitalist politicians and the Generals were represented out of all proportion to their numbers in the population.

The Bolsheviks boycotted the conference, leafleted it from the outside and organised a general strike in Moscow in protest at its undemocratic nature. This was convincing proof, were it needed, that Bolshevism was still very much alive and kicking, even if its voice was not heard inside the Moscow opera house where the State conference was taking place. A number of speeches from the extreme right—notably from General Lavr Kornilov, commander-in-chief of the army—made it clear that Kerensky was under pressure from the right to get rid of the soviets, curb the far left and impose greater discipline on the army.

The days immediately following the Moscow State conference proved how astute Lenin was when he described Kerensky's regime as increasingly unstable. On 21 August the Baltic port of Riga fell to the German Army and the Northern front threatened to collapse entirely, endangering red Petrograd. With the Bolsheviks still subject to persecution and apparently in disarray, right-wing elements convinced Kornilov the time was ripe for a military coup to save Imperial Russia. Kerensky was implicated. Kornilov had begun secret negotiations with him to introduce military rule in the capital under the General's personal command.

Kerensky's purpose had been to shore up his administration by getting the armed forces on the German front to send a large contingent to suppress the Petrograd Soviet. Kornilov readily agreed. Kerensky was eager that Kornilov crush both the soviets and the Bolsheviks. But at the last moment he learned that the retribution of Kornilov's counter-revolution would be extended to him and his government as well as the Bolsheviks and the soviets.

The General was not content with the plan to suppress Bolshevism. In collusion with the French and British military, he wanted Russia rid of the soviets, the moderate socialists and Kerensky as well as the intransigent Bolsheviks. Inflated with a sense of his own mission as saviour of society, he withdrew his allegiance from Kerensky's government and, having surrendered Riga to the Germans, ordered his troops to move on Petrograd by train on 27 August. Having plotted with Kornilov, Kerensky now tried to sack him.

But the commander-in-chief, convinced of support from all his generals, big business and the allied powers, defied Kerensky, boasting to his fellow officers that he "would not hesitate to hang them all if need be".[212]

As Kornilov advanced his battalions on Petrograd, Kerensky now felt obliged to offer at least formal opposition to a self-appointed military dictator. But Kerensky, his government, the leaders of the soviets, the Menshevik and Social Revolutionary committees and executives were now in a state of panic. They were in no position to defeat Kornilov's coup without help from the Bolsheviks, without arming the workers who followed Lenin, without reviving the soviets and the Red Guards suppressed after the July Days.

Kerensky himself asked the Bolsheviks to induce the sailors of Kronstadt, who had been at the forefront of the July mutiny against him, to "protect the revolution". Keeping their own grievances and resentments under control, the Bolsheviks responded to the appeal and fought in the first ranks against Kornilov. The counter-revolution over-reached itself and drove all the socialist factions and groups to unite against it.

A united front against Kornilov

Despite the fact they were semi-illegal and had been suppressed and persecuted by Kerensky, the Bolsheviks called for a united front against reaction and took the lead in building resistance. They offered no political support to the government whatsoever. What they did do was organise an energetic mobilisation against Kornilov and in defence of the revolution. This meant fighting alongside Kerensky and his supporters, but without subordinating themselves to Kerensky either politically or militarily. Although still in hiding, Lenin was instrumental in shaping this Bolshevik response. He insisted the real goal must not be lost sight of:

> It would be wrong to think in all this that we have moved away from the task of the proletariat winning power. No. We have come very close to it, not directly, but from the side. At the moment we must campaign not so much directly against Kerensky, as indirectly against him, namely by demanding a more active, truly revolutionary war against Kornilov. The development of this war alone can lead us to power.[213]

The Bolsheviks demanded Kerensky arm the workers and summon regiments loyal to the soviets back to the city. In doing so they were clear not to sow illusions in Kerensky but to speak over his head to the workers of Petrograd. Trotsky recalls a discussion with sailors from the cruiser *Aurora* who visited him in prison: "Isn't it time to arrest the government?" asked one of them. "No, not yet", was his answer. "Use Kerensky as a gun-rest to shoot Kornilov. Afterwards we'll settle with Kerensky".[214]

Committees for the revolutionary defence against Kornilov were organised everywhere. The Bolsheviks helped establish them and took part as a minority. Being the most consistent and energetic force, they were confident in their ability to play a leading role and were well used to punching above their weight. Historian David Mandel describes the fantastic response to their call for unity:

> News of Kornilov's march on Petrograd broke on the working class districts on the night of 27-28 August in an atmosphere of pent up rage and frustration. The workers' response was far from panic. In fact the howl of the factory horns announcing the emergency seemed to dispel in one swoop the sluggish, depressed mood of the preceding two months. There followed a show of enthusiasm, the like of which had not been seen since February.[215]

The Petrograd Soviet set up a Military Revolutionary Committee to co-ordinate resistance to Kornilov. Trotsky was released from jail to help lead and co-ordinate it.

Factory committees all over Petrograd quickly organised detachments of Red Guards. Led in the main by Bolsheviks, they encompassed over 40,000 workers. The Shlüsselburg explosives factory sent a barge load of grenades to the capital, which the central council of Factory Committees distributed among the workers of the Vyborg district.

The giant Putilov factory became a centre of resistance. Fighting companies were hastily formed and there was a sorting out of new cannon for the formation of proletarian artillery divisions. Factory worker Minichev said: "we worked 16 hours a day and got together about 100 cannon".[216] The newly formed railway workers' trade union had special reason to fear a Kornilov victory. He wanted to impose martial law on the railroads so the railway workers tore up the tracks and barricaded them to halt his army's advance.

Kornilov's army units would find themselves moving along the wrong tracks. Regiments would arrive in the wrong place, artillery would be sent up a blind alley. All the big stations had their own soviets, their railroad workers and their military committees. The telegraphers kept them informed of all movements, and changes. They held back Kornilov's orders. The machinists, the switchmen, the oilers, became agitators. "It was in this atmosphere that Kornilov's echelons advanced—or what was worse, stood still".[217]

The wonderful response of the workers and soldiers meant Kornilov's march on Petrograd collapsed in four days. He then fled but was arrested by the soldiers' committees. Generals were dismissed, government ministers who were implicated were suspended from their posts and the Cabinet fell. Kerensky tried to form a new government that would include the Kadets, the party of the bourgeoisie. But Kerensky's own party, the SRs ordered him to exclude the Kadets. At first he threatened to resign but popular feeling against the Kadets was so high that he dared not oppose it. Instead a temporary directorate of five of the old cabinet with Kerensky in charge assumed power in the hope of getting their way at a later date once the popular anger had abated.

Now the situation was transformed again. The Bolsheviks were out in the open, rapidly gaining mass support while Kerensky had no reliable force he could use against them after Kornilov's defeat. The united front against Kornilov brought a new lease of life to the soviets, which had become dormant since the persecution of Bolsheviks after the July Days. In September, against the overwhelming sentiment of the population, Kerensky and the moderate socialists established a new coalition with the propertied classes, and as result, "the Mensheviks and Socialist Revolutionaries lost the confidence of the people forever".[218]

Now the balance between the soviets and the Kerensky government shifted decisively and class polarisation sharpened considerably. Morgan Phillips-Price of the *Manchester Guardian* wrote, "the masses throughout the country won't endure a coalition government which betrays the revolution behind their backs any longer". John Reed records how the rejection of dual power was becoming self-evident:

> Along a thousand miles of front millions of men in Russia's armies stirred like the sea rising, pouring into the capital their hundreds upon hundreds of delegations, crying, 'Peace! Peace!'
>
> I went across the river to the Cirque Moderne to one of the great popular meetings, which occurred all over the city, more numerous night after night. The bare, gloomy amphitheatre, lit by five tiny lights hanging from a thin wire, was packed right up the steep sweep of grimy benches to the very roof—soldiers, sailors, workmen and women, listening as if their lives depended upon it.
>
> A soldier was speaking—from the Five Hundred and Forty-Eighth Division, wherever and whatever that was: 'Comrades', he cried, and

there was real anguish in his drawn face and despairing gestures. 'The people at the top are always calling upon us to sacrifice more, sacrifice more, while those who have everything are unmolested.

'We are at war with Germany. Would you invite German generals to serve on our Staff? Well we're at war with the capitalists too and yet we invite them into our government.'[219]

Menshevik support melted away and the split in the SRs deepened with the left everywhere gaining ground. The army became more and more radicalised; the authority of the officer corps had been fatally damaged by its support for General Kornilov. Sukhanov, a Menshevik representative in the Petrograd Soviet admitted, "it was obvious to any honest observer that our army, even though it was pinning down 130 German divisions on the Eastern front, could not hold out the winter, not even the autumn."

In his personal history of the revolution he recounts a session in the Petrograd Soviet on 21 September, when an army officer from the front spoke out against the war: "The soldiers in the trenches want only one thing now—the end of the war. Whatever you may say here the soldiers are not going to fight any more. I'm telling you what I know and what the soldiers have sent me to tell you".[220] In the countryside, according to the deliberations of the new coalition government, "disorders are now taking place on absolutely unendurable, really menacing proportions across Russia—there are riots in Zhitomir, Kharkov, Tambov, Orel, Odessa, etc, etc".[221]

There were shootings and martial law but repression could not quell them. The peasants, finally losing patience with the latest Provisional government, began settling the agrarian question in the manner the Bolsheviks had suggested, by their own methods. The estates and cattle herds of the rich were broken up and divided. Country houses were destroyed and set on fire. Arms were seized and stores were plundered. These were no longer "excesses", as the government had called them in May; it was now a mass movement, tidal waves of land seizures through-out the country.

Increasingly the Bolsheviks were able to pull the movement towards them. Not, as many historians would later suggest, because the leader-ship manipulated the party and the party manipulated the movement. Actually it was the other way round. Bolshevik organisation in 1917 was the most democratic internally and the most insistent on democracy from below.

The leaderships of the other socialist parties were far less accountable to their members, who had very little influence over a remote leadership whose policies many ordinary members felt lukewarm about, at best. Consequently the Mensheviks and SRs—the acknowledged peasant party—haemorrhaged support in the late summer and autumn of 1917. Most of it shifted to the Bolsheviks as their arguments developed throughout the course of 1917. The SRs split into the Right SRs and Left SRs and the Left worked alongside the Bolsheviks.

The popular radicalism from below continually pushed against the bourgeois limits of the February revolution, proving these limits too narrow. Instead an alternative base of power was built on the new factory committees and soviets. In *State and Revolution* Lenin made concrete this idea, outlining the possibility of a far higher form of soviet democracy.

The Bolsheviks were steadily increasing their delegation and support in the Petrograd Soviet of Workers' and Soldiers' Deputies, where, according to Kollontai, "in one brilliant speech after another, Trotsky was calling for power to pass to the soviets".[222] The Bolshevik central committee had swung to the left since the July Days. As well as Kollontai, Trotsky and Lunacharsky, it now included: Nikolai Bukharin; Adolf Joffe, a close ally of Trotsky and a former Menshevik; Karl Radek; Georgi Piatakov, a former anarchist who had worked with Shlyapnikov in Stockholm; and Christian Rakovsky, another ally of Trotsky.

On 31 August the Petrograd Soviet overturned its executive, carrying the Bolshevik resolution that argued the majority soviet parties must take power. When the old executive walked off the platform, fresh elections took place, which for the first time gave the Bolshevik party a substantial majority in the Petrograd Soviet. Trotsky was elected chairperson, the post he held in the 1905 revolution. Many delegates changed to the Bolsheviks and, significantly, delegates from the army regiments who had previously voted solidly with the SRs now defected in large numbers and voted for the Bolshevik position. Five days later the Bolsheviks won the majority of the Moscow Soviet. By the middle of September the soviets of Kiev, Kazan the old Tartar capital, Baku in the middle of the oil fields, and Finland and other industrial centres had all followed suit.

The Federated All Units Soviet of the Baltic Fleet held a congress against the wishes of its own Executive. It went ahead with 731 delegates. The supporters of the Provisional government got 42 votes. The rest went Bolshevik or Left SR. Thanks to the influence of the Bolsheviks, the struggle inside the soviets gave the rank and file soldiers and sailors the confidence to speak out and challenge their officers.

John Reed's description of a meeting of the Congress of Soviets gives a taste of the new kind of rank and file democracy being demanded inside the army and the navy. "An army officer attacked the Congress and claimed to be speaking for 'delegates at the front'. Soldiers in uniform began to stand up all over the hall. 'Who are you speaking for? What do you represent?' they shouted. 'You represent the officers, not the soldiers. What do the soldiers say about it?' There were jeers and hoots".[223]

Without that struggle in the soviets and the victory inside them of a revolutionary party over the parliamentary parties, the October Revolution would never have taken place. In his autobiography *My Life*, written after he had been expelled from the Russian Communist Party[224] and exiled to Turkey by the Stalin clique that rose to power after Lenin's death in 1924, Trotsky recounted the great significance of Lenin's *April Theses*:

> Lenin's stand at that period—that is before 4 April 1917 when he appeared on the Petrograd stage—was his own personal one, shared by no one else. Not one of the leaders who were in Russia had any intention of making the dictatorship of the proletariat, the social revolution, the immediate object of their policy.
>
> A party conference on the eve of Lenin's return showed none of them even imagined anything beyond bourgeois democracy. No wonder the minutes of that conference are kept a secret! Stalin was in favour of supporting the Provisional government of Guchkov and Miliukov and of merging the Bolsheviks with the Mensheviks.[225]

Trotsky, a fantastic orator, writer and agitator, by joining the Bolsheviks in July finally conceded to Lenin's constant mantra: that without an independent revolutionary workers' party, no revolution could succeed. Such was the force of Trotsky's personality and the clarity of his politics that within months of his arrival back in Russia in May 1917 he was elected onto the Bolshevik central committee. He stood second only to Lenin in the eyes of its massively expanding support. From July onwards, with Lenin forced underground, Trotsky would become the public face of Bolshevism.

There was a massive swing to the left and the Bolsheviks were growing fast. The estimate of membership in January, before the emergence from underground activity and the return of its exiled members, was 23,600. This was a broad enough base for further expansion during the more favourable months of revolution.

The Bolsheviks grew to 79,000 at the end of April; to over 240,000 by the end of July; and to 400,000 by mid October.[226] The vast majority of newer members were workers and soldiers. The slogan, "Peace, Land and Bread—All Power to the Soviets", matched the popular mood. By October there were more than 900 soviets in Russia.

The rights of oppressed nationalities in the old Tsarist Empire remained unresolved. The February Revolution established a republic of sorts and brought about a great awakening and a yearning for freedom. The formal equality only emphasised the extent of their real oppression. The Provisional government's repeated refusal to grant the right of self–determination, increased the opposition of the oppressed nationalities. Lenin's clear policy on the right of self-determination, which he had to fight for inside the leadership of the party, cut through the equivocation of the February regime and was a powerful lever in the October Revolution. That the soviets in Finland, an oppressed nation, went pro-Bolshevik in September proved it. John Reed describes the popular mood in September:

> A foreign professor of sociology visiting Russia came to see me in Petrograd. Businessmen had informed him the revolution was slowing down. He wrote an article about it and then travelled around the country, visiting factory towns and peasant communities.
>
> To his astonishment, the revolution seemed to be speeding up. Among the wage earners and those working on the land it was common to hear talk of 'all land to the peasants, all factories to the workers'. The professor was puzzled but he need not have been. The property owning classes were becoming more conservative, the masses of the people more radical.[227]

It was now obvious from the arithmetic as well as the politics, that a majority of the delegates attending the Second All-Russian Congress of

Soviets, due to convene on 20 October, would back a soviet takeover of power. But leading Bolsheviks, notably Kamenev and Zinoviev, opposed this, while Stalin hedged his bets, arguing instead for discussions with leaders of the Mensheviks and SRs. But Lenin and Trotsky were convinced further delay in challenging for soviet power could prove fatal.

In July Lenin had resisted those who wanted to seize power, holding back the party from a premature insurrection. Now, still in hiding, he was bombarding the Bolshevik central committee with letters demanding plans for one! His argument was based on the new balance of forces and the rapidly deteriorating military and economic situation. In mid September, because he was still in hiding, he felt compelled to write a series of urgent letters to the Bolshevik central committee under the title, "The Bolsheviks must assume power". At first the majority, chastened by the fiasco of the July Days and the repression it had brought on the party, rejected his call, but that did not deter him. (Actually they decided to burn the first one after reading it but they did not dare tell him.)

Fortunately Lenin took the argument outside the central committee, bombarding the whole party with a flurry of letters, articles and pamphlets arguing that Bolshevism was no longer isolated in Petrograd. The party, he argued, had already won a majority of workers and was backed by substantial numbers of the peasantry. The army was in ferment. The soldiers not only detested the war, Kerensky had been forced to issue a proclamation against the lynching of officers. Lenin stepped up the pressure with another article, *Can the Bolsheviks Retain State Power?*

> We have not yet seen the strength of resistance of the proletarians and poor peasants, for this strength will become fully apparent when power is in the hands of the proletariat, when every labourer, every unemployed worker, every cook, every ruined peasant sees, not from the newspapers, but with their own eyes that the workers' state is not bowing to wealth but is helping the poor.
>
> They will be convinced when they see that it confiscates surplus from the parasites to feed the hungry, that it puts the homeless in the houses of the rich, that the land is transferred to the working people, that the factories and banks are placed under workers' control. And that punishment

is meted out to millionaires who conceal their wealth. When the poor see this, no capitalist will vanquish the peoples' revolution.[228]

In a last ditch attempt to bolster its support, Kerensky's government convened a "Democratic Conference". It was rigged and unrepresentative. But instead of boycotting it and preparing a struggle for power, as Lenin argued, the Bolshevik central committee sent a delegation to it and proceeded to waste a week in futile discussion. This only spread confusion. Lenin and Trotsky had argued against participation in this fake conference and its successor, the "Pre-Parliament". Belatedly on 5 October the Bolshevik leadership agreed to the boycott.

The masses had gained confidence they could change Russia. For the Bolsheviks to declare they did not share their confidence would only undermine it. The economic crisis was growing worse by the day, threatening to turn hope into despair. Lenin predicted if the Bolsheviks did not move quickly, the ruling class would move to destroy the revolution, either by launching another military coup or by allowing the advancing German armies to capture Petrograd and drown the revolution in blood.

Trotsky put it like this: "the masses saw with their own eyes the danger of counter-revolution. They came to the conclusion it was now up to the Bolsheviks to find a way out of this situation. Neither the disintegration of the state power nor the confidence of the masses in the Bolsheviks could endure for a protracted period of time. The crisis had to be resolved one way or the other. 'It is now or never!' Lenin kept repeating".[229]

Finally, at a special central committee meeting on 10 October lasting ten hours, the decision was taken to plan for insurrection. Lenin, in disguise to evade arrest, was present and there was a sharp argument between him and Trotsky, over whether it should be the party or the soviets that should call it. Lenin, who had dedicated his political life to building the Bolsheviks for this very moment, argued the party itself should call the insurrection. Trotsky agreed with Lenin on the urgent need for an insurrection but was sure a call by the party alone was a non-starter. Backed by other Bolshevik leaders, notably Sverdlov, Bukharin and Kollontai, Trotsky had the advantage over Lenin of being better placed to gauge the mood on the streets, in the factories and barracks. Lenin was at a disadvantage; in hiding, he could not move around openly or attend meetings to hear the debates.

Soundings had been taken, and the general sense of those comrades who were for insurrection and hadn't got cold feet, was that the time was right but only if the call came from the soviets. Trotsky later made an astute analogy about the relationship between the party and the working class: "Without a guiding organisation the energy of the masses would dissipate like steam not enclosed in a box. But nevertheless what moves the locomotive is not the piston or the box but the steam." The February Revolution had already shown this. It was the action of the masses, not led by a revolutionary party. They were powerful enough to overthrow the Tsar and create soviets but not to prevent the coming to power of Prince Lvov's Provisional government.

Trotsky convinced Lenin that the party alone would not be a broad enough base from which to deliver the motive force required to drive the insurrection; that to pull most workers and soldiers behind it, the locomotive would have to be the soviet, not simply the Bolshevik party.

Lenin was not a bully, not a prima donna and certainly no fool. His willingness to listen and learn was what really made him a great leader. The Bolsheviks had majority support in all the major soviets and this meant the All-Russian Congress of Soviets, at this point scheduled for October 20, would back the call for insurrection. The Petrograd Soviet's massive authority would be a crucial factor in winning the 200,000 soldiers and sailors garrisoned around Petrograd. In an insurrection force is decisive and the soldiers and sailors who were crucial to it would be putting their lives on the line: if the insurrection failed they would be court martialled and shot.

At this late stage a small minority of the Bolshevik leadership still opposed insurrection. They entertained the dangerous illusion that the situation would go on becoming more and more favourable; that power would simply fall into their hands like a ripe apple, without any further party initiative. Zinoviev and Kamenev, backed by Stalin, who kept his options open, argued that the time was not right. They said there was a deepening process of radicalisation and by encouraging it, the Bolsheviks would win a majority in the Constituent Assembly, which the Provisional government kept promising to convene. Lenin poured scorn on this idea, saying the government had delayed the Constituent Assembly so many times it could not be trusted to convene anything; and that delaying the insurrection was inviting the generals to stage another coup. In his polemic *Can the Bolsheviks Retain State*

Power? Lenin quotes Marx on the danger of trying to disarm the ruling class while assuming a defensive posture:

> The defensive is the death of every armed rising; it is lost before it measures itself against its enemies. Surprise your opponents while their forces are scattered, prepare the way for new successes, however small; keep up the moral superiority which the first successful rising gives you; rally the vacillating elements to your side, which always follow the strongest impulses and are always on the lookout for the safer side; force your enemies to retreat before they can gather their strength against you. In the words of Danton, the greatest master of revolutionary tactics yet known: 'de l'audace, de l'audace, encore de l'audace'.[230]

Kamenev, Zinoviev and Stalin were clinging to the old, pre-April perspective of the Democratic Republic, pleading for more time to reform the Provisional government and establish a Constituent Assembly. A number of revisionist historians have cited their argument, claiming the revolution should have restricted itself to establishing a parliamentary democracy in 1917: a bourgeois revolution. While accepting that the Kerensky government was weak and ineffectual, they seem to believe a different coalition could have resolved Russia's crisis at the end of 1917.

But the choice in 1917 was not between workers' power and parliamentary democracy; it was not even a choice between soviet power and a Constituent Assembly; it was between workers' power and military dictatorship. There was no middle road. The Bolsheviks were preparing to defend the revolution by ending dual power in favour of the soviets, while at the same time the right was moving to crush the Bolsheviks, the soviets and the Provisional government. The choice was stark: revolution or counter-revolution. That was what was at stake when Kornilov moved against Kerensky. Kornilov was a figurehead for powerful forces out to crush all forms of democracy inside Russia.

These forces included Russia's imperialist allies Britain, France and the USA. Later Trotsky is reported to have said that had Kornilov succeeded, the word for fascism would have come into the world not as an Italian word but a Russian one.[231] These forces had not gone away. In October they were preparing to butcher Russia's fledgling democracy.

History since 1917 has repeatedly shown that in the middle of a revolutionary crisis there is a very high price to pay for illusions in the parliamentary road to socialism. As the great French revolutionary leader St Just cautioned, "those who half make a revolution dig their own grave." Fortunately the majority of the Bolshevik central committee finally grasped what was at stake and had the nerve and the audacity to act. In *Ten Days That Shook The World* John Reed explains it thus:

> It was the propertied classes who, when they realised the growth in power of the popular revolutionary organisations, undertook to destroy them and to halt the revolution. To this end the propertied classes finally resorted to desperate measures. In order to wreck the Kerensky ministry and the soviets, transportation was disorganised and internal troubles provoked; to crush the factory committees, plants were shut down and fuel and raw materials diverted; to break the army committees at the front, capital punishment was restored and military defeat connived at.
>
> This was all excellent fuel for the Bolshevik fire. They retorted by preaching the class war, and by asserting the supremacy of the soviets.[232]

On 9 October Trotsky, now chair of the Petrograd Soviet, persuaded it to revive its Military Revolutionary Committee, the same body that had coordinated Kornilov's downfall in August. And on 13 October the Soviet voted to instruct this committee to meet and lay plans for an insurrection in the imminent future. Also on that day the soldiers' section of the Petrograd Soviet voted to transfer all military authority from Army HQ to the Soviet Military Revolutionary Committee, and the Petrograd army regiments passed the following resolution: "The Petrograd garrison no longer recognises the Provisional government. The Petrograd Soviet is our government. We will obey only the orders of the Petrograd Soviet, through its Military Revolutionary Committee".[233]

In Petrograd rumour and speculation was rife: that Kerensky was considering the use of elite army units against the soviets; that Kornilov and the right were poised to install a military dictatorship, sponsored and funded by Britain, France and the USA to keep Russia in the war; that the Provisional government was about to abandon Petrograd to the Germans. John Reed's account confirms these intrigues were very real.

> Certain newspapers began to sigh for a Russian Napoleon. There were signs everywhere that the forces of reaction were gaining confidence.

On 15 October I had a conversation with the great Russian capitalist Lianozov, known as the 'Russian Rockefeller'—a Kadet.

'Revolution', he said, 'is a sickness. Sooner or later the foreign powers must intervene here, as one would intervene to cure a sick child and teach it how to walk. The nations must realise the dangers of Bolshevism in their own countries—such contagious ideas as proletarian dictatorship and world revolution. There is a chance that this intervention may not be necessary. Transportation is chaotic, the factories are closing down and the Germans are advancing. Starvation and defeat may bring the Russian people to their senses'.

Liazonov was emphatic that whatever happened it would be impossible for merchants and manufacturers to permit the existence of workers' committees or to allow the workers any share in the management of industry. 'As for the Bolsheviks' he said, 'they will be done away with by one of two methods. The government can evacuate Petrograd then a state of siege declared and the military commander of the district can deal with these gentlemen without legal formalities. Or if, for example, the Constituent Assembly manifests any utopian tendencies, it can be dispersed by force of arms'.[234]

Counter-revolution was afoot and in response the Soviet Military Revolutionary Committee met and decided it was now do or die. It began preparing for an insurrection in October with the date to be kept secret meantime; there was no point in alerting the class enemy too far in advance. On 16 October an enlarged plenum of the Petrograd Soviet, its Military Revolutionary Committee, the Petrograd trade union committees, the factory committees and the various military organisations all re-affirmed the decision for an insurrection. Although they did not make it public for obvious reasons, the plan was to synchronise the insurrection to coincide with the Second All-Russian Congress of Soviets, then scheduled by its outgoing, defeated Menshevik-SR executive, to meet on 20 October. The Bolshevik central committee then agreed to move to "technical preparations" for an insurrection after assessing the mood of the districts.

But shortly after the 16 October meeting it was discovered the Menshevik-SR dominated Executive had decided to delay the opening of the Second Soviet Congress yet again by another five days until 25 October. With Lenin in hiding and while everyone else was dithering, the Petrograd Soviet's Military Revolutionary Committee, under Trotsky's guidance, moved into action mode.

Zinoviev was still unhappy, claiming, "the mood in the factories is not what it was in June". Two days later he and Kamenev spilled the beans. Acting as the minority of the Bolshevik leadership opposed to insurrection, they wrote a joint letter to this effect and had it published in a non-party newspaper edited by Maxim Gorky. An angry Lenin claimed they were acting like "strikebreakers" and that "any worker would understand this". He demanded the expulsion from the party of two of his oldest comrades, but again, Lenin was outvoted; instead the two reluctant revolutionaries were censured, forced to resign from the central committee and prevailed upon to keep a diplomatic silence.

The October insurrection

On 21 October the Petrograd Soviet let it be known it had instructed all army units in the city to disobey any order not countersigned by its Military Revolutionary Committee—for it was the real authority as far as the Petrograd garrison and the Kronstadt naval base were concerned. This was a direct provocation to the government and its generals and was intended as such.

Sunday 22 October was designated "the day of the Petrograd Soviet". Workers, soldiers and sailors openly flooded into mass meetings at different venues and workplaces across the city under the guise of "a review of soviet resources". It was really a rallying of soviet forces and a deliberate and open show of strength to intimidate the class enemy. Trotsky's political opponent Sukhanov recalled how on that day,

> Trotsky, tearing himself away from the work of the revolutionary staff, rushed from the Obukhovsky plant to the Trubochny, from the Putilov to the Baltic works, from the cavalry school to the barracks; he seemed to be speaking at all points simultaneously. His influence among the masses and the staff was overwhelming. He was the central figure of those days and the main hero of this remarkable page of history.[235]

The only thing needed was to lure Kerensky's government into an act of provocation against the revolution, so that a defensive mantle could be thrown over the activities of the Military Revolutionary Committee. The government fell into the trap carefully prepared for it. Kerensky finally summoned what he hoped would be loyal army units from the Northwest front. On 23 October his regime issued the orders that it hoped would forestall its own downfall.

At dawn on 24 October, amid widespread talk of a plan to transfer all revolutionary regiments from Petrograd to the front, Kerensky's commander in Petrograd ordered soldiers to close down the Bolshevik printing presses. Detachments of officer cadets loyal to Kerensky were sent to guard government institutions and railway stations. The bridges across the river Neva were raised to isolate the workers' districts from the city centre. The battle cruiser *Aurora*, whose crew had been solidly for insurrection against the Provisional government ever since June, was ordered out to sea for training exercises. Telephone lines to the Soviet headquarters at the Smolny Institute were cut.

Next, Kerensky issued arrest warrants for all members of the Military Revolutionary Committee including Trotsky. Kerensky planned to arrest the entire executive of the Soviet and this was all the provocation the Military Revolutionary Committee needed, to go over to the offensive. The moment Kerensky's orders were issued, the Soviet agitators were out round the army units with the message: "no government orders to be obeyed!" The Bolshevik printing press was forcibly re-opened by Red Guards and by noon presses were running again. The orders to the *Aurora* were countermanded. Its crew then drove Kerensky's troops from the Neva bridges and re-opened them to the workers.

The plans of the Military Revolutionary Committee, which all the military units including the Red Guards, army regulars and the new conscripts accepted, were issued simultaneously. They had been worked out in advance, in great detail and with great precision. The clash of forces moved to its climax.

The garrison of the Peter and Paul Fortress wavered. Built on an island in the river Neva, its guns commanded the approaches to the Winter Palace on one side of the river and the city garrison on the other. For the insurgents it was critical they take the fortress quickly before Kerensky's government stopped debating and started doing something to protect itself. Sukhanov describes how, "two methods were proposed for taking the fortress. Antonov-Ovseyenko, Secretary of the Military Revolutionary Committee, proposed to send a reliable battalion to disarm the garrison. Trotsky had another proposal—that he, Trotsky, go to the fortress, hold a meeting there and capture not the body, but the spirit of the garrison".[236]

Trotsky set off at once with Lashevich, another member of the Military Revolutionary Committee. Their appeal was enthusiastically received. There and then the garrison passed a resolution supporting the soviets, affirming its readiness to rise up against the bourgeois government. A Soviet Commissar was installed in the fortress, under the protection of the garrison after it refused to recognise its official Commandant. A hundred thousand extra rifles from the fortress arsenal were now in the hands of the Bolsheviks.

On 24 October an anxious Lenin, in the dark and impatient to find out if the insurrection was really going to happen at all, threw caution to the wind and came out of hiding to arrive unexpectedly that evening at the Smolny Institute. He feared he would find evidence of insufficient urgency. He need not have worried. Once a residence of the Romanov Empress Katherine the Great, it was now the HQ of the Petrograd Soviet, for it had long outgrown its former meeting place in the Tauride Palace. The following afternoon Lenin appeared at the Petrograd Soviet, now in permanent session for the duration of the insurrection.

The insurrection itself was planned and orchestrated by Trotsky and Antonov-Ovseyenko, a former Tsarist naval officer and a staunch Bolshevik. In the early hours of 25 October detachments of armed workers, soldiers and sailors occupied all the bridges crossing the Neva, the railway and power stations, telephone exchanges, telegraph agency, ammunition dumps, banks and printing works. Other detachments were sent to mop up resistance anywhere the Provisional government still had forces. Morgan Phillips-Price, a British diplomat, wrote eyewitness accounts for the British press. His report for the *Daily Herald* from the Soviet headquarters on 25 October highlights the role of ordinary workers:

> During a quiet interval I went outside again. Soldiers with red cockades in their hats and sailors from the Kronstadt naval base had brought up a field gun. Detachments of Red Guards were arriving from the factories. A motorcycle came along. Someone in a leather overcoat from the Military Revolutionary Committee called to one of the soldiers, 'What detachment is this?'
>
> 'We are from the Putilov works', replied a young civilian with a rifle on his shoulder and a red armband on his arm. 'Who is your

officer?' asked the Commissar. 'There is none. We are all officers', said the Red Guard.[237]

Women played a keyrole in the events. Young female Bolsheviks, including the party's youth workers, Liza Pylaeva and Evgenia Gerr, took up arms as members of the Red Guard for the attack on the Winter Palace. There the Provisional government was installed, nervously hoping for early news to confirm that Kerensky's forces had succeeded in crushing soviet opposition.

Other prominent Bolshevik women, Nadezhda Krupskaya, Alexandra Kollontai, Konkordia Samoilova, Ludmilla Stal, Klavdiia Nikolaeva and Praskovya Kudelli, all had city-wide responsibilities, while others concentrated on local preparations: "Thus, Slutskaia played a key role in organising the Moscow district of Petrograd as Menzhinskaia and Lazurkina did in the first city district and Kruglova in the Okhta district".[238]

Fifty women workers prepared for the insurrection by spending the night at the Vyborg Soviet, taking instruction in first aid from a female doctor. Tram conductor Rodionova was a member of the detachment defending the city centre and was responsible for making sure that trams with machine guns left the depot for storming the Winter Palace. She also had to ensure the tram service operated during the night of 25-26 October, to assist the seizure of power and to check the Red Guard posts across the city.

Early on 25 October the Military Revolutionary Committee was able to issue the following proclamation:

> To the citizens of Russia: The Provisional government is deposed. State power has passed into the hands of the organ of the Petrograd Soviet of Workers' and Soldiers' Deputies, the Military Revolutionary Committee, which stands at the head of the Petrograd proletariat and garrison.
>
> The cause for which the people were fighting—immediate proposals for a democratic peace, abolition of landlord property rights over the land, workers' control over production, creation of a soviet government—that cause is securely achieved. Long live the Revolution of the Workers, Soldiers and Peasants![239]

There were hardly any casualties because there was virtually no resistance in the city.[240] The Kerensky regime went down without a shot except at the Winter Palace.

It was still held into the late evening by units that the Revolutionary Committee thought would obey Kerensky's orders, including the special Women's Battalion of patriots.

The battleship *Aurora* was brought up the river Neva and anchored outside the Winter Palace as a clear threat to encourage them to surrender. Both the Red Guard units and the regular units from the garrison had surrounded the Palace. The officer cadets inside were blasting away. They had lots of ammunition and were firing aimlessly as inexperienced soldiers do, but there were few casualties. Then the Revolutionary Committee brought up the cannon.

They fired the first of three blank rounds to convince the cadets inside they could reduce the Palace to a heap of rubble. They still wouldn't surrender so the sailors on the *Aurora* fired more duds and threatened to shell the palace with live ammunition. That threat was enough and most of the troops guarding the perimeter of the Palace surrendered. After this the pro-government forces melted away in the night—including Kerensky. Groups of armed workers, sailors and soldiers cleared the Winter Palace and arrested what few government ministers were left. By the time the Second All-Russian Congress of Soviets convened an hour before midnight, the news was pouring in of support for the insurrection.

When the Menshevik Sukhanov arrived at the Smolny Institute in the afternoon before the final seizure of the Winter Palace, the Petrograd Soviet was already in session and he recounts Trotsky's report to it: "We were told that the insurrection would provoke a pogrom and drown the revolution in blood. So far everything has gone off bloodlessly. We don't know of a single casualty. I don't know of any examples in history of a revolutionary movement in which such enormous masses participated and which took place so bloodlessly." Sukhanov then explains how Trotsky introduced Lenin to the meeting and goes on to recount Lenin's speech:

> The oppressed themselves will form the government. The old state will be destroyed and a new administration created in the form of soviets. Now begins a new era in the history of Russia and this third Russian Revolution. One of our tasks is to end the war; for that capitalism must be conquered. In this we shall be helped by the world working class, which has already begun to develop in Italy, Germany and Britain.

Within Russia an enormous section of the peasantry has said, 'enough of fooling around with the capitalists; we will go with the workers'. We must set out at once on the construction of a proletarian, socialist state.[241]

Was it a coup?

October was not like February; it did not involve such huge numbers on the streets. Some historians claim this means it was merely a 'coup'— a Bolshevik conspiracy; that the masses stayed home. But Trotsky explains, the opposite was the case: "If the Bolsheviks did not now call a general strike, it was not because they were unable, but because they did not feel the need. The Military Revolutionary Committee before the uprising already felt itself master of the situation".[242]

Compared to the February revolution, October was bloodless. Support for the Provisional government simply melted away. Yet the contrast between the spontaneous mass uprising of February and the alleged "Bolshevik coup" of October is one of the staple right-wing myths about the October revolution. Even according to liberal historian Robert Service, no fan of Lenin and the Bolsheviks, "the image of a tightly knit bunch of inveterate conspirators so assiduously cultivated by their enemies, was a cruel mockery".[243]

From the narrative it should be obvious to the reader that the Bolshevik Party was not an autocratic clique that seized power behind the backs of the workers. Had that been the case, the Russian Revolution could not have lasted a week.

Robert Service agrees: "What really counted was that the Bolshevik political programme proved steadily more appealing to the mass of workers, soldiers and peasants as social turmoil and economic ruin reached a climax in late autumn. But for that there could have been no October revolution".[244]

The revolutionary organisations, especially the soviets, were organically connected with the class that led the revolution. Between the aspirations and intentions of their members and those of the workers and soldiers who elected them, there could be no gap. While the majority of the masses were Menshevik, the soviets were Menshevik; when the majority began to follow the Bolsheviks, so did the soviets.

The Bolshevik Party was simply a party of class-conscious militants who could frame policies and suggest action alongside other such parties, in the soviets as in the factories themselves. Their coherent agitation and self-discipline meant they could implement policies quickly—but only if the workers and soldiers were prepared to listen and follow them. Even consistent opponents of the Bolsheviks recognised this. Sukhanov, an opponent who witnessed it first hand, dismisses the claim that the insurrection was nothing more than a military conspiracy as "an absurdity".

> Was the proletariat in sympathy or not with the organisers of the October insurrection? Yes the Bolsheviks acted with the full backing of the Petrograd workers and soldiers. To talk about military conspiracy instead of national insurrection, when the overwhelming majority of the people followed the Bolshevik party, when the party had already de facto conquered all real power and authority, was clearly an absurdity.
>
> On the part of its enemies it was a malicious absurdity but on the part of its 'cronies', Zinoviev and Kamenev, it was an aberration based on panic. Here Lenin was right.[245]

The truth about the Bolsheviks, a remarkable workers' organisation that proved indispensible as the mass of the population moved into action and reached out for power over their own lives, is buried under a mountain of lies and slanders, the work of conservative historians and anti-communists eager to prove 1917 has no bearing on the present—except to prove revolutions are bad and should be avoided like the plague. So Richard Pipes argues, "Lenin, Trotsky and their associates seized power by force... The government they founded derives from a violent act, carried out by a minority", while Orlando Figes in *A People's Tragedy* calls the October insurrection "a coup d'état".[246]

Fortunately more accurate and better-researched accounts paint a truer picture of Bolshevism in 1917. Alexander Rabinowitch's *The Bolsheviks come to Power* was written and researched in the 1970s when he was Professor of Russian Politics at Indiana University, and republished in 2004. It drew on newly unearthed material and includes the following portrait of Lenin's party:

> A major source of the Bolsheviks' growing strength and authority in 1917 was the magnetic attraction of the party's platform embodied in the slogans 'Peace, Bread and Land' and 'All Power to the Soviets'. The

Bolsheviks conducted an extraordinarily energetic and resourceful campaign for the support of the Petrograd factory workers and the Kronstadt sailors. Among these groups the slogan 'All Power to the Soviets' signified the creation of a democratic socialist government, representing all parties and groups in the soviet and committed to a programme of immediate peace, internal reform and the early convocation of a Constituent Assembly...

Perhaps even more fundamentally, the phenomenal Bolshevik success can be attributed in no small measure to the nature of the party in 1917. Here I have in mind neither Lenin's bold and determined leadership, the immense historical significance of which cannot be denied, nor the Bolsheviks' proverbial though vastly exaggerated organisational unity and discipline. Rather I would emphasise the party's relatively democratic, tolerant and decentralised structure and method of operation, as well as its essentially open and mass character.[247]

Rabinowitch reveals an organisation completely at odds with the top down monolith supposedly demanded by Leninist doctrine:

Amid the chaotic, locally varying, constantly fluctuating conditions prevailing in Russia throughout 1917, the central committee at the top of the Bolshevik organisational hierarchy was simply unable to control the behaviour of major regional organisations and except in a broad way, it rarely tried. The relative flexibility of the party, as well as its responsiveness to the prevailing mass mood, had at least as much to do with the ultimate Bolshevik victory as did revolutionary discipline, organisational unity or obedience to Lenin.[248]

Internal debate took place at every level of the party and leading members differed publicly. Lenin often found himself in the minority on key issues such as the party's opposition to the Provisional government, the October insurrection, the issue of a coalition government, elections to the Constituent Assembly and the peace treaty of February 1918. These arguments often divided the party as any serious disagreement in a democratic organisation is bound to do.

During the spring and early summer of 1917 the Vyborg local committee in Petrograd sent out its own agitators to tour the area around the Baltic arguing against what they rightly saw as their Petrograd Committee's over-tolerant attitude towards the Provisional government.

According to Robert Service, there was no tradition of subordination and top down discipline in the Bolsheviks. "Insubordination was the rule of the day, whenever the lower party bodies thought questions of importance were at stake... If anything Committees tended to be called into account from below rather than from above. Rank and file members and activists could not only make their views known but also re-elect their representatives at frequent intervals...few leaders succeeded in acting against the viewpoint of their colleagues over a lengthy period".[249]

The Bolsheviks could tolerate a high level of internal debate because the party's experience over two turbulent decades plus a high level of argument and discussion had led to clarity, agreement and trust. Even more important, they had used every opportunity to root themselves in the working class and its organisations, training their members never to stand aside or aloof from the struggle, and to express the party's ideas not in an abstract fashion, but in the context and experience of those struggles.

As Marc Ferro's account acknowledges, "a challenging of institutions and a radicalisation of opinion and behaviour" among workers, soldiers, peasants and subject nationalities, allowed the Bolsheviks to give "a movement that was both incoherent and convergent, the will to overthrow the regime".[250]

The first workers' government

The Second All-Russian Soviet Congress, the most democratic government institution in the history of the world, began at the Smolny Institute very late in the evening of 25 October—just as the storming of the Winter Palace was about to reach its climax.

The Congress delegates were overwhelmingly workers, soldiers, sailors and poor peasants from across Russia. Gone were the well-heeled intellectuals, the army officers and the moderate leaders who had dominated the First Congress held at the start of June. The October Congress was much younger and more proletarian. John Reed was there to see the new delegates arrive at the Smolny:

> Burly, bearded soldiers, workmen in black blouses, a few long-haired peasants. The girl in charge—a member of Plekhanov's group—smiled contemptuously. 'These are very different people from the first Congress',

she remarked. 'See how rough and ignorant they look, the Dark People!' It was true, the depths of Russia had been stirred, and it was the bottom that came uppermost now.[251]

Its political composition was different too. The majority of the delegates were supporters of Bolshevism. The party held 390 seats out of a total of 650. The strength of the Social Revolutionaries (SRs) was estimated between 160 and 190 but most of them were supporters of the Left SR party, which was now pro-Bolshevik.

The Mensheviks, who in June had more than 200 delegates, were reduced to less than 70. The Right SRs and Mensheviks could count on less than 100 votes. The Congress elected a new executive consisting of 14 Bolsheviks, seven SRs, three Mensheviks and one United Internationalist from Maxim Gorky's group.[4] The Right SRs and Mensheviks at once declared they would refuse to share executive power with the Bolsheviks, bluntly rejecting coalition as "collaboration with the party of insurrection."

After their spokesperson read a contemptuous statement to this effect, the minority of moderates, the Mensheviks and right SRs, decided to ignore the resolution they had just voted for, denounced the Bolsheviks for overthrowing the Provisional government and walked out of the Congress to the accompaniment of loud jeering from the vast majority who remained.

The meeting elected a new Central Executive Committee of the Soviet Congress—a legislative committee empowered to meet and act between sessions of the All-Russian Congress, but still subject to it. On this body the Bolsheviks were allowed 67 seats, the Left SRs 29; 20 seats were divided among the minor groups, including six United Internationalists.

The Congress also elected the new government, the Council of People's Commissars. Initially the Left SRs refused to join it, arguing their non-participation would enable them to mediate between the Bolsheviks on the one side and the Mensheviks and Right SRs on the other, so as to promote and obtain a wider coalition. Three weeks

---

4   The United Social Democrat Internationalists—also called Novaya Zhin (New Life) from the name of their influential paper—was a group of intellectuals with a small following among the workers and the personal followers of Maxim Gorky, its leader. Their programme was very similar to the left Menshevik Internationalists but they refused to be tied to either the Bolsheviks or Mensheviks. Opposed to the Bolshevik tactics, they remained in the Soviet government.

hence, when it became clear that many of the Mensheviks and right SRs were in fact lining up alongside the forces of reaction, the Left SRs would join the Soviet government in coalition with the Bolsheviks.

But for now the new Commissariat of People's Commissars appeared before the Congress of Soviets and asked for its endorsement. Lenin was asked to address the Congress and, according to John Reed, when he stood up to speak, after a prolonged ovation from the floor, he began, simply: "We shall now proceed to the construction of a new socialist order."

Lenin then read the Declaration of Peace "to the peoples of all the warring countries," calling on governments to open negotiations and agree to the soviets' demands for an immediate three-month armistice and an end to all secret diplomacy. Suddenly peace was no longer a dream.

Congress delegates agreed the following declaration: "Guided by the overwhelming majority of the workers, soldiers and peasants, by the victorious Petrograd revolution, which has been brought about through the efforts of the Petrograd workers and its garrison, the Second All-Russian Congress of Workers' and Soldiers' Soviet Deputies now takes the government power into its own hands. Long Live the Revolution!"[252]

According to John Reed's watch it was exactly 10.35 when Kamenev asked all in favour of the proclamation to hold up their hands. It was carried unanimously. In *Ten Days That Shook the World* Reed records: "Suddenly we were all on our feet mumbling together in the smooth lifting unison of the *Internationale*. A grizzled soldier sobbed openly and Alexandra Kollontai rapidly blinked back the tears, as the immense sound rolled through the hall. 'The war is ended, the war is over', said a young worker next to me, his face shining. Then someone at the back of the hall shouted, 'Comrades, let us remember those who died for liberty!' So we sang the Funeral March, that slow, melancholy and yet triumphant chant, so Russian and so moving".[253]

With its agenda completed and the Soviet government now in place, the delegates returned to their local areas scattered across Russia. In her later writings Alexandra Kollontai recalled that as she walked home through the streets of Red Petrograd that night, "extreme happiness and an awareness of our responsibilities merged into a resonant choir of sensations".[254] She remembered seeing outside the Smolny Institute a poster on the wall announcing that the Bolsheviks were in power and then turning to read a large poster beside it for *The Committee to Save the Country*, a body formed earlier that day by the collapsing Provisional government in an attempt to bring down the revolution.

While Russia's masses were hoping for peace, bread and land, its rich propertied classes, its generals and their British, French and US allies were already plotting to crush the new soviet regime. The battle lines were drawn. The next morning the Bolshevik newspaper *Pravda* reported defiantly, "so they wanted us to take the power alone, so that we alone should have to contend with the terrible difficulties confronting the country. So be it! We take the power alone, relying on the voice of the country and counting upon the friendly help of the European proletariat. But having taken the power we will deal with the enemies of the revolution and its saboteurs with an iron hand. They dreamed of a dictatorship of Kornilov; we will give them the dictatorship of the proletariat".[255]

8

War and Revolution: The international impact

The Bolsheviks always insisted socialism could not be built in any single country, certainly not in backward, war-ravaged Russia. The essential precondition for ending class society required the pooled resources of a number of the more advanced capitalist states—just as it would today. Having led the October Revolution to success, the Bolsheviks staked everything on international socialist revolution and looked in particular to the German working class. Lenin was clear: "It is not open to the slightest doubt that the final victory of our revolution, if it were to remain alone, if there were no revolutionary movement in other countries, would be hopeless. Our salvation from all these difficulties is an all European revolution".[256]

Later Trotsky put it like this: "Having, by virtue of historical necessity, burst the narrow bourgeois-democratic confines of the Russian revolution, the victorious proletariat would be compelled also to burst its national and state confines; that is to say, it would have to strive for the Russian revolution to become the prologue to a world revolution".[257] Because mass opposition to the war was already underway in Europe, the Bolsheviks were confident revolution would spread. Working class radicalisation under the conditions of war production was not confined to Tsarist Russia. Every major imperialist power passed through a similar experience.

1914 brought the first ever "total war" and to meet its challenge every one of the belligerent states was forced to intervene on an unprecedented scale in its economy, imposing rationing, conscription of labour, commandeering key firms and banning strikes. In this they received the loyal assistance of the leaders of the traditional workers' organisations—the social democratic parties and the trade unions. "Social Peace" was proclaimed across Europe as the leadership of the workers' movement in every country did its bit for the slaughter.

In Britain the war eventually consumed 70 percent of everything produced and this kind of war economy was replicated across Europe. In Germany Generals Hindenburg and Ludendorff exercised a virtual dictatorship over the economy.

Within the process of production workers were subjected to a draconian state discipline backed by their own trade union officials. In Britain strikes were made illegal and strike leaders faced imprisonment under the Defence of the Realm Act, while in Italy and Germany agitators like anti-war Reichstag deputy Karl Liebknecht were conscripted to the front. Wages were controlled while rents, prices and profits were allowed to soar. Labour historian James Hinton coined the term "the Servile State" and described its British manifestation:

> The collaboration of employers, state and trade union officialdom presaged the growth of a bureaucratic regulation of every aspect of economic life and the withering away of social and political freedoms. It was a war whose fate was decided as much in the workshops of Britain and Germany as it was in the trenches of France. The context of blood and iron is at the same time the context of intensified social discipline, of domestic repression.
>
> War brutalised and simplified social relations—at home as well as on the front. It lent some of its own violence and urgency to the workers' perennial fight for economic security and for class power.[258]

By the end of 1917 workers across Europe were clamouring for peace and ready to fight for a better world instead of each other. There was indeed the "whirlwind of struggle in the West" Trotsky had hoped for—a stormy revolutionary movement that swept across Europe. The February Revolution of 1917 had been preceded by the Dublin Easter Rising in 1916. The overthrow of the Tsar was followed by two massive strike waves centred on Berlin in April 1917 and January 1918 that were punctuated by strikes of 200,000 British engineering workers in May 1917 and a mass uprising in Turin in August 1917. In May that year the entire French army on the Western front mutinied.

The October Revolution was followed by the German Revolution at the end 1918. It toppled the Kaiser, ended the war and led to a situation of dual power. Soviet regimes were actually established in Hungary,

Bavaria, Finland and Latvia and there was an uprising in Vienna. The opening shots in the Irish war of independence against British rule were fired in January 1919 and throughout that year there were mass strikes in Britain. September 1920 saw the occupation of the factories throughout Italy alongside land seizures by agricultural workers.

The 1916 Easter Rising had been the harbinger of what was to come. Revolutionary socialist James Connolly had anticipated the war and he fully expected the international socialist movement to live up to its pre-war resolutions and oppose it. He hoped it would use the outbreak of war to launch a general strike in all the belligerent nations and bring capitalism crashing. Instead, Connolly watched in horror as the socialist and trade union leaderships in Germany, France and Britain lined up alongside their own rulers, ditching socialism for patriotism.

When Connolly helped lead the Easter Rising his perspective was not that of a nationalist. He was determined to strike a blow for Irish freedom but he predicted that against the backdrop of the First World War, a revolt in Dublin would have worldwide significance, encouraging the anti-colonial struggle throughout the British Empire and starting a chain reaction that would end the war: "Ireland may yet set a torch to a European conflagration that will not burn out until the last throne and the last capitalist bond and debenture will be shrivelled on the funeral pyre of the last warlord".[259]

The inspiration of revolutionary Russia

In early 1917 a war-weary European working class welcomed the overthrow of the Tsar and looked to Russia for hope and inspiration. Ordinary people began to rebel in huge numbers. Following on from the mutiny of the French army, 10,000 British and Commonwealth troops mutinied at Étaples in France. Throughout 1917 there were mutinies and mass desertions in the Russian, Italian, Austrian, Turkish and German armies. The February Revolution in Petrograd inspired huge peace demonstrations in Britain, Germany, France, Italy and Austro-Hungary. In March 1917, 12,000 packed into the Albert Hall in London to support the Russian Revolution. Another 5,000 supporters were locked outside.

In the spring of 1917 women textile workers in Paris went on strike and their struggle became famous among French troops taking part in the huge mutiny at Chemin des Dames. One machine gunner wrote home, "we are emulating the Midinettes", referring to the seamstresses' strike. When the French government threatened to send a prominent anti-war union activist to the front, 200,000 workers took strike action and won his reprieve. In May Renault workers struck over pay and against the government's planned military offensive. Within two days the strike spread to the Peugeot and Citroen plants to involve 200,000 workers. A strike rally at Billancourt ended in chants of "Down with the war!"

In May 1917 after news of the February Revolution arrived in Austria, 42,000 metal workers struck in Vienna. After the October Revolution the favourite slogan among the militant Viennese workers was "Speak Russian".

In Britain a mood of optimism generated by the Russian Revolution lifted the gloom. In 1914 the shock of the war and an initial wave of patriotic fervour had brought four years of bitter, mounting industrial struggle, the great unrest, to a juddering halt. But within a year the struggle began to revive. Although 5 million workers were away in the army, Britain's trade union membership grew from four to six and a half million between 1914 and 1918.

By the end of the war the annual figure of 6 million working days lost to strikes showed how much things had changed—for it happened in a period when striking meant defying the government, the bosses, the courts, the police, the army, the press barons, the trade union officials and the Labour Party. Many of the militants who led this activity, as in the pre-war days, were revolutionaries who rejected the parliamentary road to socialism. In munitions the new intake of women took part in industrial action alongside the men, and independently when necessary.

In 1916 women munitions workers on Tyneside staged a sit-down strike over pay. They went to their machines but sat knitting, sewing or reading. When management appealed to them to remember the men at the front they were told: "don't mention the soldiers. England at two and a half pence an hour isn't worth fighting for".[260] This general revival in working class confidence, already underway, was boosted by news of the February Revolution in Russia. There had already been illegal, unofficial mass strikes on Red Clydeside, across the South Wales coalfield and in Sheffield. In May 1917 200,000 engineering workers struck throughout the midlands and the industrial north of England. On

May Day 70,000 marched through Glasgow in solidarity with the February revolution, and at the end of May another demonstration of 90,000 marched to Glasgow Green to demand the release of jailed anti-war socialists John Maclean and the Russian refugee Peter Petroff, a hero of the 1905 Revolution now exiled in Scotland. Two hundred Russian sailors left their warship as it lay at anchor on the Clyde to join this march.

Labour responds to the Russian Revolution

The problem for the government, according to Arthur Henderson, leader of the Labour Party, was that discontent at home was being "deepened by the Russian Revolution". At the outbreak of war Ramsay MacDonald was Labour's leader. A pacifist who voiced his doubts about the war, he was quickly deposed by the patriotic trade union bureaucracy and replaced by Henderson, whose pro-war stance earned him a cabinet post in the National Coalition government formed in 1915.

At the beginning of 1917 Labour was mired in class collaboration. Yet by the end of the year it was championing a socialist programme and in 1918 adopted Clause IV. It seemed that Labour was poised to bid for power on a socialist programme. The Russian Revolution, its popularity and its massive impact on working class struggle had forced Labour leftwards. Clause IV, later ditched by Tony Blair, claimed Labour's aim was "to secure for the workers by hand or by brain the full fruits of their industry and the most equitable distribution thereof that may be possible upon the basis of common ownership of the means of production, distribution and exchange, and the best obtainable system of popular administration and control of each industry and service".

The party had barely existed as an independent force until late in the war. Its adaption to the rising struggle and its need to renew its organisation and enhance its appeal in the wake of the Russian Revolution led to the Leeds Convention. In June 1917 this brought together 1,300 delegates representing all the organisations critical of the war. There was a strong pro-Russia mood among workers in Britain, who contrasted the democratic sensitity of Russia's soviets with the entrenched and reactionary parliamentary system that still denied all women and many working class men the vote.

At the Leeds conference there were revolutionary speeches and calls to establish workers' and soldiers' councils across Britain. But Ramsay

MacDonald and Phillip Snowden proposed the main resolutions. MacDonald described the con he played at Leeds in an article written soon afterwards: "Before the war I felt that what was called 'the spirit of the rebel' was to a great extent a stagey pose. It was now required to save us." MacDonald's first gambit was to pay tribute to Russia's February revolution. Addressing the Convention he said: "when this war broke out, organised labour in this country lost the initiative. It became a mere echo of the governing classes' opinions. Now the Russian Revolution has given you the chance to take the initiative yourselves".[261]

The Leeds gathering promised great things but delivered nothing. Henderson, MacDonald, Snowden and the other Labour fakers used both Clause IV and the Leeds Convention in a deliberate, conscious attempt to stave off revolution. Henderson went to Russia representing Lloyd George's coalition cabinet, arriving in Petrograd in June 1917. His job was to encourage the Provisional government to continue the war. When he returned he determined to ensure the Labour Party was ready to oppose any revolutionary developments at home, describing revolution as "alien to the British character" and arguing "only Labour can rehabilitate parliament in the eyes of the people".

But the October Revolution made an even bigger splash in Britain than the February events. The new Soviet government was greeted across Europe with wild enthusiasm. John Maclean, along with the German anti-war socialist Karl Liebknecht, was made an honorary president of the Soviet government and appointed Soviet Consul in Glasgow. Anti-war socialist Harry McShane, a close comrade of Maclean, recalled:

> I was a shop steward and working at A W Smith's factory when the second Revolution occurred and the Bolsheviks took power through the soviets. The Liberals went stone mad; Winston Churchill toured the country speaking against the Bolshevik 'beasts', losing any popularity he ever had among the working class.
>
> Labour wouldn't support the Bolsheviks either. Like the Liberals, Ramsay MacDonald had been supporting Kerensky, who wanted a parliamentary 'Duma'—not soviets. Of course the revolutionary element, including some in the ILP, began to understand workers' democracy. For the Glasgow socialist movement the October Revolution and the new soviet system was a revelation. From Phillips-Price's reports in the *Manchester Guardian* we got to know the slogan "All Power to the

Soviets" and a better idea of what they were—workers' and soldiers' councils, a new kind of rank and file organisation.

In Russia they had discovered something new: a system of working class self-government, through which the old crowd could be completely destroyed. We began to realise what was meant by revolution. We could now talk of working class power, before we had only known working class revolt.

For the first time the ordinary worker saw something being gained by revolution; and with the kind of fight that we had in Glasgow for workshop organisation it was easier for them to understand what was happening in Russia. People were sympathetic to revolution and we could get our ideas across. Lenin's *State and Revolution* helped us enormously.[262]

In January 1918, with strikes mounting, prominent Fabian Beatrice Webb wrote in her diary that Labour's leadership was "distinctly uneasy about the spirit of revolt amongst the rank and file, which openly declares its sympathy with the lurid goings on in Petrograd". Arthur Henderson warned "at no period during the war had the industrial situation been so grave and so pregnant with possibilities. The temper of the workers is dangerous and the unyielding attitude of the government brings the country to the verge of industrial revolution".[263] According to Lloyd George the police strike brought the country "nearer to Bolshevism than at any other time." For Lloyd George things were about to get worse.

Britain and its empire

1919 was the worst year for the British ruling class since the Chartists. In January 10,000 soldiers demonstrated at Folkestone against being sent back to France. They set up a soldiers' union and refused to sail. The strike spread and so did their popular chant, "Come on you Bolsheviks".[264] At Dover 2,000 soldiers, ordered to embark for France, mutinied, formed a soldiers' union and went on strike. The boats sailed empty. Twenty thousand British soldiers mutinied at Calais, electing strike committees and a soldiers' council.

Churchill wrote, "under the present pressure the army is liquefying fast." He cabled prime minister Lloyd George to say that if demobilisation were not speeded up, there would be nothing left of the army but a "demoralised and angry mob". General Haig complained that "if things went on in the same vein, he would have no army left in France by February".[265]

The British ruling class was in big trouble: they could not get their troops to fight abroad and they couldn't be confident about using them against strikers on the domestic front. And they needed to, for throughout 1919 UK strike figures reached unprecedented numbers. The year began with the 40 hours strike that brought Clydeside and Belfast to a standstill. Miners struck, railway workers struck, sailors mutinied and even the police went on strike. When the London Metropolitan force struck, flying pickets hundreds strong went from police station to station forcing others to join them.

From July 1917 the British government was actively involved in the Western powers' intervention against revolutionary Russia and although every effort was made by the state to cover up the extent of this, mass opposition soon prevailed. In January 1919 the revolutionary left, the ILP and the National Shop Stewards Movement organised a Hands off Russia conference in London. The *Daily Herald* backed the campaign and in June a national Hands off Russia conference was held in Manchester, at which John Maclean spoke along with Sylvia Pankhurst.

Even the leaders of the Labour Party, although completely opposed to anything that smacked of revolution, condemned Churchill and Lloyd George's intervention. Philip Snowden for example poured scorn on the idea that "the government was waging a war against Bolshevik excesses". After all "they were bosom buddies of the late Tsarist regime, which committed more diabolical outrages in a day than the Bolsheviks have committed in a year of revolution".[266]

The Hands off Russia campaign pulled out the stops when London dockers, ordered to load supplies and munitions for the Russian offensive onto the *Jolly Roger* in the East India Docks, walked out in protest. When the government threatened to use troops to load the ship, the unions told them the whole port would shut, so they promptly backed down. In August 1920 as Lloyd George again threatened military intervention against revolutionary Russia, protest meetings were held all over Britain and the government was panicked into thinking the unions might call a general strike against such a move. For the first time the *Daily Herald* produced a special Sunday edition to condemn the intervention, its editorial claiming: "The workers only had to fold their arms for forty eight hours to bring down the wickedest government that has ever betrayed this country".[267] In 1919 General Sir Henry Wilson, chief of the Army, told King George and his cabinet; "A Bolshevik rising was likely".[268]

To cap it all the Irish War of Independence had begun, and it was igniting rebellion across the Empire. In 1919 a soviet was declared in Limerick. The year before 10,000 had attended a May Day rally in Dublin, at which a resolution was passed paying tribute to "'our Russian comrades who have waged such a magnificent struggle for their political and social emancipation'. A year later the same workers borrowed the Russian term 'soviet' as the name for their own protests against British rule".[269]

Tory leader Bonar Law told Lloyd George: "The King is in a funk about the labour situation and is talking about the danger of revolution".[270] No wonder; his cousins Tsar Nicholas and Kaiser Wilhelm had been toppled, along with the Hapsburg dynasty that had ruled central Europe for generations and the Ottoman Empire that ruled Turkey and the Middle East.

So scared of revolution was the British monarchy that King George, counselled by his cabinet, refused his relative the deposed Nicholas II and his family, political asylum and safe residence in Britain. Their later execution by the Bolsheviks in June 1918 provoked "horror and outrage" on the part of the establishment, but Royalty and government here were willing to sacrifice the Romanovs to save their own skins.

If Britain had been defeated in General Ludendorff's spring offensive of 1918 on the Western front—and for a period such a catastrophe was perilously close—it would have brought the downfall of the Saxe-Coburg-Gotha dynasty. In panic they changed their name to Windsor during the war, largely because of anti-German sentiment stirred up primarily by the British government and the capitalist press. Haig, the British commander-in-chief on the Western front recorded in his diary: "The Kaiser is in Holland and if the war had gone against us no doubt our king would have had to go".[271]

Germany: the key centre

Germany, the industrial power house of Europe, was the key centre of the European revolt. From 1916 onwards it saw bread riots, mass strikes, mass desertion of German troops from the Western front, mutinies in its North Sea Fleet and the formation of workers' councils right across Germany.

The toppling of the Tsar and the collapse of Russia's military machine put paid to the feeble excuse used by the leaders of German Social Democracy (SPD) that Germany was fighting "a war for national defence against Russian tyranny". To increasing numbers of German workers and soldiers, the real menace was the war policy of their own German state. Karl Liebknecht and Otto Ruhle, elected as Reichstag deputies for the SPD, had opposed their party's line and agitated against the war. For his continued opposition Liebknecht was conscripted into the army. In May 1916 he was re-arrested for treason as he condemned the war from the rostrum at the Berlin May Day rally while wearing his army uniform.

His arrest provoked a wave of street clashes with the police and Germany's first mass political strike of the war. At the start of his trial mass demonstrations took place in Berlin: when he was sentenced to four years hard labour, 55,000 munitions workers came out on strike. Although broken by the German state, the strike reflected the growing anti-war mood which split the SPD, leading to the foundation of the German Independent Social Democratic Party (USPD).

Famous names associated with the "Great Betrayal" of 1914, Kautsky, Bernstein and Hilferding, left the SPD and joined its left breakaway. The Berlin revolutionary shop stewards who led the May strikes, and the Spartakists, a small revolutionary group of SPD members associated with Rosa Luxemburg and Karl Liebknecht, joined the newly-formed USPD too.

By the start of 1917 real wages had fallen drastically and food was so scarce that the German winter of 1916-17 became known as the turnip winter. Despite press censorship German workers became aware of two important events: the February Revolution in Russia and bread riots in Leipzig, both led by working class women. The Berlin shop stewards decided it was time to strike against the war but the police tried to pre-empt the strike by arresting Richard Müller, its leader.

Yet three days later Berlin was paralysed as 200,000 workers came out on strike. On 16 April the Leipzig bread protest escalated into a political challenge to the state.

Strikes erupted in the city as Leipzig produced the first German workers' council. As well as demanding bread, the strike raised political demands: for peace without annexations, the abolition of anti-labour laws, the end of censorship and freedom for political prisoners. In Berlin the 10,000-strong workforce at the DWM engineering plant elected a factory council and other factories followed suit. For a time it looked like the shop stewards' initiative would transform the strike from a food protest into a challenge to the war.

But in 1917 the Prussian state machine was still intact. Police arrested the key militants, all the factories were placed under martial law and the strikers began drifting back to work. Müller's arrest had weakened organisation and the top union officials stepped in to defuse the unrest. But what had begun as a bread strike far surpassed the earlier action of 1916.

Finally a third series of mass strikes began in Austro-Hungary in January 1918 and spread rapidly to Germany, acting as the curtain raiser for the German Revolution itself. The action started in Budapest at the biggest munitions factory in Hungary. It spread to the factories in lower Austria and Vienna. Days later the Berlin munitions workers followed suit.

> On the morning of 28 January 1918, the lathe operators and shop stewards signalled the start of the action by striking their hammers onto the oxygen tanks used for welding. Within a few hours Berlin's entire armaments industry was at a standstill. By the afternoon 414 delegates representing 400,000 workers gathered for a meeting in the Berlin union halls. Richard Müller led the assembly and received their demands: peace without annexations, democratisation of the entire state apparatus.[272]

An action committee was elected, which included Clare Casper, its only woman member, itself a revolutionary breakthrough. Two million workers took part as the movement spread to the docks in Hamburg and the coalmines in the Rhine-Ruhr region. At one of the many mass rallies the speaker argued, "we are not fighting for ten grams of butter but for all who hate the war."

In Nuremburg strikers went from factory to factory shouting "peace", to persuade those not already on strike to join in. A vast demonstration took place in which tens of thousands, many of them youngsters and many of them soldiers in uniform, took part carrying posters with the slogans "Bread, Peace" and "Liebknecht must be freed".[273]

But the movement was contained and eventually collapsed. The shop stewards' networks were important but they were not enough. It was not state repression that contained the strike but the chicanery of the leading SPD politicians who sabotaged the strike by negotiating a rotten compromise that only addressed its economic demands. The left USPD leaders also undermined the strike by deferring to the SPD and refusing to put out leaflets supporting the strikers. Although the revolutionary shop stewards and the Spartakists around Rosa Luxemburg had joined the USPD, its centrist leadership ensured it remained primarily a parliamentary party.

Revolution in Berlin

The German Revolution began in November 1918. The Kaiser's war machine was collapsing under the sheer weight of mutinies and mass desertions in his army and navy. In November 1918 the "bodies of armed men" Engels had pointed out are the essential core of the state machine, began to turn on their masters.

The port of Kiel was at fever pitch. The High Command and the officers of the navy surrendered, while some on the battleship Koenig and other vessels were killed. The sailors had become masters of the situation and the army units in the area joined them. In Kiel there was only one authority, the Council of Workers', Sailors' and Soldiers' Deputies. From Kiel the rebellion spread to Hamburg and on the night of 8 November the worried authorities in Berlin learned the insurgents had triumphed with little or no resistance, in Hanover, Magdeburg, Cologne, Stuttgart, Munich, Frankfurt-am-Main, Brunswick, Oldenburg, Wittenberg and other cities.

On the morning of 9 November the general strike broke out in Berlin. The Kaiser fled and the German workers, through their councils of deputies, found themselves in power. The German Revolution brought the war to an abrupt end. The Prussian monarchy had reigned for hundreds of years, and ruled the whole of Germany for half a century. Now it had collapsed in a few short days.

The German High Command had been scrambling to make new friends, especially the leadership of the SPD, by promising democracy. They even released Karl Liebknecht, who was greeted as a hero by thousands of triumphant workers and soldiers in Berlin. The task now was to consolidate a revolutionary, democratic workers' republic. But the right-wing SPD, who controlled the largest block of delegates on the workers' councils, were determined to avoid this at all costs. They had become the junior partners of the German ruling class during wartime and they were setting out to save German capitalism.

Europe ablaze

As well as Germany, the years 1918-20 saw revolution in Austria and the setting up of soviet republics in Hungary, Bavaria, Finland and Latvia. The victorious powers were also embroiled in the revolt. For "two red years" Italy was convulsed by massive struggles, including a wave of factory occupations and land seizures.

Even before the October Revolution militant workers in Turin knew about Lenin and the Bolsheviks, who were still largely unknown throughout the rest of Europe. News of the February Revolution and the overthrow of the Tsar brought widespread hope to Italian workers that the February events in Russia would go further and bring an end to the war. On May Day 1917 anti-war demonstrations were held in the northern cities with women and youth playing a key role. They continued over the early summer and reached their peak in Turin. A delegation from Kerensky's Provisional government came to the city in August to address a mass rally of 40,000 munitions workers. Comprised of Mensheviks and other moderates, the delegation was there to urge the Italian workers to work harder and produce more weapons for the war effort. The Russian delegation was astonished at being heckled as large sections of the crowd kept chanting: "Viva Lenin!"

Two weeks later the city was gripped by food riots initiated by working class women. Like their counterparts in Petrograd and Liepzig they were expected not only to queue for hours for meagre food rations but also to work a 12-hour day in the factories. What started as a bread riot turned into insurrection as the women made links with other factory workers.

In August eight of Turin's bakeries failed to open and women and children demonstrated across the city to demand bread. Workers at the Diatto-Frejus factory blocked its gate, chanting: "We haven't eaten. We can't work. Give us bread!" Management promised bread if they would immediately return to work. In response the workforce shouted: "To hell with the bread! We want peace! Down with the profiteers! Down with the war!"[274] They stayed out on strike.

Three days later angry crowds converged on the city centre and were driven back by tanks and machine guns. Four days of rioting followed, and at the end of it 50 demonstrators were dead and 800 jailed. Other workers were arrested and sent to the frontline trenches.

The Russian Revolution set the whole of Europe ablaze. Victor Serge described the conflagration:

> Revolution descended on the streets of Vienna and Budapest. From the North Sea to the Volga the councils of workers' and soldiers' deputies— the soviets—are the real masters of the hour. Germany's legal government is a council of People's Commissars made up of six socialists...
>
> The newspapers of the period are astonishing...riots in Paris, riots in Lyon, revolution in Belgium, revolution in Constantinople, victory of the soviets in Bulgaria, rioting in Copenhagen. The whole of Europe is in movement. Clandestine or open soviets are appearing everywhere, even in the allied armies; everything is possible, everything.[275]

At the opposite end of the political spectrum, Britain's prime minister David Lloyd George wrote to French premier Clemenceau with similar news, though his tone was more sombre: "The whole of Europe is filled with the spirit of revolution. There is a deep sense, not only of discontent, but also of anger and revolt amongst the workers. The whole existing order, in its political, social and economic aspects, is questioned by the mass of the population from one end of Europe to the other. Bolshevism is gaining ground everywhere".[276]

Impact in the USA and beyond

The impact of the October Revolution was not confined to Europe. Big Bill Haywood, the inspirational leader of the USA's Industrial Workers of the World (IWW or Wobblies) embraced the Russian Revolution: "It was the greatest event in our lives. It represents all we have been dreaming of and all we have been fighting for. It is the dawn of freedom and industrial democracy".[277]

It inspired other great American working class leaders: Eugene Debs, James P Cannon and Elizabeth Gurley Flynn; and it inspired hundreds of thousands of ordinary American workers too. 1919 saw a dramatic explosion of industrial unrest throughout the United States with over 4 million workers involved in over 3,600 strikes. In February 1919 there was a general strike in Seattle. Later in the year there were strikes by streetcar operators; textile and clothing workers; telephone operators; and many other groups including the Boston police, who struck in September.

The American ruling class responded to this explosion with the fiercest repression imaginable and a "red scare". For trade unionists at the time America was like a police state. During the steel strike civil liberties and free speech were suspended in the strike districts. Labour journalist Mary Heaton-Vorse wrote, "it was not a strike—it was warfare." The American ruling class were so determined to eradicate militant trade unionism and the threat of Bolshevism that the Attorney General rounded up and jailed 5,000 US workers in the infamous, anti-Communist "Palmer" raids of 1919.

The spirit of the Russian Revolution was also present in the 1919 strike wave in Australia and in the general strike and workers' uprising in Buenos Aires. The Bolshevik Revolution with its message of anti-colonialism also reached out to both the developing nationalist movements and the newly emerging working class in China, India and Egypt during the riots, strikes and demonstrations that swept these countries after 1918.

Achievements of the Revolution

Let us suppose for a moment that the Bolsheviks do gain the upper hand. Who will govern us? The cooks perhaps—those connoisseurs of cutlets and beefsteaks? Or maybe the firemen? The stable boys? The chauffeurs? Or perhaps the nursemaids will rush off to meetings of the Council of State between the diaper-washing sessions?

Who then? Where are the statesmen? Perhaps the mechanics will run the theatres; the plumbers foreign affairs; the carpenters the post office. Who will it be? History alone will give a definitive answer to this mad ambition of the Bolsheviks. [278]

Such were the jibes of the conservative daily newspaper *Novoe Vremia*, the morning after the Bolsheviks took control of Petrograd. The situation facing the new Soviet government after four years of war was grim: the complete breakdown of administration and transport; the break-up of the war front; a hostile German army in the Ukraine; and a hostile internal opposition from the rich.

Lenin had never doubted the crucial role of the working class in the revolution or its ability to rule. Under threat and with its future uncertain, the revolutionary government held its nerve and acted boldly by launching a programme of immediate, far-reaching, radical reform. To spell out that these were not just the empty promises of a self-seeking elite, it was decided all government officials would be paid the average wage of the skilled industrial worker and, following the example of the Paris Commune, that all elected representatives would be subject to the right of recall. On 21 November the new government issued the following decree:

No elective institution or representative assembly can be regarded as being fully democratic and really representative of the people's will unless the electors' right to recall those elected is accepted and exercised. This fundamental principle of true democracy applies to all representative assemblies without question.[279]

The Paris Commune of 1871 had seen the workers of Paris take control of their city for two months. But the Commune was isolated then drowned in blood by the French ruling class. This was different; what had happened was momentous and without precedent. Now a congress of workers, soldiers and peasants had taken state power in a country of 150 million stretching from the Pacific coast to the Baltic, from the Arctic Circle to the Black Sea.

Never before was such radical change carried out in so short a time and under such straitened circumstances. Despite the huge and mounting difficulties the Soviet government faced, decrees of world historical importance were issued and acted on. The first introduced workers' control in the factories. Virtually all the factories, mines and other valuable resources of the country were taken over by the workers to prevent the old bosses from sabotaging the economy or from moving assets, like the global steel barons do today.

Between the February and October revolutions many factory owners had tried to sabotage or block change. The overthrow of the Tsar in February was seen as the signal for workers to democratise factory life and improve their lot. Decrees were fine but decrees on their own were just bits of paper. As Lenin argued: "Socialism cannot be decreed from above. Its spirit rejects the mechanical, bureaucratic approach. Living, creative socialism is the product of the masses themselves. Decrees are instructions which call for practical work on a mass scale." Real, practical change had to come from below.

Workers had no option but to take over the workplaces and run them for themselves. John Reed, living in Petrograd during 1917, described this:

> When the February Revolution broke, the owners and administrators of many plants either left or were driven out by the workers. In the government factories, where labour had long been at the mercy of irresponsible bureaucrats appointed by the Tsar, this was particularly the case. Without superintendents, foremen, engineers and bookkeepers, the workers found themselves faced with the alternative of keeping the work going or starving.

A committee was elected, one delegate from each shop or department; this committee attempted to run the factory. Of course at first it seemed hopeless. The functions of the different departments could be co-ordinated in this way but the lack of technical training on the part of the workers produced some grotesque results.

Finally there was a committee meeting in one of the factories, where a workman rose and said, "Comrades, why do we worry? The question of technical experts is not a difficult one. Remember, the boss wasn't a technical expert; the boss didn't know chemistry, engineering or book-keeping. All he did was to own. When he wanted technical help he hired men to do it for him. Well, now we are the bosses. Let's hire bookkeepers and so forth to work for us".[280]

The old Tsarist legal code was torn up and the legal system completely reformed. Courts were established with elected judges who were subject to popular recall. The death penalty was abolished.

Semi-feudal land ownership was swept away, far more radically than even in the French Revolution of 1789. The decree on land transferred the property of the rich landlords to the millions of poor peasants who worked on it and fed the people. Like all the early Soviet decrees it was clear and straightforward, ordering the immediate expropriation of the big landlords and the transfer of land to the peasants, not after the Constituent Assembly was scheduled to meet, not after six months working out who gets what, but immediately.

In February 1918 the Soviet government adopted the new Western calendar. In March the Bolshevik Party became the Communist Party.

Women and the revolution

The Russian Revolution provides the best answer so far on the question of how women's liberation can be achieved. After the defeat of the 1905 revolution, increasing numbers of women had been drawn into the workforce. Patronisingly the capitalists calculated they would be meek, compliant and more strike-averse than the men. But entering the workforce gave women collective organisation and economic muscle. Between 1885 and 1911 the number of women workers increased six-fold.

The onset of war and military conscription meant that by January 1917, 130,000 women worked in the factories of Petrograd, with even more working in the metal industries than in textiles. This compared to 83,000 domestic servants, nearly all women, who worked in much worse conditions and for much lower wages than the women in the factories.[281] For single women who left their families or left domestic service, factory work brought a measure of economic independence. But for married women the burdens of being a housewife and mother as well as a wage worker, were onerous in the extreme. City life might be less oppressive than the village but "domestic labour remained as much the responsibility of the women in the 'proletarian' family as it was in its peasant counterpart".[282]

Alexandra Kollontai was prominent in the revolutionary movement for over 20 years, leading the struggle to organise working class women and win them to the fight for socialism and women's liberation. Soon after the February revolution she wrote for *Rabotnitsa*, the Bolshevik paper for working class women:

> Much depends on us, the women workers. The days are passed when the success of the workers' cause depended only on the organisation of the men. As a result of this war female labour can now be found everywhere. In 1912 there were only 45 women for every 100 men working in factories, now it is not uncommon to find 100 women for every 75 men.[283]

Kollontai was the elected delegate of the women textile workers in both the 1905 and 1917 Petrograd soviets. In 1917 she was elected to its executive. She served on its Military Revolutionary Committee and played a key role throughout the insurrection that removed the Provisional government.

Tsarist Russia was a fiercely religious society, subject to the darkest superstitions and prejudices: "I thought I saw two people," went an old Russian joke, "but it was only a man and his wife". Patriarchal attitudes were particularly strong in the countryside where peasant wives were deemed the property of their husbands. The peasant's inventory of belongings invariably listed his wife with the livestock: women literally treated like cattle.

Yet despite these most difficult of circumstances, the revolution carried through a programme of women's liberation never attempted anywhere else. "Revolution", argued Trotsky, "does not deserve its name if with all its might and all the means at its disposal it does not help the woman—twofold and threefold enslaved as she has been in the past. In order to change the conditions of life we must learn to see them through the eyes of women".[284]

Kollontai was elected Commissar for Social Welfare in the new Soviet government. She presided over the enactment of the most progressive legislation in the world, aiming at the full emancipation of women. Women won the vote, equal pay, equal employment rights and universal paid maternity leave. Less than a month after taking power the new government introduced decrees that swept away the old marriage and divorce laws and marriage became a free, voluntary relationship. The distinction between legitimate and illegitimate children was eliminated. Free divorce could now be had for the asking, by either partner. Kollontai explained:

> By virtue of the decree of the People's Commissaries of 18 December 1917, divorce has ceased to be a luxury accessible only to the rich; henceforth, the working woman will not have to petition for months, or even years, for a separate credential entitling her to make herself independent of a brutish or drunken husband, accustomed to beat her. Henceforth, divorce may be amicably obtained within a week or two.[285]

When interviewed by an American journalist who asked, "Is it true a divorce may be had for the asking?" Trotsky replied, "Of course it's true. It would have been better to ask a different question; 'Is it true there are still countries where divorce cannot be obtained for the asking by either party to a marriage?'"[286]

Adultery was decriminalised; so too was homosexuality as homophobia was challenged and all laws against gays abolished. Under Tsarism being gay was punishable by five years in Siberia but was tolerated in the imperial court. According to Cathy Porter, the spirit of the 1905 Revolution had encouraged "a lively gay subculture in the cities".[287] After the 1905 Revolution liberal reformers had argued it should be decriminalised but this did not happen until a month after the Bolshevik Revolution in 1917. Dan Healey's *Homosexual Desire in Revolutionary Russia* shows convincingly that this was a conscious, not an inadvertent decision and was influenced by the early radicalism of revolutionary Russia.

Until the late 1920s the Director of the Russian Institute for Neuropsychiatry, Lev Rozenstein, one of the government's leading clinical psychiatrists, influenced by German socialists Wilhelm Reich and Magnus Hirschfeld, continued to conduct counselling and sex education programmes for LGBT+ people. Healey argues, "his view of female sex and gender was frankly emancipationist" and that he judged it "appropriate to assist patients in accepting same-sex desire and finding suitable and productive social roles."

Rozenstein invited "lesbians, militia women and Red Army members in uniform to give their histories to his students" and asserted that, "women in Soviet Russia may legally take men's names and live as men".[288]

By the early 1930s what remained of the earlier moves towards genuine sexual liberation was swept away by the victory of Stalin and the final overturn of the remaining gains of the revolution. Homosexuality was made a crime again in 1933 as his regime re-asserted motherhood and family values. Under Stalin Russia became in the words of one sociologist, a society with "a pathological animosity to sex".

Yet in the period immediately after 1917 socialists everywhere had looked to Russia as the freest society on earth, eliminating not only exploitation and oppression but also sexual repression. Conservatives have always accused revolutionaries of "immorality and free love" and while it is true socialists challenge the hypocrisy of conventional society, there is a bit more to it than that. At the end of 1917 the new Russia sought to create the possibility of new human relationships developing, in which by liberating women real gender equality would be possible and a free choice of heterosexual and/or homosexual love would develop without interference from church or state.

The attitude of the Revolutionary government was not just about changing the laws but challenging attitudes. If women were really going to be able to play a role in building a new society, passing laws would not be enough. In Britain the Equal Pay Act was passed in the late 1960s yet women still don't have equal pay.

In Russia the new government decided the material basis for women's oppression would have to be ended and the traditional family transformed to free women from domestic drudgery. As Kollontai insisted: "Separation of the kitchen from marriage is a reform no less important than the separation of church and state, at any rate in the history of women. Separation of the kitchen from marriage and the care of children as a social obligation were the guiding principles".[289]

The workers' state moved to take over "women's work", which had enslaved the great majority of women in the home. Kollontai and other leading Bolshevik women, including Nadezhda Krupskaya and Inessa Armand, fought to ensure that the new workers' state set up collective education, communal restaurants, laundries and nurseries, to shift the burden of childcare and feeding from individual women so they could play a full part in building a new society. Soon these facilities became commonplace. In Petrograd during 1919-20 almost 90 percent of the entire population ate communally; in Moscow more than 60 percent. In 1920 the communal eating centres served 12 million town dwellers.

Trotsky was asked by *Liberty* magazine if Bolshevism was destroying the family and encouraging bigamy and polygamy; he responded, "If one understands by family a compulsory union based on the marriage contract, the blessing of the church, property rights and the single passport, then Bolshevism has destroyed this policed family from the roots up".[290]

In 1920 Russia became the first country in the world to legalise abortion and make both it and contraception safe and freely available. All sorts of special provisions were made for pregnant and nursing mothers and a special department of health was established. Socialist feminist Sheila Rowbotham points out: "These seem like unspectacular reforms now, but in the Russian context they were an extraordinary achievement".[291]

In Britain the 1967 Abortion Act came almost 50 years after it had been introduced in revolutionary Russia. The long campaign to legalise abortion was inspired by the policy of Bolshevik Russia, initiated by women committed to the labour movement and the liberation of working class women.

In Russia the pressure for change had come from the socialists and from a new self-confidence among women. In her pamphlet, *Towards a History of the Working Women's Movement in Russia*, Kollontai challenged the notion of women as passive objects and wrote about "the transformation of the proletarian women into women of a new type."

It is the challenging of attitudes and the economic independence of women that will break oppression. The revolution boosted this process. One young soldier interrupted a women's street meeting to ask: "Does this mean I can't hit my wife?" The crowd shouted back, "None of that here. You just try it! Let ourselves be beaten anymore? Not on your life! Nobody has that right now".[292]

This really was a revolution—a massive upheaval in which those at the bottom of society rose up and fought to control their own destinies. They could not do so unless they shook apart every hierarchy and challenged every element of oppression. Of course many male workers resisted this challenge to their traditionally dominant role in the family. And of course that state of affairs and many other things didn't change overnight. But what was impressive was that many male workers understood the need to break with such divisive prejudice and how they were able to win a majority of the class to their standpoint. As Marx insisted: "Revolution is necessary not only because the ruling class cannot be overthrown in any other way, but also because only in a revolution can the class overthrowing it rid itself of the muck of ages and become capable of rebuilding society anew".[293]

During the revolution the Bolsheviks had fought hard for commitment to equal pay in the workplaces, the trade unions and the soviets. The magnificent role of the women workers in February 1917 convinced the Petrograd committee of the Bolsheviks to make extra special efforts to organise women. Vera Slutskaia, in charge of agitation, was asked to prepare a report for action. Days later she brought the committee her recommendations: the creation of a Women's bureau as part of the Petrograd committee and the re-launch of *Rabotnitsa*, the Bolshevik newspaper for working women. Each district committee was to select a woman representative and send her to work in the bureau.

The study of female Bolsheviks and women workers in 1917, *Midwives of the Revolution*,[294] shows how the Bolsheviks, as well as organising women factory workers, paid close attention to and helped organise low paid women service workers such as laundresses, hotel and catering workers and shop assistants. Bolshevik opposition to the war led them to highlight the miserable situation of the soldiers' wives.

Agitation bureaus were established throughout the party, and clubs were founded with the aim of drawing non-party women into activity. In May 1917 the Bolshevik newspaper for working women *Rabotnitsa* was re-launched as a weekly with seven women editing and producing it. The first issue sold out immediately and the print run increased to 50,000. Mass *Rabotnitsa* rallies were held at which Kollontai and others would address huge audiences of women. One of Lenin's first acts on returning to Petrograd from exile in April 1917 was to write to the Bolshevik central committee demanding its full support for increasing political work among women: "Unless women are drawn in to taking an independent part, it is idle to speak not only of socialism, but even of complete and stable democracy".[295]

In 1918 Kollontai planned the First All-Russian Congress of Working Women. Not everyone thought it would succeed; some thought her expectations too high: "We were told, 'don't bother it's not worth it, you'll never get that many. Plan for 80 and no more'. In fact 1,147 delegates came".[296] Now the question was how to mobilise not just thousands but hundreds of thousands of women. In 1919 the Bolsheviks set up a special department aimed at involving more working class women in the revolutionary process. Headed by Inessa Armand, it was known by its Russian acronym *Zhenotdel*.

Thousands of women volunteered and male revolutionaries were also expected to help. When Armand died of cholera, Kollontai became Commissar for Propaganda and Agitation and helped pioneer Agitprop and the special Agit-trains and Agit-ships including the *Red Star* which took the message of socialism and women's liberation to some of the remotest areas across the great land mass of Russia.

The modernist *Blue Blouse* theatre group played a key role in this work. They travelled with poster art and song and dance groups; held meetings, showed films and plays and taught literacy. They also travelled among the Muslim populations in the east, wearing hijabs so they could mix and work with veiled women. As Inessa Armand argued: "If the emancipation of women is unthinkable without communism, then communism is unthinkable without the emancipation of women".[297] On the second anniversary of the revolution Lenin could write:

> In the course of two years of soviet power in one of the most backward countries in Europe, more had been done to emancipate women, to make her the equal of 'the strong sex', than has been done during the past 130 years by all the advanced, enlightened, 'democratic' republics of the world.[298]

In the 1930s, after the defeat of the revolution, Stalinism re-imposed the stereotyped family, anti-abortion and anti-gay laws, and restrictions on divorce. The later Stalinist image of liberated womanhood was not a picture of emancipation at all. It was a picture of women forcibly drawn into production outside the home and ruthlessly exploited in order to meet the needs of an expanding state-capitalist economy.

Of course the right to work is a necessary precondition for emancipation, but it is not in itself emancipation. That is shown by what happened to Russian women after the isolation and defeat of the revolution. When a shortage of skilled labour became apparent in the late 1920s, workers had to be found within the existing population. Between 1929 and 1936 millions of women were conscripted into the workforce, but this work did not emancipate women. At the same time as they went to work, housework was individualised instead of being socialised, motherhood was glorified and parents were made responsible for the behaviour of their children. At the same time the sexual liberation of the revolutionary period was wiped out and replaced with spurious, backward theories of sexuality.

Fighting national oppression

For Lenin, Tsarist Russia was "the prison house of nations"—an immense tract of conquests within which 20 enslaved nations were penned—nations ruled by Russian bureaucrats, subject to Russian law, and occupied by Russian troops. Russian Orthodox was the state religion and the sole official language of the Tsar's empire was Russian. Yet of its 150 million population only 43 percent were Russian and the non-Russians included Finns, Ukrainians, Poles and White Russians, the archaic name for what is now Belarus.

The national question was an explosive one and this was especially true in the eastern part of the empire where the national minorities were far more oppressed than those in the more advanced west. Some 10 million of the peoples and tribes along the Volga, in the Caucasus and central Asia, had been deprived of their best lands by colonising Russian landlords and wealthy peasants: the kulaks.

When the revolution began in 1917 the masses took centre stage, including the oppressed nationalities. Lenin fought for the right of oppressed nations to self-determination and this was a key element in the revolutionary mobilisation between February and October 1917. Shortly before the October insurrection, he promised: "When we win power we shall immediately and unconditionally recognise this right for Finland, the Ukraine, Armenia and any other nationality oppressed by Tsarism and the Great Russian bourgeoisie.

On the other hand we do not favour secession. We desire proletarian unity. We want free unification; that is why we must recognise the right to secede".[299]

The decree on self-determination gave the right of secession to the oppressed nations of the former Tsar's empire: "In its Declaration of Rights the new government invited each nation in Russia 'to decide independently at its own plenipotentiary Soviet Congress whether and on what basis to participate' in federal government".[300] The constitution adopted in July 1918 clarified that district soviets "distinguished by a particular way of life and national composition could come together and choose whether to enter the Russian Socialist Federative Soviet Republic".[301]

In the next few years, five independent states were created, including Poland and Finland. Within the new Russian federation, 17 autonomous republics and regions were established. Revolutionary Russia became a federation of free and equal peoples with the right to use their own languages and practice their own religion. Despite the great difficulties they were facing during the civil war, the Bolsheviks renounced all of the Tsar's colonial possessions.

This stands out in sharp relief to the Tsarism that preceded 1917 and the Stalinist reaction that came in the late 1920s. The Bolsheviks made mistakes but they owned up to them and tried to correct them; their policy on the national question has to be judged in the difficult context of the civil war. The sheer size and diversity of the Soviet Union means the legacy of the Bolshevik policies on the national question and the debates around them provide a rich experience for today. They show the potential for a future free of national prejudice and division.

Stalin reversed the start that Lenin and the Bolsheviks had made in overturning centuries of oppression. Stalin's imperative was not workers' internationalism but the creation of a new Russian Empire that could compete as an imperialist power. Lenin had insisted on the workers' state giving independence where necessary. He also insisted on real autonomy for the national minorities. With Stalin's rise to power Great Russian chauvinism saw a return to national oppression on a par with Tsarism. In 1939 Stalin went as far as signing a deal with Hitler in order to annex the Baltic States, Moldavia and Western Ukraine, in return for allowing the Nazis to invade Poland.

Fighting religious discrimination

Religious freedom was an important aspect of national freedom for the oppressed peoples of the former Tsarist Empire. Bolshevik policy aimed as far as possible, to make amends for the crimes of Tsarism against national minorities and their religions.

The Tsar's empire had been home to 16 million Muslims, some ten percent of its population. They suffered terribly at the hands of Russian imperialism and their anger erupted after conscription was imposed in central Asia during the First World War, when a mass rebellion in 1916 saw over 2,000 Russian colonists lose their lives.[302] The revolt was followed by ferocious Tsarist repression with 83,000 Muslims massacred. The February revolution radicalised millions of Muslims, as they demanded religious freedom and national rights denied them by the Tsars.

Soon after the February overthrow of the Tsar, the first All-Russian Congress of Muslims was held in Moscow. Of the 1,000 delegates more than 200 were women. After heated debates the congress voted for an eight-hour working day, the abolition of private landed property, confiscation without indemnity of large properties, equality of political rights for women, and an end to polygamy and purdah. This meant that Russia's Muslims were the first in the world to free women from restrictions typical of Islamic societies at that time.

Within weeks of taking power the new Soviet government issued its Declaration "to all the Muslim workers of Russia and the East" on 24 November 1917: "Muslims of Russia...all you whose mosques and prayer houses have been destroyed, whose beliefs and customs have been trampled on by the Tsars and oppressors of Russia; your beliefs and practices, your national and cultural institutions are forever free and inviolate. Know that your rights, like those of all the peoples of Russia, are under the mighty protection of the revolution".[303]

The Bolsheviks were atheists yet because they understood the appeal of religion is rooted in oppression and alienation, they welcomed left-wing Muslims into the Communist parties. By 1923 in some former colonies as many as 15 percent of the Communist party membership were believers in Islam. In parts of central Asia it was as high as 70 percent.[304]

The Bolsheviks took a very different approach to Orthodox Christianity, the official religion of the brutal Tsarist colonists and missionaries. Orthodox Christianity and the Russian language ceased to dominate in the Caucasus and in central Asia. Native languages returned to the schools and to local government. Indigenous people were promoted to leading positions in the local state and given preference over Russians in employment. Universities were established to train a new generation of non-Russian leaders. This was part of a Bolshevik policy that sought to redress the crimes of Tsarism. Islamic monuments, books and objects looted by the Tsars were returned to the mosques. Friday, the day of Muslim celebration, was declared the legal day of rest throughout central Asia.

At the Baku Congress of the Peoples of the East, held in 1920, the Bolshevik leaders issued a call for "a holy war" against Western imperialism. Two years later the Communist International endorsed alliances with pan-Islamism against imperialism. In the years immediately after the October revolution the Bolsheviks succeeded in winning large numbers of Muslims to fight for socialism. Historians agree that a majority of Muslim leaders supported the soviets, convinced that soviet power meant religious liberty.

Fighting anti-semitism

Anti-semitism had been rampant in Tsarist Russia for centuries. In 1881 500 pogroms were carried out against Jews. Under Tsarist rule Jews were not allowed to live in either of the two capitals, St Petersburg or Moscow, without the special permission of the state. The Tsar and his officials were openly anti-semitic. The man who headed the Russian Orthodox Church for 25 years announced the "Jewish problem" would only be solved when one third of Jews had been converted to Christianity, another third had emigrated and the rest had "disappeared".

The Bolsheviks fought anti-semitism and the revolution led to a big change in attitudes. In 1917 the President of the Petrograd Soviet, Trotsky, was a Jew. The President of the Moscow Soviet, Kamenev, was a Jew. And the President of the Soviet Republic, Sverdlov, was a Jew.

Shlyapnikov, the leading Bolshevik worker intellectual who was central to building and maintaining the party's underground networks during the First World War, came from an 'Old Believer' background—a highly oppressed, minority Christian group. The Bolshevik attitude to minority rights was one of the things that attracted Shlyapnikov when he was a young engineering apprentice in the early 1900s.

In his book *Reconstructing Lenin*, Tamas Krausz writes: "Lenin and the Bolsheviks had the courage to take up the fight on theoretical, political and military levels against the racist, anti-semitic tide that later steeped the 20th century in blood. The pogroms were in one sense a forerunner of the Holocaust because the Whites exterminated the Jews en masse".[305]

The Jewish socialist parties were among the first to work in co-operation with the Bolsheviks and move towards full unity with them. Although at first he opposed separate Jewish organisation within the Bolshevik Party, in January 1918 Lenin became concerned at the distance between the assimilated minority of Jews in the Russian Communist party and the mass of non-assimilated Jews. Thus the Jewish Section of the Russian CP was established for Yiddish speakers for whom language was a barrier to active party membership.

Although Western Jewish historians concentrate on the role of the pogroms in driving Jews over to the Bolsheviks, there were also many positive reasons for Jewish people to join the party. The Jewish socialist organisations, such as Poale Zion and the Bund, continued to operate and, in contrast to the other Russian socialist parties, the Bolshevik Party sought to concentrate its criticisms on the Zionist and right-wing Jewish parties, not on the Jewish socialists.[306]

Literacy and education

The 1897 census revealed only 21 percent of the population of European Russia was literate. Twenty years later in 1917 two thirds were still illiterate. During and after the revolution hundreds of thousands of leaflets, pamphlets, newspapers and books were distributed across Russia.

The new government revolutionised the education system. It reformed teaching methods in a progressive, libertarian spirit, using Marxist concepts and the best ideas from abroad. The illiterate learned to read. John Reed wrote: "The thirst for education, so long thwarted, burst into a frenzy of expression. Russia absorbed reading matter like hot sand drinks water—it was insatiable".[307] Within the year the number of schools was up by 50 percent. Libraries were expanded and a huge education programme was underway. Examinations and learning by rote were discouraged. University fees were abolished to allow greater access to higher education. Decades before the Western liberal democracies, schools for children with learning difficulties and adult education courses were established.

The revolution brought a co-operative, socialist spirit into education and encouraged experiment and innovation. It saw an explosion of interest in politics and ideas. Ordinary people were involved in the big debates of the day:

> Thousands flooded to the public squares to watch everything from poetry to Greek drama. There were lectures, debates, speeches—in theatres, circuses, schools, clubs, soviet meeting rooms, union headquarters, and army barracks. In Petrograd and all over Russia every street corner was a public tribune.[308]

Anatoly Lunacharsky was Commissar for Education and Soviet spokesperson on cultural affairs. A brilliant orator, he held meetings that attracted up to 30,000 people in huge public arenas and would speak for two hours on Shakespeare, Greek drama and art, enthralling huge audiences of workers. Lunacharsky's preamble to the first-ever Soviet Education Act of 1918 expressed the new regime's concern for the development of the human being:

> The personality shall remain as the highest value in the socialist culture. This personality however can develop its inclinations in all possible luxury only in a harmonious society of equals. We do not forget the right of an individual to his or her own peculiar development. It is not necessary for us to cut short a personality, to cheat it, to cast it into iron moulds, because the stability of the socialist community is based not on the uniformity of the barracks, not on artificial drill, not on religious and aesthetic deceptions but on an actual solidarity of interests.[309]

Art and revolution

This sense of liberation and social progress that characterised the Soviet Republic in its early years, underpinned the enormous artistic flowering of the ensuing decade.

Revolutionary Russia saw mass literacy campaigns alongside a ferment of innovation and experimentation in literature, painting, cinema, photography, music, drama and architecture. The revolution had to take over the cultural heritage of the past, to preserve it and make it accessible to ordinary people and to develop them culturally.

The explosion of new art that followed the revolution has become known as the Golden Age, a period that introduced Symbolism and Futurism among many other cultural movements. "Rodchenko, Kandinsky, Eisenstein, Meyerhold and Mayakovsky are just some of the great artists linked with this period... The 'Golden Age' of Russian art and culture became the inspiration for the young Shostakovich to create his first musical masterpieces".[310]

The government sponsored Picasso's works in Russia; appointed Mark Chagall director of the popular Academy of Art and allowed the same scope to his opponent, Malevsky the constructivist. The government also sponsored Mayakovsky the poet; Tatlin the great modernist architect; and Sergei Eisenstein's epic film projects. The early years of the Soviet Republic showed what socialist revolution could achieve, even in the most unfavourable circumstances. As Trotsky pointed out:

> The October revolution laid the foundations of a new culture taking everyone into consideration, and for that very reason immediately acquiring international significance. Even supposing for a moment that owing to unfavourable circumstances and hostile blows the Soviet regime should be temporarily overthrown, the indelible impress of the October revolution would nevertheless remain upon the whole future development of mankind.[311]

Consolidating Soviet power

It would be demanding something superhuman from Lenin and his comrades if we should expect of them that under such circumstances they should conjure forth the finest democracy, the most exemplary dictatorship of the proletariat and a flourishing socialist economy.[312]
—*Rosa Luxemburg*

With the Provisional government overthrown could the new Soviet regime consolidate power? Capitalist, Menshevik and Socialist Revolutionary circles inside Russia were convinced it would not last long. "We are absolutely certain that the Bolsheviks will not be able to organise state power," wrote *Izvestia*, now controlled by the Mensheviks. Stankevich, former military commissar of the Provisional government, wrote: "The conviction grew with every hour that the Bolsheviks would soon be liquidated." Three days after the insurrection, the daily newspaper *Delo Norado* wrote: "The Bolshevik adventure like a soap bubble will burst at the first contact with the hard facts."

John Reed, who moved around in a far wider variety of social circles than any other journalist in Russia probably got it right when he wrote: "That the Bolsheviks would remain in power longer than three days never occurred to anybody—except perhaps Lenin, Trotsky, the Petrograd workers and the simple soldiers".[313] The new regime was already fighting for its life against heavy odds. Laid waste by three and a half years of war, revolutionary Russia was about to face a new onslaught from its many enemies abroad. In the words of Winston Churchill, Britain's minister of war, their stated aim was "to strangle Bolshevism in its cradle."

Though their own populations were never informed, France, Britain and the USA had seen military dictatorship under General Kornilov as their best option for Russia. In August 1917 French and British officers donned Russian uniforms to march with him against both Kerensky's government and the revolution, handing out leaflets in Russian that hailed "Kornilov the Hero". These leaflets had been printed at the British military mission in Petrograd. But the defeat of Kornilov's putsch meant a change of plan.

The day after the October insurrection, armed with weaponry supplied by Britain, Kerensky and the arch-right-wing General Krasnov ordered 8,000 Cossacks and officers to march on Red Petrograd. En route they defeated a small force commanded by Bolshevik sailor Dybenko and then headed towards the capital. A hastily assembled army of workers, soldiers and sailors from Petrograd, Kronstadt and Helsingfors, all under the command of Antonov-Ovseyenko, confronted Krasnov's forces on the Pukovo Heights just outside the city, after tens of thousands of Petrograd's citizens had built barricades and dug trenches.

> Hundreds died in the battle—including 27 year old Bolshevik Vera Slutskaya, killed by an enemy shell as she tried to get medical supplies across the enemy lines. But it was there the Bolsheviks scored their first military victory and on 9 November Petrograd was saved.[314]

After the triumph in Petrograd on 25 October, it took another eight days for the revolution to triumph in Moscow, where the resistance was fierce, the street fighting bitter and there were many more casualties. But the weakness of the old order meant a peaceful transition in most other places. With a makeshift army of Red Guards, sailors and soldiers from the disbanded army, the Bolsheviks were able to quickly defeat military resistance in the northern Caucasus, southern Urals and the Ukraine, where generals and bourgeois politicians fleeing from central Russia briefly reinforced counter-revolutionaries.

By the end of January 1918 it appeared the civil war had been won relatively painlessly, and had it not been for the major imperialist powers it would have been. But direct military intervention by Western governments would give Russian reaction the encouragement, arms and troops to launch its counter-revolution.

The coalition crisis

Right from the start the new Soviet government also had to deal with cynical opposition from the discredited Mensheviks and Right SRs as they tried to block the new government's programme and topple it, to hand back power to the property owners and the industrialists.

Conservative historians have always sided with right against the left in the Russian Revolution, but some liberal historians blame the Bolsheviks for failing to compromise with the moderates and in particular for rejecting a coalition government with the Mensheviks and the Right Social Revolutionaries. Even on the left, one-time supporters of the Russian Revolution Eric Hobsbawm and Robin Blackburn adopted this position soon after the USSR collapsed over 25 years ago. In doing so they either forgot or ignored some important facts.[315] Alexander Rabinowitch's *The Bolsheviks Come to Power* shows that the Bolsheviks repeatedly tried conciliation with the Mensheviks and SRs.

Lenin was not against an All-Socialist government provided it was accountable to the soviets and accepted the Bolshevik minimum programme. Even before the insurrection, in early September, Lenin and the Bolsheviks had proposed a peaceful transfer of power to the soviets so long as the moderate socialists were willing to draw the lessons of the previous six months and break with the Kadets and the other ruling class parties. The offer was flatly rejected and it was one of the reasons Lenin fought so hard for the October insurrection, fearing an imminent counter-revolution.

Weeks later when the Provisional government was overthrown, the Second Congress of the Soviets voted unanimously to form a coalition government of parties represented in the soviets—including the Mensheviks and the SRs. The minority moderates then immediately chose to ignore the resolution they had just voted for, denounced the Bolsheviks for overthrowing the Provisional government and stormed out of the Congress. Victor Serge tells how the Right SRs and Mensheviks, after walking away on 25 October, immediately united with the Kadets and some key industrial magnates to form a Committee of Public Safety, which openly appealed to the troops to overthrow the new Soviet power.

When not one single regiment heeded this call the Right SRs, supported by the Mensheviks, then attempted to organise a "Junker Mutiny": an odd alliance of monarchists, military officers and antisoviet socialists. Indeed the Right SRs would offer military assistance to the Cossack warlord and future Nazi collaborator Krasnov, who was marching on Petrograd. The Menshevik, Dan, later admitted that they had hoped the Bolsheviks could be "liquidated by force of arms." Serge commented "Nothing is more tragic at this juncture than the moral collapse of the two parties of democratic socialism".[316]

After all this, at the Soviet Congress on 29 October, four days after the soviets had taken power, the representative of the All-Russian Executive Committee of the Union of Railway Workers, a union leadership controlled by Mensheviks and SRs that no longer represented the mood of their own rank and file, declared opposition to the seizure of power by the Bolsheviks. In his call to replace the new government, the Railway Workers' representative demanded a government composed of all socialist parties.

He claimed his union would strike unless this demand was conceded. The ultimatum panicked a number of leading Bolsheviks into opposing Lenin and Trotsky and to demand the party should relinquish power in favour of such a coalition.

This move came from the same small group on the central committee that had argued against the October uprising, claiming it was premature and would be defeated. At their insistence negotiations were begun with the Mensheviks and SRs, the parties that had been propping up the Kerensky government. Interestingly, Lenin again made it clear he did not oppose negotiations with the Mensheviks and SRs, provided that in any coalition the Bolsheviks were assured a stable majority and that all coalition parties would recognise the Soviet state, its peace decree, its land decree, workers' control, the right of self-determination for oppressed nationalities and so forth.

Lenin was sure nothing would come of more negotiations because this was simply another Menshevik-SR manoeuvre, and they remained intransigent against a workers' government. He felt further negotiations would expose this and serve as a lesson for those Bolshevik leaders who wanted conciliation and a coalition with people who would turn out to be scoundrels. And he was proved right. Historian Alexander Rabinowitch confirms that during these coalition discussions the Mensheviks and Right SRs displayed little interest in coming to terms with the Bolshevik regime. They again proved utterly disingenuous, pulling the rug out from under the Bolshevik conciliators with the following ultimatum: "(1) The Red Guards be disarmed, (2) Petrograd's garrison be placed under the orders of its city council, and (3) an armistice be declared, offering for their part to secure a pledge that the troops of Kerensky on entering the city would not fire a single shot or engage in search and seizure. A socialist government would be constituted, but without Bolshevik participation".[317]

Three days later at the Railway union conference, the whole truth emerged when, "the Mensheviks said that one should talk to the Bolsheviks with a gun and the central committee of the right Socialist-Revolutionaries was against any agreement with the Bolsheviks".[318]

So the negotiations were terminated and the Bolshevik conciliators embarrassed: there could be no coalition with traitors. The only positive outcome was that the Left SRs, keen on a genuine socialist coalition, were now so angry and resentful at the Menshevik and Right SRs that they decided to join the Bolsheviks in a Coalition government. It was now clear that for the leaders of the Mensheviks and Right SRs, talk of coalition was simply the prelude to participation in a counter-revolution that aimed to roll back the soviets and bring the bourgeoisie to power.

The Constituent Assembly

Having resolved the coalition crisis the new regime would have to decide whether elections to a Constituent Assembly, originally envisaged as a bourgeois parliament that would emerge from a successful bourgeois revolution, should go ahead. The call for a Constituent Assembly had now become the rallying cry for all the forces that had opposed the October Revolution and the new Soviet government: the same forces that had opposed or deferred convening a Constituent Assembly between February and October. It was an unholy alliance of Mensheviks, Right SRs, Kadets, Monarchists and the Generals. The Bolsheviks faced a dilemma: having campaigned vigorously for a Constituent Assembly before and throughout 1917, they were now completely unprepared for a conflict between it and the Soviets.

They had not considered the possibility of such a conflict because the Provisional government and the forces behind it had opposed both soviets and a Constituent Assembly. Lenin wanted the forthcoming Constituent Assembly elections postponed so the voting age could be extended to 18; the old out-dated electoral lists updated to match the new extended franchise, and the Kadets and Kornilov supporters banned from voting. But other Bolshevik leaders insisted a postponement was unacceptable. It would look bad, they argued, since the Bolsheviks had regularly lambasted the Provisional government for continually delaying the Constituent Assembly. Bolshevik secretary Sverdlov argued that to avoid isolating Petrograd from the rest of the country, the election must not be delayed again. Lenin's response was:

> Nonsense! Deeds are important, not words. In relation to the Provisional government the Constituent Assembly might represent progress; in relation to the soviets, and with the existing electoral lists, it will inevitably mean regression. Why is it inconvenient to postpone it? Will it not be more inconvenient if the Constituent Assembly turns out to be composed of a Kadet-Menshevik-Right SR alliance? You are wrong. It's a mistake that can be very costly. Let's hope the revolution won't have to pay with its life.[319]

Only with the success of the October Revolution was it possible for the Constituent Assembly elections to be called. But now all those parties that had delayed the Assembly suddenly became its most ardent supporters because the electoral dice were loaded in their favour. The Assembly and the soviets were mutually antagonistic, one representing the continuation of capitalism and accommodation to the remnants of the old Tsarist state, the other the overthrow of capitalism and the rule of the working class and peasantry.

But Lenin lost the argument and the election went ahead. The Right SRs won a majority because they garnered all the SR votes, despite the fact that the SRs had subsequently split into a right wing and a left wing that supported the Bolsheviks. The Right SRs used their rigged majority to block the Soviet government's radical programme. Lenin argued the election result was not a true reflection of the real mood. Voting was based on an obsolete law that disenfranchised the young and gave an unfair advantage to the Right SRs. American historian O H Radkey, who carried out a detailed study of the election returns in *Elections to the Russian Constituent Assembly 1917*, verified Lenin's claim.[320] The Bolshevik vote plus the Left SR majority share of the overall SR vote should have combined to win the popular vote and achieve a majority for the Soviet government. The result was indeed a fix.

Nonetheless the Constituent Assembly was convened on 5 January 1918 and Sverdlov, on behalf of the soviets, moved that it endorse the declaration summing up all the main decrees agreed by the newly elected Soviet government: all power to the soviets, land to the peasants; the decrees on peace and workers' control over production, and so forth. But the Assembly majority voted down Sverdlov's motion and the programme of the Soviet government and this sealed its fate; after a day in existence the Soviet government dissolved it. The dispersal of the Constituent Assembly demonstrated the antagonism between bourgeois and socialist democracy.

Kautsky the renegade

The leading German Marxist Karl Kautsky was outraged. He attacked the dissolution of the Constituent Assembly in his publication *Dictatorship or Democracy*. He insisted bourgeois democratic institutions were absolutely necessary if the working class was to mature sufficiently, especially in Russia, where the workers lacked culture and education. Despite his Marxist reputation Kautsky was a gradualist. His fixation with parliamentary democracy stemmed from his prejudice that workers could not change their ideas through struggle and that the educated middle class was a key force the Bolsheviks had ignored: "The importance of the educated classes was not recognised by the Bolsheviks at first.

At the beginning they merely served to increase the blind passion of the soldiers, the peasants and town labourers; the educated were from the beginning hostile to the Bolsheviks".[321]

Polish-German socialist Rosa Luxemburg had argued against such snobbery, pointing out working people have always had to prove they were "mature enough for political freedom. Only when God's Anointed on the Throne together with the noblest Cream of the Nation felt the calloused fist of the proletariat on their eye and its knee on their breast, only then did belief in the political maturity of the people suddenly dawn on them".[322] Before the war Lenin rated Kautsky and German social democracy highly. Until 1914 he was "the Pope of Marxism", his authority stemming from his membership of the prestigious German Social Democratic Party (SPD).

The SPD was the first major organisation to claim allegiance to Marx's politics. Founded in 1869 it became the party of the German working class, surviving through years of semi-legality. In the 1912 election, the SPD polled over 4 million votes, winning 111 seats with 35 percent of the total vote. It was a mass party at the centre of a burgeoning international socialist movement, the Second International, and it was held up as the model of what a Marxist party should be.

When in 1914 its Reichstag deputies voted en bloc for war credits and backed the Kaiser's war machine, Lenin's illusions in Kautsky and the SPD were shattered. But with the benefit of hindsight it is possible to see the shambles coming years, even decades before. The post-1914 Kautsky was not just a renegade from pre-1914; the "Pope of Marxism" had feet of clay all along. According to Trotsky:

> Kautsky at one time wielded very great authority as the theorist of Marxism. The war soon showed it was only a method for passive inter-pretation of the process of history, not a method of revolutionary action. But when war and the after-war period brought the problems of revolution onto the field, Kautsky took up his position definitively on the other side of the barricade. Without breaking away from Marxist phraseology he made himself instead the advocate of passivity, of a crawling capitulation before Imperialism.[323]

Rosa Luxemburg, Kautsky and the fight against reformism

Rosa Luxemburg, the bravest and ablest figure in the SPD, jailed throughout the war for her revolutionary opposition to it, had been arguing and challenging the SPD's rotten leadership since the late 1890s. Luxemburg, an eye-witness and participant in the waves of mass strikes in Russia 1895-1905, wrote about them and their historic, inter-national significance. The mass strike was, "not a specifically Russian phenomenon but a universal form of the proletarian class struggle resulting from the present stage of capitalist development and class relations".[324] When she applied its lessons to the German labour move-ment, the top leaders of the SPD and the union bosses attacked her. When again in 1910 she raised the issue of the mass strike, it was Kautsky who argued against her and his opposition wasn't simply one of tactics or timing.

For Kautsky mass strikes were secondary and only useful in supple-menting parliamentary work. He saw the general strike as something the official leadership could turn on and off like a tap. The same reformist politics lay behind his attack on the Bolsheviks for curtailing the Constituent Assembly and choosing soviet democracy in 1918. Two decades earlier Luxemburg had delivered a devastating attack on Bernstein, the leading theorist of the revisionist wing of German social democracy. Now it applied to Kautsky too:

People who pronounce themselves in favour of legislative reform in place of and in contradistinction to the conquest of political power and social revolution, do not really choose a more tranquil, calmer, and slower road to the same goal, but a different goal. Instead of taking the stand for the establishment of a new society they take a stand for the surface modifications of the old society. Our programme becomes not the realisation of socialism, but the reform of capitalism.[325]

At his most radical in 1908, Kautsky had argued that because of the way capitalism was developing, "a world war was now threateningly close." But when the war arrived he changed his tune, arguing it was a mistake and that "out of the world war of the imperialist powers, there can now result a federation of the strongest among them, which will eliminate the arms race."[326]

Centrism

Adopting a pacifist position, Kautsky saw the war as an interruption of normal political life and when things returned to normal the problems could be patched up. Like Trotsky, Lenin realised that while Kautsky might talk revolutionary socialism, when it came to action he was a long way removed from it. That's why Lenin regarded him as an obstacle during the war.

As German workers and soldiers began to break from their right-wing SPD leaders in 1918, Lenin knew that Kautsky, by opposing soviet power, would prevent or delay them drawing revolutionary conclusions. Lenin called him a "centrist" because he fudged between reform and revolution. Reacting furiously to his attack on the dispersal of the Constituent Assembly and his haughty attitude to the first working class in history to have taken power into its own hand, Lenin replied to Kautsky:

Only Soviet Russia has given the proletariat and the vast labouring majority of Russia a freedom and democracy unprecedented, impossible and inconceivable in any bourgeois democratic republic, by replacing a bourgeois parliamentarianism with the democratic organisation of the soviets, which are a thousand times nearer the people than the most democratic bourgeois parliament.[327]

While Kautsky was lecturing the Bolsheviks on *Dictatorship or Democracy*, the German imperial army was storming into Russia and ignoring the Bolshevik offer of peace. All the major capitalist states were already funding counter-revolutionary terror, and were about to invade in order to restore a dictatorship. Throughout 1918 to 1920, the years of the civil war in Russia, the slogan of the Constituent Assembly served as a screen for the dictatorship of the landowners and capitalists. Admiral Kolchak's banner was that of the Constituent Assembly and it was carried for him by the right-wing SRs, until he suppressed them.

Rosa Luxemburg, concerned at the prospect of the Russian revolution becoming isolated, wrote from prison to her friend Luise Kautsky, Karl's wife, at the end of November 1917:

> Are you happy about the Russians? Of course they won't be able to maintain themselves in this witches' Sabbath, not because statistics show economic development in Russia to be too backward, as your clever husband has figured out, but because social democracy in the highly developed West consists of miserable, wretched cowards who will look on and let the Russians bleed to death. But such an end is better than 'living for the fatherland'—it is an act of world historical significance whose traces will not be extinguished for aeons.[328]

At the start of 1918, Luxemburg was stressing over and over again the decisive importance of the German Revolution, if Revolutionary Russia was to survive: "Everything that happens in Russia is comprehensible and represents an inevitable chain of causes and effects, the starting point and the end term of which are: the failure of the German proletariat and the occupation of Russia by German imperialism".[329] It is instructive to contrast the Russian Revolution with the German events a year later in November 1918.

After the October Revolution the Bolsheviks dispersed the newly elected Constituent Assembly, with its unfairly contrived right-wing majority, in favour of handing over power to the soviets of workers', soldiers' and peasants' delegates. After the November Revolution in 1918, the German Social Democratic Party (SPD) dissolved the workers' and soldiers' councils, in which it had a majority, in favour of the National Assembly, in which it did not. In both cases the question of constitutional forms was really a question of class power. The effect of the Bolsheviks' action was to create a workers' state, whereas the effect of the SPD's action in Germany was to create a reconstituted bourgeois state, the Weimar Republic.

The German revolution had come in spite of the social democrats but they determined to bend all their efforts to restoring the bourgeois state. Twenty years before Luxemburg had argued,

> the entry of socialists into a bourgeois government is not, as is thought, a partial conquest of the bourgeois state by the socialists, but a partial conquest of the socialist party by the bourgeois state... Within bourgeois society the role of social democracy as an opposition party is prescribed by its very essence. It can come forward as a ruling party only on the ruins of the bourgeois state.[330]

When this issue became a concrete matter during the German Revolution, Luxemburg lambasted the leaders of the left-wing breakaway from the SPD, the Independent Social Democratic Party (USPD), for joining the government. She knew their participation would be used by the right as a mask to lull workers into a false sense of security while the counter-revolution prepared behind the mask for the restoration of a stable bourgeois regime.

Soviets after the revolution

The controversy surrounding the Soviet dispersal of the Constituent Assembly in December 1918 revealed the antagonism between bourgeois and socialist democracy. How was Russia to be organised after 1917? Blueprints for a socialist future cannot be drawn up in advance. As Russia in 1917 shows, millions of people engaging in a real revolution will be infinitely more creative than a few self-proclaimed experts drawing up detailed plans beforehand; or as Lenin put it, "the intelligence of millions of creators provides something infinitely superior to the most gifted individual insights".

It is claimed that when asked what socialism would look like, Lenin replied: "Soviets plus electricity!" According to Alexandra Kollontai Lenin was an enthusiast for electricity because it would "free millions of domestic slaves from the need to spend three quarters of their lives in smelly kitchens".[331] Like electricity, the soviets didn't come out of Lenin's brain. As he said: "it is not anybody's invention. It grows out of the proletarian class struggle as it becomes more widespread and intense. The new apparatus of state power, the new type of state power, is soviet power".[332]

The Bolsheviks were determined that soviets should be the foundation of the new workers' state and the embodiment of workers' democracy. On the eve of October Lenin quoted Engel's remark that universal suffrage is "an index of the maturity of the working class. It cannot be anything more in the modern state".[333]

John Reed, whose *Ten Days that Shook the World* is acknowledged as the classic account of the October Revolution, also wrote a separate account on the organisation of revolutionary Russia during 1918 that highlights the role and functions of the soviets.

Locally based and sympathetic to the revolution, Reed was able to find out not only what the Bolsheviks were up to, but to move on the streets and write down the experiences of ordinary Russians, including individuals and groups who opposed or were suspicious of the revolution. His account of the soviets first appeared in the US magazine *The Liberator* in October 1918. The following excerpts give a sense how the Russian workers and peasants organised during the hey day of the revolution, before isolation, civil war and foreign intervention ruined the economy and decimated the Russian working class:

> Through all the chorus of abuse and misrepresentation directed against the Russian soviets by the capitalist press there runs a voice shrill with panic: 'There is no government in Russia! There is no organisation among the Russian workers! It will not work! It will not work!' There is method in their slander. As all real socialists know, and as we who have seen the Russian Revolution can testify, there is today in Moscow and throughout all the towns and cities of Russia a complex political structure upheld by the vast majority of the people and which is functioning as well as any new-born popular government ever functioned.
>
> The workers of Russia have fashioned from their necessities and the demands of life an economic organisation that is evolving into a true industrial democracy. The soviet is based directly upon the workers in the factories and the peasants in the fields; the Petrograd Soviet of Workers' and Soldiers' Deputies serves as an example. It consisted of about 1,200 elected deputies and held plenary sessions every two weeks.
>
> It elected a central executive committee of 110 members based on party proportionality and this central executive committee invited delegates from all the political parties, from the union committees, the factory shop committees and other democratic organisations.
>
> Besides the big City Soviet there were also ward soviets made up of the deputies elected from each ward to the City Soviet that administered

their part of the city. In some parts of the city there were no factories and therefore normally no representation of those wards, either in the City Soviet or the ward soviets of their own. But the soviet system is extremely flexible, and if the cooks and waiters, or the street sweepers, or the courtyard servants or the taxi drivers of that ward demanded representation, they were allowed delegates.

Elections of delegates are based on proportional representation, which means the political parties are represented in proportion to the number of voters in the whole of the city. And it is political parties and programmes that are voted for, not candidates. The political parties designate the candidates and can replace them with other party members. The delegates are not elected for any particular term, but are subject to recall at any time. No political body more sensitive and responsive to the political will was ever invented. And this was necessary, for in time of revolution the popular will changes with great rapidity.

At least twice a year delegates are elected from all over Russia to the All-Russian Congress of Soviets. An extraordinary session of the Congress can be called at any time on the initiative of the All-Russian Central Executive Committee, or upon the demand of soviets representing one third of the working population of Russia.

This body of 2,000 delegates meets in the capital in the form of a great soviet and settles the essentials of national policy. It elects a central executive committee, like the Central Committee of the Petrograd Soviet, which invites delegates from the leading elected bodies of all democratic organisations. This augmented central executive committee of the All-Russian Soviets is the parliament of the Russian Republic. It consists of 350 people. Between All-Russian congresses it is in supreme authority but must not act outside the lines laid down by the last congress, and is responsible in all its actions to the next congress.[334]

Peace or war?

On taking power, the priority for the new Soviet government was taking Russia out of the war. True to their word the Bolsheviks offered an immediate armistice to all states at war with Russia pending a permanent peace based on "no annexations, no indemnities".

Like an early 20th century Wiki-Leaks with direct access to Russian state secrets, the new government publicly exposed the secret treaties behind the war, the secret deals agreed between the allied powers: Britain, France, Italy and Russia. In doing so the Bolsheviks were widely hailed as finally nailing the lie of a just war and proving beyond any doubt that ruling classes everywhere had gone to war for empire, profit and plunder.

But in February 1918 the Kaiser and his generals spurned the Bolsheviks, offer of peace and declared Germany was still at war with "Red Russia". In two weeks German troops drove 125 miles into Russia, arming white counter-revolutionary forces and sweeping aside remnants of the old Russian army units at Narva, within 100 miles of Petrograd. The German forces invaded Finland and backed the White Terror that smashed the revolutionary government there, costing 20,000 lives. The new government in Russia, less than three months old, faced enormous danger. Germany demanded huge tracts of territory in return for halting its advance. Lenin argued: "We are now powerless. German imperialism has us by the throat. Give me an army of 100,000, a strong, steadfast army that will not tremble at the sight of the foe and I will not sign the peace treaty".[335] But that was something the revolution did not have.

Here the word "peace" is a misnomer. The terms demanded by the Kaiser's negotiators were so harsh that despite the overwhelming desire for a genuine peace, continuation of the war suddenly seemed preferable to probably more than half of the Bolshevik Party and certainly to a majority in the soviets. "Peace" was one thing, abject humiliation and terms which could wreck the revolution was an entirely different proposition.

Trotsky led the Bolshevik delegation at the Brest Litovsk talks with the German High Command. By using delaying tactics, he sought to encourage socialist revolution in Germany and throughout the Austro-Hungarian Empire. Trotsky's outstanding role in prolonging the negotiations while fanning anti-war sentiment amongst front line German troops; the first stirrings of a revolutionary strike movement against the war in Germany, Hungary and Austria; and the arguments between Lenin and Trotsky on tactics, important though they were, were secondary to Lenin's absolute insistence on ending the war as soon as possible.

Like Trotsky and the other Bolsheviks, Lenin viewed ending the war as the potential trigger for the expected German socialist revolution, the taken for granted precondition for the survival of the Russian Revolution; but he was adamant the Bolsheviks could not wait on it. He knew that if they tried to continue with a revolutionary war against mighty German imperialism, they would be defeated and overthrown and reaction installed in Russia. Lenin knew peace with the Germans had to be achieved to allow a breathing space for the revolution, but at first Lenin was again in a minority.

The robber's peace

After a lengthy debate Lenin convinced a sizeable majority of the delegates attending a specially convened Soviet congress in March to accept his position and a Brest Litovsk peace treaty was reluctantly agreed. Still leading left Bolsheviks, including Kollontai, Bukharin and Shlyapnikov, remained opposed to it. Before signing the Bolsheviks issued this statement: "The German proletariat is as yet not strong enough to stop the attack of German imperialism. We have no doubt the triumph of militarism over the international proletariat will prove temporary. Meanwhile the Soviet government, unable to resist the German armed offensive, is forced to accept peace terms to save revolutionary Russia".[336]

The terms were catastrophic and the Bolsheviks knew it was a "robber's peace". It was estimated that Russia lost territories and resources approximately as follows: 1,227,000 square miles, with 62 million population, or one fourth of territory and 44 percent of population; one third of crops and 27 percent of state income; 80 percent of sugar factories; 75 percent of iron and 75 percent of coal. Of the total 16,000 industrial undertakings, 9,000 were situated in lost territories.[337] The next day the Soviet government issued a decree for the formation of the Red Army and Trotsky was tasked with building it. The revolution would quickly have to learn how to defend itself from internal reaction and the intervention of predatory capitalist states until such time as the European revolution could come to its aid.

The conduct of the Bolshevik Party throughout the tense debates over Brest-Litovsk left a lasting impression on the former anarcho-syndicalist Victor Serge:

> This party, so disciplined and so unencumbered by abstract democracy, still, in these grave hours, respects its norms of internal democracy. It puts its recognised leader in a minority: Lenin's tremendous personal

authority does not hinder the militants in the central committee from standing up to him and energetically maintaining their point of view. The most important decisions are settled by vote, often by small majorities—a margin of one vote—to which the minorities are willing to defer without abandoning their ideas.

Lenin, when in the minority, submits while waiting for events to prove him right and continues his propaganda without breaking discipline. Even though impassioned, the discussion remains objective. Gossip, intrigue or personality plays no important part. The militants talk politics, without trying to wound or discredit the comrades on the opposing side.

Since the opposition is never bullied, it shows only the minimum of emotion that one would expect in events of this order, and soon recovers from its rash decisions. At this hour the party really is the courageous "iron cohort" of Bukharin's later description. It is a living organism, teeming with initiative from the lowest to the highest ranks.[338]

News of the Bolsheviks' initial peace offer and the Kaiser's rejection enraged those fed up with the war in Germany and Austria. German anti-war socialist Karl Liebknecht expressed this from his prison cell: "Thanks to the Russian delegates, Brest Litovsk has become a revolutionary platform with reverberations felt far and wide. It has denounced the central European powers and exposed the German spirit of brigandage, lying, cunning and hypocrisy. It has delivered a crushing judgement on the peace policy of the German Majority, a policy which is not so much hypocritical as cynical".[339]

The leaders of the Soviet republic knew better than anyone that a backward Russia, ravaged by war and surrounded by reaction, could not create socialism. The Bolsheviks looked to international revolution. As Lenin said in 1918: "We have always emphasised the fact that in one country it is impossible to accomplish such a work as the socialist revolution."

When in November 1918 news reached Russia of the German Revolution, the fall of the Kaiser and the end of the war, eyewitness Karl Radek described the mood of euphoria:

"Tens of thousands of workers burst into wild cheering. Never have I seen anything like it. The world revolution had come. Our isolation was over".[340]

Revolution one year on

On New Year's Day 1919, 14 months after the October Revolution, John Reed wrote his preface to *Ten Days that Shook the World*:

> Instead of being a destructive force, it seems to me that the Bolsheviks were the only party in Russia with a constructive programme and the power to impose it on the country. If they had not succeeded to the government when they did, there is little doubt in my mind that the armies of Imperial Germany would have been in Petrograd and Moscow in December 1917 and Russia again would be under a Tsar.
>
> It is still fashionable after a whole year of the Soviet government to speak of the Bolshevik insurrection as an 'adventure'. Adventure it was, and one of the most marvellous mankind ever embarked upon, sweeping into history at the head of the toiling masses and staking everything on their vast and simple desires.
>
> Already the machinery had been set up by which the land of the great estates could be distributed among the peasants. The factory committees and the unions were there to put into operation workers' control of industry. In every village, town, city and province, there were elected Soviets of Workers', Soldiers' and Peasants' Deputies, prepared to assume the task of local administration.[341]

The German Revolution of November 1918 and the sudden end to the First World War meant the robber's peace of Brest Litovsk imposed by the Kaiser's Generals would eventually be annulled. Russia's future now hinged on what the European working class would do.

The armies of Britain, France, the USA, Japan and ten other capitalist states were already invading Russia to assist the reactionary White armies, which the Western powers had been covertly funding: in the case of the USA and Britain since before the October Revolution. Their aim was regime change, the destruction of the new Soviet republic and the overthrow of the first workers' government in history.

Revolution under siege
and how it was lost

The USSR Ltd was ended in 1991. It was a strange paradox: the product of a revolution in 1917 led and supported by the working people; yet by the end of the 1920s the revolutionary generation had been marginalised and the revolution turned on its head. By the end of the 1930s Russia had become one of the 20th century's bloodiest dictatorships.

Under Stalin, Russia emerged as a Great Power. The regime continued to call itself socialist and communist but although it built statues to Marx and Lenin, it had become the opposite of socialism: a bureaucratic state capitalist tyranny. In destroying the soviets along with the social and cultural gains of 1917, the regime became increasingly undemocratic and repressive.

When the group around Stalin finally took control of Russia at the end of the 1920s, they defended their control by developing a military apparatus as powerful as that of any potential foe. That was only possible by imitating Western military potential: building up heavy industry by squeezing the living standards of workers and peasants. Once these methods were adopted, it was logical to copy the West in other ways as well: to reach out beyond the USSR's borders for further resources for accumulation. Hence the division of Poland with Hitler in 1939 and the division of Europe with Churchill and Roosevelt in 1944-45.

Towards the end of the Second World War nuclear weapons were developed to fulfil the irrational needs of an irrational system. From the capitalist standpoint even the most horrific weapons of mass destruction are rational—a view shared by Stalin and his henchmen. Bizarrely, some on the left tried to argue that Soviet militarism, although there had been no soviets since the 1920s, was different; that armed force was a neutral instrument and what mattered was which state wielded it. So the Western atom bomb was condemned and the 'socialist' atom bomb celebrated.

From the late 1920s Russian foreign policy blocked and hindered wider social change, helping to set the bloody pattern of the 20th century and trapping the larger part of the international left, who identified more or less critically with Stalinist Russia and the Eastern European satellite states it created after 1945. In 1985 Duncan Hallas wrote:

> The small clique of bureaucrats who run the USSR, together with their allies, satellites and imitators, and even more so the ruling class of the USA, with their allies, satellites and ideologists, habitually refer to 'the Soviets' doing this or that. There are no soviets in Russia and have been none since the 1920s. The 'Supreme Soviet' and other bodies in the USSR that are given the name of soviet are in no way organs of workers' power as set up by the revolutionary workers in 1917.[342]

The rulers of the USSR, by claiming the inheritance of the workers' revolution of 1917 for six decades, validated their rule over the workers. It also suited the interests of the ruling classes in the West to identify soviets, workers' power, with its complete opposite—bureaucratic dictatorship over the working class.

The collapse of the Eastern European satellites, thanks to pressure from below in 1989, finally destroyed any lingering illusions on the left. Then in 1991 the Soviet Union itself collapsed. US President George Bush senior told a meeting of the IMF and the World Bank: "Today leaders around the world are turning to market forces to meet the needs of their peoples. The jury is no longer out. History has decided".[343]

But *Observer* economic editor William Keegan was soon pointing out; "It is rather unfortunate that capitalism should have celebrated the collapse of communism by arranging a crisis of its own".[344] According to the White House and the Kremlin, the history of post-revolutionary Russia was either unbroken tyranny or unbridled progress. The refusal of both camps to acknowledge the deep chasm that separated the Bolshevik revolution from the Stalinist dictatorship that crushed it was deliberate; it suited both sets of rulers, east and west. It is difficult to exaggerate how important this was. The existence first of one state, then a whole series of states claiming to be socialist, but which were repulsive caricatures of socialism, was a major factor in the survival of Western capitalism. Right-wing propagandists argued Stalinism, or something like it, was the inevitable result of trying to get rid of capitalism. Social democrats on the other hand, argued Stalinism was the inevitable consequence of Bolshevik centralism; that Stalin was "Lenin's heir".

Both groups are proved wrong by the facts. Stalin's counter-revolution was preceded by a tremendous working class victory in 1917, which still stands as testament to the power of a popular, revolutionary movement from below. But the Bolsheviks knew in advance that ultimate success depended on whether their revolution could spread to the more developed West, enabling Russia to break out of its isolation and overcome its economic backwardness.

A cautious Lenin said it depended on successful working class revolutions, "in at least one or two advanced countries". Trotsky, speaking on behalf of the new Soviet government in 1918, also made clear there was no possibility of building socialism in one country, and certainly not in war ravaged, backward Russia: "If the peoples of Europe do not arise and crush imperialism, we shall be crushed".[345]

Missed opportunities: lost revolutions

Despite the difficulties, the Bolsheviks anticipated October would spark a wave of revolutions in the West; and it did. The abrupt end to the First World War proved their prognosis was sound. The most striking episode in the European crisis was not the Russian Revolution but a series of upheavals that engulfed the most industrially developed European power, Germany, from the revolution of November 1918 that toppled the Kaiser through to the Communist Party's abortive attempt to seize power five years later in October 1923.

The victorious powers were also affected: 1919 was the most dangerous year the British state had ever faced, while Italy experienced two years of mass struggle culminating in the factory occupations and land seizures of 1920. But despite coming desperately close with a whole series of revolts and workers' insurrections, the European insurgency was contained.

To triumph, the revolutionary crises that developed in a whole number of European states required, in advance, effective revolutionary organisations on the ground and a decisive break with the unreliable leaders. Only in Russia was this achieved. The defeat of the Berlin uprising in early 1919 emphasised the need for an effective revolutionary international to replace discredited social democracy; the Third or

Communist International (Comintern) was launched at a founding conference in March 1919 on the back of the revolutionary wave at the end of the war.

Though neutered by Stalin in the years following the defeat of the German Revolution and Lenin's death in 1924, there was a period in the early 1920s when the new International started to make real progress.

It helped turn revolutionaries in western Europe and in the USA towards the construction of mass parties. In Britain Lenin was instrumental in bringing together the various competing factions of the revolutionary left, together with the leaders of the shop stewards and workers' committee movement, to form the Communist Party of Great Britain in 1920-21.

There were of course many bigger, more important achievements in other countries. The Third Annual Congress of the Comintern, held in March 1921 was attended by 600 delegates from 55 countries, including China, India, Palestine, the United States and Australia. Its delegates represented millions of workers across the world.

Lenin's project of welding together the most militant, class conscious sections of the European and international working class into a current that could play a leading role in the class struggle, acting both with and against the reformist leaders but without becoming sectarian, was real and impressive.

But by 1924 Russia was left isolated and exhausted and Lenin, incapacitated for over a year by a series of strokes, was dead. Even then the stabilisation of Western capitalism was at best precarious and temporary. In virtually every European state the workers' movement at some point over the next dozen or so years, would seriously threaten the existing social structure. In addition a Chinese workers' revolution appeared on the horizon. China, the vast, populous landmass bordering Russia, was a semi-colony partitioned between Britain, France, the USA and Japan. The Chinese Communist Party (CCP) was founded in 1921 against the backdrop of an anti-imperialist struggle and working class militancy. By 1925 it was the effective leadership of the growing Chinese labour movement.

Trotsky, still a member of the politburo but effectively isolated and excluded from influence by then, attacked the Stalin clique that promoted an alliance between the CCP and the Kuomintang (KMT), the party of China's bourgeois nationalists. Recalling the fight over "permanent revolution" in Petrograd in April 1917, Trotsky wrote: "The new and absolutely false theory promulgated by Stalin about the 'immanent revolutionary spirit' of the colonial bourgeoisie is, in substance, a translation of Menshevism into the language of Chinese politics".[346]

Trotsky's warnings were ignored. Chiang Kai Shek, leader of the Kuomintang and Stalin's supposed ally, turned his forces on the Communist-led workers' movement and butchered it. As a result imperialist domination of China was given a further 20-year lease of life. Strangely such defeats and debacles for the international revolutionary movement strengthened Stalin's hold and the crazy lie of "socialism in one country".

From Lenin to Stalin

Opponents of the Russian Revolution have tried to blame October 1917 for the later horrors of Stalinism. They ignore the most important fact: the basis of Stalin's power from 1928 was the antithesis of that established in 1917.

The government of 1917 was based on elected delegates to the All-Russian Workers', Soldiers' and Peasants' Council. The first Soviet government had the support of 67 percent of the delegates elected in October 1917 and 74 percent of those chosen in the elections three months later. Elections took place against the backdrop of unfettered debate with different newspapers and periodicals supporting different parties. Within the Bolshevik Party, overwhelmingly made up of workers, there was free and open debate for at least the next four years. The revolutionary years were characterised by a profound social transformation. Revolutionary Russia was no one party state.

Victor Serge described how, even "in the years of the greatest peril the soviets and the central executive committee of the soviets includes Left Social Revolutionaries, Maximalists, anarchists, Menshevik social democrats and even Right Social Revolutionaries. Far from fearing discussion, Lenin seeks it. He feels he has something to learn from merciless criticism".[347]

By contrast under Stalin there were no workers' councils and no workers' democracy. The Supreme Soviet of his 1936 constitution was a sham and the elections to it were rigged. There was only one party and all the newspapers slavishly followed its line. The majority of the party members were not workers but managers, state bureaucrats and full-time party officials. No party member high or low was allowed to present any policy different to Stalin's. Anyone who tried was imprisoned and usually executed or deported.

Stalin's party continued to call itself the Communist Party of the Soviet Union (Bolshevik) but it had nothing in common with Lenin's party of 1917. Only 1.3 percent of the 1.5 million members in 1939 had been members in 1917; only one in ten of the 200,000 surviving Bolsheviks of 1918 were still in Stalin's party by then. Of the 15 members of the first Soviet government, ten were murdered on Stalin's orders, four died naturally and only one, Stalin, survived. Hundreds of thousands of revolutionaries were killed by the secret police or died in labour camps. As Trotsky himself put it before Stalin had him assassinated, "there was a river of blood between Bolshevism and Stalinism."

Trotsky was exiled and later murdered in Mexico in 1940 by Stalin's assassin. Even Krupskaya was targeted in an obscene whispering campaign. At one point Stalin muttered that he could "make someone else Lenin's widow".[348] In the years to come this tireless veteran of the revolutionary underground and a lifelong socialist, was gagged. Her rich experience of the real Lenin was too dangerous for Stalin to allow and even her memoirs could not be published until they were purged of Trotsky's name.

Zinoviev was shot in 1936 as was Kamenev. Shlyapnikov, the skilled metalworker who joined the party as a young apprentice, the most prominent of the Bolshevik worker intellectuals who were the backbone of Lenin's party, was shot in 1937 for his supposed involvement in Zinoviev's so-called conspiracy. Stalin had Bukharin executed in 1937 for supposedly planning to kill Lenin and Stalin in 1918.

Vladimir Antonov-Ovseyenko, who served on the Military Revolutionary Committee of the Petrograd Soviet and planned and directed the October insurrection alongside Trotsky, was also murdered in 1937 in Stalin's purge of the 'old Bolsheviks'. His wife later committed suicide in one of Stalin's labour camps. His son Anton spent his youth there. In his history of Stalinism Anton denounced the dictator who murdered his parents far more furiously than any antisoviet historian, but for quite different reasons:

> My father fought against the Tsarist regime, took part in the October insurrection and commanded red battalions in the civil war. He did

not do so that a filthy criminal could entrench himself in the Kremlin. Stalin murdered my father, just as he murdered thousands of other revolutionaries.[349]

What Antonov-Ovseyenko's parents and the countless other murdered revolutionaries had fought for did not come to pass. Most of what they did achieve was wiped out and reversed by Stalin's counter-revolution. But it was not because of Lenin or the nature of Bolshevism. Stalin was not the rightful heir of 1917; he was its gravedigger.

Four years of imperialist war followed by three years of civil war left revolutionary Russia prostrate by 1922. Industrial production had declined massively and the working class base of the Bolshevik Party virtually disappeared from the factories. Most had fought and died in the Red Army; others had been co-opted into the government and party administration. Popular democracy diminished and the bureaucracy around the party functionary Stalin increasingly wielded power. Stalin displayed talents of an exceptionally high order for this type of skullduggery.

The monumental problems of reconstruction in a siege economy meant ideals were necessarily subordinated to expediency. So between 1918 and 1921 "War Communism" was imposed on Russia not by choice but by international capitalism. Lenin acknowledged the Bolshevik's plight in 1921: "What we actually have is a workers' state, with this peculiarity: firstly it is not the working class but the peasant population that predominates in the country; and secondly it's a workers' state with bureaucratic distortions".[350]

Retreat: the New Economic Policy
In March 1921 the New Economic Policy (NEP) replaced the War Communism of the civil war. It was adopted not as a development of socialism but as an attempt to conciliate the peasantry by making material concessions to them. It was also an attempt to restore some dynamism into a devastated economy and buy time to allow international solidarity to come to the aid of revolutionary Russia. It is significant that Lenin used the term "state capitalism" for these measures—but the need to make such compromises was seen as a temporary expedient.

Every day the soviets extended their life it brought them that much closer to revolution in the West. The internal situation, while Lenin was at the helm, was conditioned by the hopes for international revolution. The Third or Communist International launched in 1919 had by 1922 gained the support of new mass Communist parties in Germany, France and other European countries, on the basis of an uncompromising, internationalist, revolutionary perspective.

But by then the post-war crisis had passed, European capitalism had temporarily stabilised and the soviets outside Russia had been crushed. As Lenin told the Comintern in 1921: "It was clear to us that without the aid of the international revolution a victory of the proletarian revolution in Russia is impossible. Notwithstanding this conviction we did our utmost to preserve the soviet system, under any circumstances and at all costs, because we know we are working not only for ourselves, but also for the international revolution".[351] It was only after Lenin's death and under Stalin that the interests of the Third International were subordinated to Russian foreign policy and the struggle inside the Bolshevik Party.

Lenin's last struggle

Lenin was badly wounded in an assassination attempt by a member of the SRs in April 1918. In May 1922 he suffered a stroke that left him weak and unable to return to work until October that year.

Then in March 1923, another stroke paralysed his right side and affected his speech, removing him from any active role. From then on his political activity was ended. It was during this period of illness that Lenin tried to fight the bureaucratic and authoritarian tendencies developing inside the party. At first he was slow to grasp their full import but as he realised the extent of the problem, he saw the need to curb the bureaucracy.

The demobilisation of the Red Army after the civil war made a massive contribution to the ranks of the Bolshevik Party. Army officers were able to achieve high rank in the party and the government machine on the basis of administrative skill and organising ability. But such skills are not entirely conducive to working-class democracy. It was on these sections and lower-rank leftovers from Tsarism that the Stalinist bureaucracy was based.

In the course of Lenin's illness Stalin elevated the post of General Secretary far beyond the routine administrative functions intended for it. He abused it to place his supporters in key positions and to isolate his critics and opponents, notably Trotsky. He also kept news of developments from the ailing Lenin. Stalin even issued Lenin's doctors with instructions not to let him work or read. It was only by delivering an ultimatum that he would ignore their advice that Lenin was allowed a few minutes each day to read reports and dictate notes and letters. At one stage Stalin felt so cocky he threatened Krupskaya, Lenin's wife, with party discipline for allowing Lenin to work in defiance of Stalin's orders.

Despite the terrible limitations deteriorating health imposed on him, Lenin could see Stalin's influence growing and spent his last months trying to end his bureaucratic stranglehold on the party apparatus. Victor Serge was one of Stalin's opponents and was imprisoned by him. He wrote this about Lenin's last struggle:

> Shortly before his death Lenin proposed to Trotsky—who was hostile to the bureaucratic system—a common action to democratise the party. As General Secretary, Stalin, obscure during the civil war, was becoming more and more influential, using his technical functions to fill the various bureaus with his own creatures. He was the obstacle to Lenin's last efforts. The last letter dictated by Vladimir Ilyich, when the finger of death was upon him, was a letter of rupture addressed to Stalin.[352]

When Lenin discovered Stalin had been bullying Krupskaya he broke off personal relations with him. Lenin's *Testament*[353] reveals the difficulty he faced. Unlike April 1917 he couldn't take his argument to the most class conscious workers: the working class was weak and small in numbers. Lenin's health was ailing and his only recourse lay inside the party structure itself. In his *Testament* the danger of a split was analysed and the character, talents and shortcomings of the leading Bolsheviks were frankly assessed. In an appendix written some days later, he argues Stalin must be removed from his post.

In the first months of 1923 Lenin was assembling his case and made it known he was preparing "a bomb for Stalin". Days later, on 7 March, Lenin suffered a final stroke that left him speechless and paralysed. Rumours abound that Stalin had Lenin poisoned, although it would be hard to prove that now.

Lenin's last struggle was important because it gives the lie to the oft-repeated claim that "Lenin led to Stalin" or that "Leninism contained the seeds of its own destruction". In fact there was a profound discontinuity between the October Revolution and the Stalinist regime that tried to claim Lenin's mantle. How then did the revolution lose its way? Bourgeois scholarship's standard response is: "Bolshevik ideology and its obsession with centralism".

This is completely contradicted by the history of the Bolshevik Party; the testimony of many participants; and by many respected historians specialising in the Russian Revolution, including Moshe Lewin, author of *Lenin's Last Struggle*. Lewin describes the Bolshevik Party during the revolution as "an authentic party of the urban masses—a legal, democratic party made up of people from diverse social strata and heterogeneous ideological horizons".[354] At all points until the 1920s the Bolsheviks were a party in which heated discussion was the norm. As Bolshevik Alexander Shlyapnikov said when battling the rise of the apparatus led by Stalin: "what bureaucratism did we know in the old underground organisation? None".[355]

The Bolsheviks were light years away from being a monolithic party controlled by Lenin. They divided over boycotting the Duma parliament and over participation in the police-inspired trade unions. They were famously divided over the very nature of the revolution and if and when to call for the second revolution. They were even split on the call for an insurrection. After the revolution they were divided over whether there should be a coalition with other socialists, over whether the elections to the Constituent Assembly should be delayed and about whether and on what basis there should be peace with German imperialism.

Victor Serge, a critical admirer of the Bolsheviks and a supporter of Trotsky's Left Opposition against Stalin, pointed out: "It is often said that 'the germ of Stalinism was in Bolshevism at its beginning'. Well I have no objection. Only Bolshevism contained many other germs—a mass of other germs—and those who lived through the enthusiasm of the first years of the victorious revolution ought not to forget it. To judge the living man by the death germs which the autopsy reveals in a corpse—and which he may have carried with him since his birth—is this very sensible?"[356]

Socialism in one country

Marx was careful, unlike many of his followers, not to completely rule out the possibility that a revolution led by its workers might enable

Russia to arrive at socialism without first going through a capitalist phase, provided "the Russian revolution becomes the signal for a proletarian revolution in the West".[357] Like Marx, Lenin and Trotsky were fully aware that the containment of a workers' revolution within Russia's borders would mean its eventual defeat, with the consequence that exploitation and oppression would return.

After Lenin's first stroke in 1922 effectively removed him from political activity, the ruling group around Stalin adapted to this state of affairs. Increasingly they came to see the interests of the Russian state as more important than those of the world and the Russian working class. In effect they were rejecting Marx and Lenin's position as well as Trotsky's.

In the period after 1925, real revolutionary opportunities in China, Britain, France and Spain were sacrificed because they clashed with the interests of Russian foreign policy. The preposterous doctrine of "Socialism in One Country" was used to justify an approach that imposed disastrous policies on the parties affiliated to the Communist International. Trotsky and other critics who launched the Left Opposition in 1923 were excluded, vilified, hounded, imprisoned, exiled and eventually murdered. Repression inside the party led to Russia being ruled by a layer of privileged bureaucrats and eventually to Stalin's dictatorship.

The unnecessary defeats and setbacks suffered by the working class abroad in the 1920s and 1930s increased the isolation of the Russian regime and the danger of another foreign invasion. To counter that threat Russia's new rulers required the latest weaponry, which could only be produced by an advanced industrial economy. The resources for that could only come from the surplus labour of Russia's workers and peasants. For that to happen the democracy of the soviets and the party was crushed. It did not happen without a struggle. In 1927 Trotsky, Zinoviev and their supporters were expelled from the Communist Party of the Soviet Union and Trotsky was expelled from Russia.

By 1928 Stalin was firmly in control and, with the last remnants of inner party democracy destroyed, he launched his "Five Year Plan". This new course forced the pace of industrialisation and land collectivisation under state control. It cut wages, outlawed strikes and sent troops to the countryside to wage war on peasant farmers. Many were forced off the land and sucked into the new factories on an enormous scale.

Millions perished in the process. As Stephen Cohen argues, Stalin's new policies of 1929-33, the "great change" as they became known, represented a radical departure from Bolshevik thinking:

> No Bolshevik leader or faction had ever advocated anything akin to imposed collectivisation, the 'liquidation' of the allegedly prosperous peasants (kulaks), breakneck heavy industrialisation, the destruction of the entire market sector, and a 'plan' that was in reality no plan at all, only hyper-centralised control of the economy plus exhortations. These years of 'revolution from above' were, historically, the birth period of Stalinism.[358]

In February 1931 Stalin addressed a special conference of managers, telling them: "No comrades, the pace must not be slackened. On the contrary, we must quicken it as much as is in our powers and possibilities. We are 50 or 100 years behind the advanced countries. We must make good this lag in ten years. Either we do it or they crush us".[359]

The horrors of Stalin's first Five Year Plan period have to be seen in context. The English, Welsh and Scottish peasantry too, were "liquidated as a class" in their time, and the casualties of the industrial revolution in Britain were certainly not lighter, proportionate to population, than in Stalinist Russia. But no one has ever pretended that late 18th and early 19th century Britain was a socialist society. This bloody work, which took two centuries in western Europe, was packed into a decade in Stalin's Russia.

Stalin's victory and his doctrine of socialism in one country was a massive defeat for the Russian working class and for international socialism. State capitalism, as it became, was also a disaster for Russia's environment. According to Martin Empson, author of *Marxism and Ecology*:

> One Stalinist planner called for 'a profound re-arrangement of the entire living world...all living nature will live, thrive and die at none other than the will of man and according to his plans'.
>
> The belief that nature was a tool for the interests of socialism would, however, have been unrecognisable to the men and women who had made the revolution. One of the foremost Bolsheviks in 1917, Nikolai Bukharin, wrote extensively on the natural world and society's relationship with it. While awaiting execution in a Stalinist prison in 1937, he wrote *Philosophical Arabesques*, which contradicted the beliefs of the

Stalinist bureaucrats and discussed the relation between human beings and the natural world.[360]

In 1991, before the old USSR finally collapsed, Alex Callinicos wrote: "The Soviet state is subject to the pressures of the world system. This is reflected in the priority within Russia's economy given to military production, which takes an enormous 12 to 14 percent of the gross national product.

"The initial decision in the 1920s to collectivise and industrialise was not the result of Stalin's malevolence and power-lust, but of the pressure of objective circumstances—the need to match Western military might. The same pressure continues to bind Russia to the world system today, to ensure that surplus-labour is not used to benefit the associated producers, but instead is ploughed back into further production".[361]

Between the late 1920s and its collapse at the end of the 1980s, the regime was never a workers' state let alone a socialist society. Rather it was bureaucratic state capitalist—a society in which the working class was exploited collectively by a state bureaucracy in competition with its Western counterparts.

Stalin's most implacable opponents were those who remembered Lenin and criticised Stalin in terms of the values they shared with Lenin, above all internationalism. Foremost were Leon Trotsky and his small band of followers in the Left Opposition. Others who lived through the First World War and the Russian Revolution, such as Victor Serge and the French socialist Alfred Rosmer, provided—along with Trotsky—the basis for a genuine socialist current to re-emerge and flourish when Stalinism crumbled after 1956.

The civil war: 1917-1921

The decay of the Russian Revolution stemmed not from flawed or evil individuals but primarily from the deteriorating material conditions when revolutionary Russia was left isolated and wrecked after a bitter three-year civil war. The monarchists and reactionaries inside Russia started the civil war, not the Soviet government. And these reactionaries were egged on and bankrolled by Western capitalism and backed militarily by 14 separate invading armies including those of Britain, France, the USA, Canada and Japan.

Even before the First World War ended the British government was actively engaged in trying to overthrow the revolutionary government in Russia. The day before the Armistice was signed, Churchill told the war cabinet they might have to rebuild the mutinous German imperial army to combat Bolshevism. British troops, warships and air force units were actively involved in the fighting in Russia, and the White generals were supplied with huge quantities of British munitions and financial support.

The Royal Navy deployed 88 warships in the Baltic for operations against the Bolsheviks; it is a little known fact that 17 of them, including a cruiser, two destroyers and a submarine, were lost and 128 British seamen killed. Unrest on the lower decks led to a rash of mutinies. But true to form, Churchill considered the operation worthwhile because it tied down the Bolshevik forces, thereby assisting the White armies.

Churchill originally pinned his hopes on the reactionary Admiral Kolchak's troops in Siberia advancing on Petrograd to crush the Reds. The defeat of Kolchak saw Churchill switch his backing to the even more reactionary anti-semitic General Denikin. His forces massacred tens of thousands of Russian Jews: men, women and small children. The British also encouraged Polish forces to attack the Russians and although Denikin's defeat delayed this plan, the Poles finally launched an offensive in early 1920, capturing Kiev.

The civil war was a continuation of the class war that started in February 1917. Throughout 1917 the Russian far right and liberals repeatedly made it clear that brute force was their class solution to the rebellion. Yet still textbook versions accuse the Bolsheviks of starting the civil war with the soviet seizure of power and the closing of the Constituent Assembly in January 1918. According to Russian history specialist Kevin Murphy, the most important revelations from recently released archives on the Russian Revolution were found not in the former Soviet Union, "but in the archives of US President Wilson".

David Foglesong's book, *America's Secret War against Bolshevism*, shows that just a few weeks after the October Revolution, the US started funnelling massive amounts of cash to White forces hostile to soviet power. The 'Russian experts' know all about this but I have yet to find a single reference in any academic study of the Russian Revolution that mentions it... Yes, let's have a discussion on the Red Terror but let's also have a sense of proportion; and let's start by discussing the Red, White and Blue Terror.[362]

The Cold War school's contention that the early Soviet regime was repressive and incarcerated large numbers of its own citizens, turns out to be a pack of lies. The same Woodrow Wilson, who was secretly channelling millions of dollars to anti-semitic bandits during the Russian civil war in his attempt to install a military dictatorship amenable to US interests, jailed 5,000 US workers in the anti-Communist Palmer raids of 1919. Some of them were deported to Russia, even people who had never been to Russia in their life! More US citizens were jailed in this eight-week period of red baiting than the Soviet regime managed to incarcerate in the entire eight years of its New Economic Policy.

Regime change 100 years ago

1917 was not the first time Uncle Sam opted for terror and regime change and as we know to our cost it wasn't the last: Iraq and Iran in the 1950s; central America and south east Asia in the 1960s; Chile and Iran again in the 1970s; Iraq again in 1991 and 2003. In the current decade we have already seen the same process attempted in Egypt, Libya, Syria, Afghanistan and Pakistan, with devastating consequences. As Christopher Read points out in his book *From Tsar to Soviets*: "Russia was the first test bed for what was to become standard western (that is initially British and French, later American) counter-revolutionary tactics based on direct armed intervention where feasible, ample funding of contras if not, and 'low-intensity' (providing one is not on the receiving end) economic warfare in any case".[363]

Too many historians treat the October Revolution and the civil war as if they were two completely separate events. Marc Ferro describes the preparation for reactionary terror that was taking place well in advance of October 1917:

> A model of anti-Bolshevism was being assembled and it was reconstituted during the civil war. It was shaped between February and October 1917 and there was some similarity between it and the fascist model that came later in Italy, then Germany: it began with resistance to social revolution, the role of the leading financiers and industrialists, with action by the army and the church, denial of the class struggle and an appeal to servicemen's masculine solidarity.

It was followed by the use of 'special action groups', the denunciation of weakness, the emergence of 'new men', with a leadership cult, anti-semitism, attacks on democratic organisations, and, finally, the sympathy and armed intervention by allied governments.[364]

Three days after the October insurrection, while the revolution hung in the balance in Moscow, Kerensky and General Krasnov's Cossacks were assembling on the outskirts of Petrograd and planning to drown the revolution in blood. They had to be driven off by revolutionary army units. When Krasnov was captured and taken prisoner by army units loyal to the revolution, he was admonished and then released unharmed upon giving a solemn undertaking that he would take no further part in counter-revolutionary activities. In no time at all he reappeared at the head of a counter-revolutionary army: so much for the tales of ruthless Bolsheviks originating the terror. If anything the Reds were initially too naïve and too conciliatory in dealing with dyed in the wool counter-revolutionaries.

In November 1917 Lenin wrote: "We are accused of resorting to terrorism but we have not resorted, and I hope we shall not resort, to the terrorism of the French revolutionaries who guillotined unarmed men. When we arrested anyone we let them go if they gave us a written promise not to engage in sabotage. Such written promises have been given".[365] These were in the days of revolutionary hope and innocence. But Lenin wasn't a pacifist. The day after the October Revolution, on Kamenev's initiative and in Lenin's absence, the death penalty was abolished. When Lenin found out he was angry with Kamenev:

> How can you make a revolution without firing squads? Do you think you will be able to deal with all your enemies by laying down your arms? What other means of repression do you have? Imprisonment? No one attaches any importance to this during a civil war when each side hopes to win. It is a mistake, an inadmissible weakness. Do you really think we shall come out victorious without any revolutionary terror?[366]

Unfortunately Lenin was correct. During the October Revolution the resistance of the counter-revolution had been greater in Moscow than in Petrograd. The street fighting was fierce and it took longer to overcome the Whites.

Victor Serge in his *Year One of the Russian Revolution* wrote:

The Whites surrendered on 2 November on the agreed terms: 'The White Guard surrenders its arms and is disbanded. The officers may keep the side arms that distinguish their rank. The Military Revolutionary Committee guarantees the liberty and inviolability of all.' Such were the principle clauses of the armistice between Reds and Whites. The fighters of the counter-revolution, butchers of the Kremlin, who in victory would have shown no quarter whatsoever to the Reds—we have seen proof—went free.

Foolish clemency! These very Junkers, these officers, these students, these socialists of counter-revolution, dispersed themselves throughout the length and breadth of Russia and there organised the civil war. The revolution was to meet them again on the Don, at Kazan, in the Crimea, in Siberia and in every conspiracy nearer home.[367]

The White Terror

The October revolution was greeted enthusiastically with a general strike in Finland and by January 1918 a workers' government had been formed there. But the German High Command backed the counter-revolutionary White Guards, sending crack troops to crush the Finnish revolution. In the brief civil war that followed the Reds were defeated and the Whites took reprisals.

In Helsinki the White generals forced workers' wives and children to walk in front of their troops as they recaptured the city street by street: 100 women and children died. Another 40 women were laid out on the ice and shot. In Lahti 200 women were shot with explosive bullets. In Viipurii (Vyborg) 600 Red Guards were lined up in rows and machine-gunned to death.[368] The Finnish White Terror claimed the lives of 23,000 Reds. These atrocities must have steeled the Bolsheviks during the civil war: they were a foretaste of what was come.

Fighting continued throughout the following months, especially in Ukraine. The catalogue of armed resistance by pro-monarchist and reactionary forces there makes a complete mockery of the claim made by former US National Security member Richard Pipes that, "the Bolshevik terror" began long before "any organised opposition to the Bolsheviks had a chance to emerge".[369]

In April 1918 the British and Japanese seized Vladivostock in the east. By the end of the year there were 73,000 Japanese, 60,000 Czech, 8,000 US, 2,500 British, 1,500 Italian, and 1,000 French troops fighting the Reds in Siberia alone; this was in addition to the German forces invading Russia from the east. The Germans did not halt their advance deep into Russia until the Brest Litovsk treaty was finally imposed in May 1918. By 1919 more than 200,000 allied troops were fighting alongside White counter-revolutionary forces.

Trotsky had to leave his post as Commissar for Foreign Affairs to become War Commissar in March 1918. He was tasked with building a Red Army capable of defending the revolution. He described the situation in August 1918 as: "a noose that seemed to be closing ever tighter around Moscow. Everything was crumbling. There was nothing left to hang onto. It seemed hopeless." At this point the Soviet state had been drastically reduced to an area that was little bigger than medieval Muscovy.

But under Trotsky's command the situation was turned around. In the summer of 1918 conscription was introduced in working class areas and those parts of Russia under immediate threat from the White Terror. Hundreds of thousands responded to the first call-ups and the new Red Army grew from 330,000 to 600,000 by the end of the year. Eventually 5 million strong, it would triumph against the odds after three years of fighting: this was the period known as War Communism.

The White generals carried out systematic terror. Wherever they gained control, brutal dictatorships of a kind only later rivalled by the Nazis held sway. "The greater the terror, the greater the victories", argued the reactionary Kornilov. "We must save Russia even if we have to set fire to it and shed the blood of three fourths of all Russians!"[370]

When the Whites recaptured Kiev in August 1919, "anti-semitic venom dripped from the public pronouncements of Denikin's generals". One of them vowed, "the diabolical force that lives in the heart of the Jew-Communists will be destroyed." W Bruce Lincoln, a historian not particularly sympathetic to the Bolsheviks, wrote: "Denikin imposed a regime marked by vicious hatred of all Jews. As the pogroms of 1919 burst upon the Jews of Ukraine with an incredible ferocity, the enemies of Bolshevism committed some of the most brutal acts of persecution in the history of the Western world".[371] Kevin Murphy writes:

> It's unfortunate there aren't many honest historians working in the field
> today like W. Bruce Lincoln. He writes about the massive Western mili-
> tary aid to the White armies and explains how this helped the civil war

drag on. I'm sure if he were still alive a revision of his book on the civil war would have included the recent findings on the secret US funding to the Whites. You won't find any mention that the US secretly funded the Don Cossack terror in an attempt to set up a military dictatorship.[372]

It is estimated that the White pogroms in the Ukraine killed as many as 150,000 Jews, a murder rate only exceeded by the later Nazi Holocaust in the 1940s. One in 13 of the entire Jewish population of the Ukraine was slaughtered. The White forces took photographs to boast of their handiwork. One dated August 1919 shows Cossacks posing over a row of dead Jews wrapped in their prayer shawls. Tens of thousands of Jews fled across Russia and beyond to other parts of Europe, the US and Palestine.[373]

The reactionaries who wanted to restore the old order ignored even the most minimal conventions of war. They issued orders to "hang all arrested workers in the streets". The *Manchester Guardian* reported on the barbarism of the counter-revolutionary officers:

> It was difficult to know what was done to prisoners. When questioned on the subject the White officers always said; 'Oh, we kill all of them that are Communists'.
>
> Jews and commissars stood no chance but it was somewhat difficult to ascertain which of the others were Communists. The system usually followed was this: from among the prisoners a man who 'looked like a Bolshevik' was led aside, accused with great violence of being a notorious Communist, but was promised his life would be spared if he gave the names of his companions whom he knew to be Bolsheviks. This ingenious scheme, which was tried on more than one victim in each group of prisoners, generally resulted in a number of Red soldiers being executed.[374]

The US commander in Siberia in 1919, General William S Graves, testified that, "I am well on the side of safety when I say that the anti-Bolsheviks killed one hundred people in eastern Siberia, to every one killed by the Bolsheviks." A US sergeant serving there said: "The majority of people here are in sympathy with the Bolsheviks—I don't blame them".[375] The question of land ownership and the right of national self-determination proved central to the victory of the Red Army. The peasants knew the Whites would take back their land and return it to the landlords. The national minorities knew a White victory would mean a return to the Russian chauvinism they had experienced under the Tsars.

It was in response to this systematic use of White Terror that the revolutionary government retaliated with its Red counter-terror. In June 1918 the popular Bolshevik agitator Volodarsky was assassinated by counter-revolutionaries. In August Right SR member Dora Kaplan shot Lenin. He was badly wounded and for a few days was in a critical condition. On the same day another Bolshevik leader, Uritsky, was murdered. The Red Terror was unleashed in retaliation.

Compared with the White Terror, however, the Red Terror was mild: "not all Communists, certainly, were saints or puritans. But their general behaviour and morale seems to have been better than those of their opponents", wrote Chamberlin in his history of the revolution.[376] When the Tsar and his family were executed in the late summer of 1918, it was only after the town of Ekaterinburg, where they were being held, was surrounded and under threat of invasion by the Whites. The Bolsheviks feared that any member of the Romanov family liberated by the reactionary White forces would become the standard bearer for the brutal counter-revolution.

The Bolsheviks had little choice but to respond in kind to the relentless White Terror. Yet despite the impression created by works such as Solzhenitsyn's *Gulag Archipelago*, the terror was very different from that employed by Stalin from 1929 onwards. In 1920 Trotsky, while on board his military train, amid the flames of civil war and besieged by imperialism, wrote this simple explanation: "History down to now has not thought out any other way of carrying mankind forward than that of setting up always the revolutionary violence of the progressive class against the conservative violence of the outworn classes".[377] Red Terror was a reaction to real, not imaginary, actions of the counter-revolution. It was never on the scale meted out by the Whites and it was ended in 1921 once the civil war was over.

As well as war and foreign invasion, Russia suffered a total blockade of investment, materials, machinery, food and medicines. By 1921 industrial output was down to an eighth of pre-war levels. The blockade reduced imports and exports to a fraction of their 1917 figures. At the end of the civil war 350,000 Russians were dead in battle and 450,000 dead from disease. During the civil war hunger, cold and disease killed 9 million people; typhus alone killed one million during 1920.[378]

The sheer effort of resistance plundered Russia and destroyed its industry. The facts are set out in great detail in the second volume of E H Carr's *The Bolshevik Revolution*.[379] As another economic expert noted:

> such a fall in the productive forces of a huge society of over 100 million people is unexampled in the history of mankind. Terms like crisis and collapse are used frequently today to describe situations when economic growth falls. There is no word of strong enough force to use when one comes to the situation of Russia in these years.[380]

Survival: but at a terrible cost

Despite the terrible hardships the revolutionary government was able to draw support from the poorer classes right across the old Empire, for it alone offered hope to the workers, guaranteed land to the poorer peasants, resisted the anti-semitic gangs working alongside the White armies and supported self-determination for the non-Russian nationalities.

The revolutionary regime held out against all the odds and by 1921 was victorious. As a woman textile worker in Moscow recalled with pride at the end of civil war, "we carried the revolution on our shoulders and we didn't give in!"[381]

According to Kollontai, by the end of the civil war there were around 66,000 female Red Army personnel. Approximately 2,000 were killed or captured. There were certainly many more women combatants in the Red Army than during the First World War, when Kerensky and a group of wealthy middle class feminists campaigned and raised money for "a patriotic women's battalion" that fought for Kerensky on the Eastern front and were feted by the wealthy.

The fact that so many women went on to defend the new Soviet republic, during the civil war, against both counter-revolutionary forces and the intervening foreign powers gives an indication of the strength and commitment of female Bolsheviks, and indeed non-party women workers, to the cause of the revolution.

The survival of the beleaguered regime was down to the revolutionary courage and the fierce endurance of the workers who still made up the bulk of the party and the Red Army, but they paid a heavy political price for survival. The regime had survived in an overwhelmingly peasant country because of the support—usually passive, sometimes active—of the peasant masses who had gained from it.

As the industrial economy collapsed, workers streamed out of the cities and back to the villages to avoid starvation and disease. The populations of Moscow and Petrograd, the heart of the revolution, were halved. The working class base of the workers' state was a fraction of its former size, no longer able to exercise collective power. There had been around 5 million industrial workers in 1917. There were less than 2 million in 1921. Of those who fought in the civil war, nine out of ten were dead. The end of the civil war left the Soviet government isolated in a hostile world and isolated from the mass of the Russian people, the peasants. So long as there was a danger the Tsarist landowners might be restored, large sections of the peasantry supported the Bolsheviks. Once this danger had passed, they became hostile to a government that had been driven to rely on the forced requisitioning of grain to feed the cities.

In 1921 sections of the peasantry and remnants of the working class began to question and challenge the regime. This was shown starkly and tragically in March when sailors at Kronstadt, the naval fort outside Petrograd, rose up against the revolutionary government, blaming it for the incredible levels of poverty. The naval base had been a great centre of Bolshevik support in 1917 but its composition had changed radically as its best militants went to fight in the Red Army and were replaced by fresh new recruits from the countryside.

The rising came from despair but had no programme to overcome it. It was not a capitalist crisis caused by the presence of wealth alongside poverty but the product of a whole country impoverished by civil war, foreign invasion and a total blockade. It was not a case of one class living in affluence and another in starvation, just different degrees of hunger.

The generals of the old regime, only just defeated in the civil war, were hovering in the wings, waiting for any chance to stage a comeback. A few had established friendly relations with some of the Kronstadt rebels. Who controlled Kronstadt controlled Petrograd and time was not on the revolutionary government's side. The ice surrounding the fortress would soon melt and it would become impossible to recapture it, posing a threat to the regime. This gave the Bolsheviks little choice but to put down the rising, a fact recognised by the workers' opposition grouping inside the Bolshevik Party, who were in the forefront of those to cross the ice and take on the rebel sailors. If the Bolsheviks had been ousted the result would have been not a more democratic society but the return of the old regime.

Kronstadt symbolised the wretched conditions to which isolation and foreign intervention had reduced the revolution. It seemed to show that the regime could only survive by methods that owed more to Jacobinism than to the Bolshevism of 1917. It was the low point of Bolshevism but there was no alternative.

Some argue that what happened at Kronstadt was the inevitable consequence of the "original sin" of revolution. Some on the left fall for a variant of this; that it was all down to Lenin's ruthlessness and the monolithic party he built. But Marx had stated the real reason 60 years earlier: "If the working class destroy the political rule of the capitalist, that will only be a temporary victory so long as the material conditions are not yet created which make necessary the abolition of the capitalist mode of production".[382]

By 1917 the material conditions had been created on a European scale but in Russia, taken by itself, they had not. The Bolshevik leadership was well aware of that but the soviets, what little was left them, were operating in a vacuum with the Bolsheviks ruling over an increasingly hostile, smallholding peasantry. Yet all the time those who led the regime, and the hundreds of thousands of volunteers who risked their lives to carry its message, looked to the workers of the industrially advanced West in the hope of badly needed relief. Historian Kevin Murphy points out that despite the utter devastation of seven continuous years of war and civil war,

> Soviet citizens could openly criticise the regime; they retained the right to practise their religion; workers continued to have considerable control in the factories; 700,000 women participated in the proletarian women's movement; the regime enacted favourable policies for national minorities, and the peasantry, for the most part, were left alone.[383]

Of course the peasantry were not always left alone by Bolshevik policies in the early 1920s. But Lenin attempted to rectify the mistakes and excesses with the ending of War Communism and the introduction of the New Economic Policy (NEP). This change staved off economic disaster. Victor Serge recounted that, "the NEP in the space of a few months was already giving marvellous results—the famine and the speculation were diminishing rapidly".[384]

All this would change drastically for the worse with Stalin's first five-year plan, when coercion and repression replaced tolerance and persuasion in every aspect of Soviet society, especially in relation to the peasantry. But decay only became inevitable when others failed to act. The various European socialist and trade union leaderships bear some of the responsibility. Had they seized even one of the recurring opportunities to topple their own ruling classes between 1918 and 1936, the history of the 20th century could have been very different and the world today would be a better place.

The October revolution put the Russian working class in power in the context of a rising tide of revolt against the old regimes in central Europe and the advanced capitalisms of western Europe. Between 1917 and 1924 the Bolsheviks would undoubtedly make mistakes but they would make them against a background of a revolutionary opportunity that could have helped them. That opportunity was never taken.

In the West there were revolutionary crises but no equivalent of the Bolsheviks to respond to them. Instead the western European equivalents of the Menshevik leaders held out against revolution, making sure the new workers' councils in Europe were either dissolved into bourgeois democracy or subordinated to it. Renegade European social democracy, which 1914 had exposed as conservative and nationalistic, was able to stall and then sabotage the European revolutionary movements. But social democracy's successes proved illusory.

Italy and Germany

In Italy and Germany the reformist leaders of the socialist parties, the PSI and SPD, rejected revolution and played a key role in helping to defeat it. They assumed a post-war recovery would see the gradual, peaceful expansion of capitalism and the continued spread of social democracy. They were in for a terrible shock. Their self-delusion assumed the First World War was an accident and the economic forces that drove the world to war in 1914 could be harnessed to bring a new age of prosperity. Events soon showed how misplaced those hopes were.

In 1919 Mussolini's fascists stood in the Italian elections but were marginalised by the factory occupations and land seizures that challenged the bosses, the landowners and the Italian state. But the ending of the occupations, sold out by the leaders of the socialist PSI and the leaders of the metalworkers' union, and the subsequent demoralisation, boosted Mussolini's fortunes. The Italian bosses hired his fascist thugs to smash a militant working class and cow the agricultural workers. The reformist socialist and union leaders were jailed and persecuted when Mussolini came to power. His success won admiration from ruling classes elsewhere in Europe.

In Germany the moderate Socialist Party (SPD) leaders fought hard to turn a burgeoning working-class revolution back into the more acceptable straitjacket of bourgeois parliamentary democracy. They created armed gangs of bitter ex-army officers called the Freikorps. Early in 1919 they unleashed these mercenary thugs to murder revolutionary workers and wreak havoc on the workers' councils across Germany. This was how some of the ablest leaders of the German working class, including Rosa Luxemburg and Karl Liebknecht, were eliminated. In 1920 the Freikorps switched from attacking the revolutionary left to target the moderate reformist leaders. Later they would form the shock troops for Hitler's Nazis when he set out to annihilate the Weimar Republic, the trade unions and the SPD, as well as the German Communist party.

Already in the summer of 1917—before the October insurrection in Russia—the German left-wing journal *Spartakus* had warned: "Here begins the fatal destiny of the Russian Revolution. The dictatorship of the proletariat in Russia is destined to suffer a desperate defeat compared to which the fate of the Paris Commune was child's play—unless the international revolution gives it support in time".[385]

The author of these lines could never have foreseen that the final defeat of the revolution would take the form of Stalin's counter-revolution. But the author of the *Spartakus* article did understand that prolonged isolation for the Russian Revolution would have fatal consequences: as did Rosa Luxemburg. She had challenged Lenin and the Bolsheviks and argued with them whenever she thought they were mistaken; but she knew what side she was on and leapt to their defence:

> Those who sent one and half million German men and youths to their slaughter without blinking an eyelid, those who supported for four years the greatest bloodletting which humanity has ever experienced—now scream about 'terror', about alleged 'monstrosities' threatened by the dictatorship of the proletariat. These gentlemen should look at their own history.
>
> Whatever a party could offer of courage, revolutionary far-sightedness and consistency, Lenin, Trotsky and the other comrades have given

in good measure. The Bolsheviks represented the revolutionary honour western Social Democracy lacked. Their October uprising was not only the actual salvation of the Russian Revolution; it was also the salvation of the honour of international socialism.[386]

Some of the recent material written about the Russian Revolution tries to argue socialist revolution was impossible then, and by extension is impossible now, because the revolutionary forces were too weak, too immature. This is the discredited position the Menshevik leaders adopted during the 1905 revolution and again in 1917. Were the Bolsheviks justified in leading the working class to power in what was a predominantly peasant country or were they simply cavalier adventurers who seized power prematurely?

Between February and October 1917 the Provisional government became increasingly unpopular with the masses and came to rely more and more on the SRs and Menshevik socialists to give it some credibility, with one of their number, Kerensky, as its leader. These moderate socialists were more than happy to run with a bourgeois government because they believed the revolution must limit itself to bourgeois horizons, even when that meant continuing the First World War. In doing so the SRs and Mensheviks turned their backs on the masses and tried to subvert the popular will. They paid the price as their support moved massively to the revolutionary left—the Bolsheviks and the Left SRs.

Kerensky's arrogance in continuing the war and increasing human sacrifice in defiance of the wishes of most of the population, including most of the soldiers, seems absolutely insane, even from a military standpoint. But as Tony Blair proves, hubris is not restricted to early 20th century moderate politicians in Russia. In May Kerensky told his war-weary, mutinous troops that, "It is not for the sake of conquest and violence but for the sake of saving free Russia that you will go forward where your commanders and the government lead you. On the points of your bayonets you will bring peace, truth and justice".[387]

Just prior to the disastrous Galicia offensive later in the summer he told them, "I summon you not to a feast but to death".[388] Many a peasant soldier must have wondered: "What's the point of getting land if I'm killed?". Kerensky's gung-ho bombast launched tens of thousands of peasant soldiers on the long trek back to their villages as they deserted in droves. The October Revolution and the Europe-wide revolt it inspired was what finally stopped the mass slaughter of the First World War.

Again it is Rosa Luxemburg who provides the best answer to the charge that the Bolsheviks took power prematurely:

> Theirs is the immortal historical service of having marched at the head of the international proletariat with the conquest of political power and the problem of the realisation of socialism—and of having advanced mightily the settling of the score between capital and labour in the entire world. In Russia the problem could only be posed. It could not be solved there. And in this sense, the future everywhere belongs to Bolshevism.[389]

Conclusion: When all things are possible

Socialism is the struggle to abolish human exploitation and oppression across the globe. Karl Marx said at the founding of the First International in 1866, "the emancipation of the working class must be won by the working class itself".[390]

Ever since, experts have periodically pronounced Marx's vision dead and buried, arguing capitalism is not inherently crisis-ridden and capitalist competition doesn't mean wars, revolutions and chaos. At every turn these experts are proved wrong.

At the beginning of the 20th century, when the system seemed buoyant, a leading intellectual in the German Socialist Party, Eduard Bernstein, announced capitalism had solved its problems; that economic crises were no longer an integral part of the system. According to Bernstein, Marx was wrong in predicting an ever-greater polarisation between the classes. He looked forward confidently to the growth of organised capitalism on a world scale, with increasingly close connections between the state and the giant trusts eliminating the system's instabilities. This led the reformist wing of German socialism—and the Labour leaders in Britain—to insist the state could be reformed and democratised to play a progressive role in colonising and civilising the "backward" parts of the world.

The First World War was history's verdict on Bernstein's revisionism. Lenin and a few others had drawn the opposite conclusion: "The state becoming merged more and more with the all powerful capitalist combines" meant not a more but a less stable system. Economic crisis and war, which Bernstein thought "organised capitalism" could abolish, are endemic to it. Lenin anticipated "an epoch of wars and revolutions". Later Bukharin, the leading Bolshevik economist, wrote: "War is nothing other than the method of competition at a specific level of development. The method of competition between state capitalist trusts".[391] History continues to prove them right and Bernstein wrong.

Just before May 1968, when the French working class launched the biggest general strike in world history, another expert, the unfortunate Andre Gorz, published his book *Farewell to the Working Class*, explaining why never again could such a thing as a general strike happen. In 1989, the year of Eastern European revolutions, Francis Fukuyama, a member of the Policy Planning staff of the US State Department, published *The End of History*. He claimed the collapse of the Stalinist states "amounted to the ultimate triumph of Western liberal democracy, the unabashed victory of political and economic liberalism"[392] and the death of socialism. But the 1990s ushered in a new and much deeper global crisis.

At the start of the new millennium Gordon Brown, Tony Blair's "Iron Chancellor", announced the end of capitalism's boom-slump cycle, while extolling the virtues of globalisation. His embrace of neo-liberalism and his devil-pact with the City of London helped to bring about the 2008 financial crash. Every temporary stabilisation of capitalism, every defeat for the workers' movement produces such experts; their theories are not original and never last very long. The world recession that began a decade ago and continues with no end in sight is the latest vindication of Marx.

As in the great depression after the Wall Street Crash of 1929, governments today are unable to change the ebb and flow of the capitalist economy. Instead, like voodoo doctors in a rowing boat, they try to command the powerful tides that rage around them. They cannot deal with a runaway system and the threat it poses for the future of humanity and planet earth.

I predict a riot

Those who think revolution has no place in the 21st century are in for a shock. 1917 is only one in a long list of revolutions against capitalism and there will be more. Throughout the 20th century there were many revolutionary upheavals in many different parts of the world and it is no exaggeration to describe it as a century of wars and revolutions.

The history of the last 100 years would be incomprehensible without acknowledging the many occasions when people challenged their rulers through collective action. Among the major revolutions and rebellions of the 20th century are those in Mexico, Russia and Turkey before the First World War; the Irish revolution of 1916-1921; revolutions in Russia, Germany, central Europe and Turkey that overthrew their respective emperors during and immediately after the war; and the upheavals that rocked Italy between 1917 and 1920.

January 1919 saw bloody battles between workers and state forces in Buenos Aires. When the government ordered the army to march on its capital city, the unions called a general strike throughout Argentina. There were mass strikes in the USA and even Britain came close to the brink of revolution in 1919 and again in 1926, when embryonic soviets appeared in the mining communities of South Wales and Fife.

In China in the 1920s and in Spain in the 1930s the course of their histories was altered by workers' revolution. There was a French general strike in 1936, triggered by widespread anti-Nazi sentiment and socialist influence inside the French working class. Mass workers' uprisings freed Paris, Athens and the cities of northern Italy from Nazi occupation in 1944.

After the Second World War the Chinese national revolution and other national liberation movements profoundly altered the global system by ending the era of direct colonial rule. Most of the non-Western governments now represented at the United Nations would not have a seat there without the revolutionary movements that ended colonial domination.

In 1952 Bolivian workers provided the force that overthrew the government, destroyed the army and broke the ruling class. The workers' revolt carried to power a populist government that was confronted with a situation of dual power and reluctantly compelled to carry out extensive structural reforms. The working class movement was unable to transform dual power into workers power but it was a valuable historical experience, for revolutionary upheaval would recur in Bolivia in the first decade of the 21st century.

In the 1950s there were revolts and uprisings against the bureaucratic state capitalist regimes Stalin installed in Eastern Europe: notably the East German uprising of 1953, a workers' uprising in the Polish city of Poznan in 1956 and the Hungarian Revolution that quickly followed it. In 1956 Budapest and every other major Hungarian town were in the hands of factory councils and local revolutionary committees. The British Communist Party, whose Stalinist leadership saw the Hungarian uprising as CIA-inspired, sent journalist Peter Fryer from the *Daily Worker* to cover the events. Fryer's honest, accurate reporting contributed to dissent inside the British Communist Party and the creation of a new anti-Stalinist left. Fryer's report from Budapest highlighted,

> the striking resemblance of these committees to the workers', peasants' and soldiers' councils thrown up in Russia in the 1905 Revolution and in February 1917. They were at once organs of insurrection—the coming together of delegates elected in the factories, universities, mines and army units—and organs of popular self-government, which the armed people trusted.[393]

But in November that year, just as Britain, France and Israel launched their combined military attack on Egypt, Russian tanks swept into Budapest. The Russian forces faced bitter armed resistance, which they eventually crushed by killing thousands and forcing 200,000 to flee across the border into Austria.

Britain's humiliation at Suez fuelled a wave of anti-British agitation throughout the Middle East. It led to the overthrow of the British-backed Iraqi monarchy two years later. The Cuban revolution of 1959 was followed by victory for the Algerian national liberation front over French imperialism in 1964.

1968: workers and students

1968 showed again how the world could be changed by rebellion from below. When millions of French workers struck in protest at police violence against student demonstrators, it soon turned into the biggest general strike in history. The resurgent workers' movement terrified De Gaulle's government and brought it to its knees. But the revolt also terrified the union bosses, who were instrumental in getting De Gaulle and French capitalism off the hook by ending the strikes in return for a general election.

1968 was the year the black ghettos of the USA exploded in protest at the murder of Martin Luther King. It also saw the Prague Spring when Czech students, workers and intellectuals challenged the Stalinist monolith and were crushed by Russian tanks. In 1968 the anti-Vietnam War movement went global and the civil rights movement in Ireland took off. The year saw strikes and demonstrations during the Italian "hot autumn" and an Argentinian workers' uprising in Cordoba.

The early 1970s saw the development of cordones or workers' councils in Chile and the staging of Pinochet's military coup to crush them and overthrow the Allende Popular Unity government. Between 1972 and 1974 the British ruling class was shaken to its core by 200 factory occupations and a series of successful national mass strikes in defiance of the Tory anti-union laws, including two miner's strikes, the second of which toppled a vicious Tory government.

1974 saw the Greek military junta toppled. The Portuguese Revolution of 1974-75 ended the fascist dictatorship that had ruled there since before the Second World War, throwing up workers' councils and raising the spectre of workers' power in Portugal and neighbouring Spain. Socialist journalist Paul Foot wrote: "Anyone lucky enough to walk the streets of Lisbon at any time between the spring of 1974 and the autumn of 1975 could not fail to be overcome by the democratic spirit that engulfed the whole city—indeed the whole country. Top of the bestseller list in Portugal for weeks on end in 1975 was Lenin's *State and Revolution*".[394]

The Portuguese revolt was triggered by national liberation struggles in its former colonies of Mozambique, Guinea and Angola. In 1975 American imperialism was driven out of Vietnam. In 1979 the Iranian revolution toppled the Shah of Iran and striking oil workers formed shoras, the Iranian equivalent of workers' councils.

The end of the Eastern-bloc

The beginning of the end for the bi-polar Cold War period came with the meteoric rise of the independent Polish trade union Solidarity in the early 1980s. The final demise of the Stalinist regimes came with the Eastern European revolutions of 1989.

1989 proved that contrary to the late great Gil Scott-Heron, the revolution will be televised. Global TV audiences witnessed both the horrors: tanks in Tiananmen Square deployed against the Chinese democracy movement; and the joys: cheering crowds in Bucharest at Christmas 1989 when dictator Ceausescu was toppled and executed. The outer empire of the USSR crumbled at its westernmost frontier in East Berlin and then unravelled eastwards from the Baltic States to the Caucasus. Nationalist movements exploded, protests spread like wildfire and two big miners' strikes shook Russia itself in 1989 and again in 1991. As Russian workers started to act independently for the first time since the 1920s, the Soviet Union officially dissolved in 1991.

Huge workers' struggles played a central role in sweeping away regimes that many on the old left defended as being "deformed" or "distorted" workers' states. Instead these societies were state capitalist dictatorships based on exploitation every bit as ruthless as their Western counterparts.

The apartheid regime in South Africa was destroyed by a combination of ANC agitation, international boycott and mass strike action by a powerful black working class. At the end of the millennium Suharto's Indonesian dictatorship fell to a popular movement from below.

Revolution in the 21st century

The new millennium opened with the rise of a mass anti-war movement and a global anti-capitalist movement. In 2001-2 Argentina was rocked by an economic crisis that saw it default on its debts, with a popular revolt that toppled five different presidents in a few days.

In Serbia and a string of central Asian states the "Velvet Revolutions", popular movements from below involving mass action by millions of people, toppled hated regimes. In 2005 Bolivia's workers, peasants and indigenous peoples drove out of office the country's second president in 21 months. Political power was in the balance before a social truce was agreed pending elections.

Then, in 2007, there was a mass popular revolt in Bolivia. Newspaper reports at the time were reminiscent of revolutionary Petrograd in the summer of 1917: general strikes; columns of peasants marching on the city of La Paz; the occupation of oil wells and airports; striking miners handing sticks of gelignite to striking teachers to throw against police lines; and attempts by workers to invade the presidential palace. What happened ten years ago in Bolivia shows how the endless uncertainty that characterises global capitalism can breed revolutionary resistance.

It's five years since Western imperialism and the Arab ruling classes across north Africa and the Middle East were terrified by the biggest revolutionary movement of the 21st century so far, the Arab Spring. Trotsky's notion of permanent revolution suddenly came to life as workers took centre stage in movements that swept away dictators in Tunisia and Egypt. It threatened the corrupt rulers in the neighbouring Arab states, brought hope to the Palestinians and terrified the rulers of Zionist Israel.

The Arab Spring showed how the working class in less economically developed societies could play a crucial role in fighting for democracy and how such struggles have the potential to develop into an international challenge to imperialism across the region. The Arab revolutions inspired the "15 May" movement in Spain and the Occupy movement that spread from Manhattan around the world.

And despite the blows of counter-revolution rained down on the Egyptian working class in 2013, the struggle there continues. The Arab revolution, like the Russian revolutions of 1905 and 1917, is a process and not a single event; it advances and retreats. In his recent book, Jack Shenker argues:

> the revolution has never been just about Mubarak, or his successors, or elections. It is not merely a civil war between Islamists and secularists, or a fight between oriental backwardness and Western modernity, nor even an event that can be fixed or constrained in place or time. In reality the revolution is about marginalised citizens muscling their way onto the political stage and practising collective sovereignty over domains previously closed to them.[395]

Shenker's last sentence is redolent of Trotsky's picture of Russia in 1917: "Revolution is the forcible entrance of the masses into the rulership over their own destiny."

Since the financial crash of 2008 and the Euro debt crisis that followed it, Greece has experienced a depression on a scale comparable with the USA in the Great Depression, when the US economy contracted by a quarter before it started to grow again in the mid 1930s. Greece too saw its GDP fall by a quarter but recovery is slower than the 1930s. Like Argentina and Bolivia before it, Greece has seen a massive explosion of working class militancy over the last decade, with mass demonstrations, a series of general strikes, the collapse of traditional parties and a polarisation between right and left.

As I write mass protests in South Korea have forced a corrupt President out of office, Greece has witnessed another general strike against government austerity and thousands of textile workers in Egypt have gone on strike.

Britain is not immune. Who knows where the Brexit crisis, the deep divisions in the British and European ruling classes and their impact on an ailing world economy, will lead? America is polarised under Trump's presidency and as the centre collapses it's clear we are living in an age of extremes. Karl Marx said revolution is the locomotive of history. The continuing relevance of revolution should surprise no one. The modern world is shaped by the most rapidly changing economic system ever known. Its motive force is blind competition to accumulate profit. Capitalism constantly reshapes agriculture and industry, transforming the conditions under which people are forced to work and live.

What is to be done?

Revolutions are not so rare or remote as our rulers would have us believe, but so far Russia 1917 remains the only victorious workers' revolution. It gave control of a major country to a workers' government for the first time. Its victory accelerated a wave of revolt across Europe that ended a world war and inspired rebellion in the colonies of the imperial powers.

Lenin died in January 1924 when the fate of Russia and the wider European revolution were still in the balance. Painted as a tyrant and a dictator by the capitalist opponents of socialism, his body was embalmed, transforming him into a peepshow and a god by Stalin and the gravediggers of the Russian Revolution: something that would have appalled him. His widow Krupskaya argued against this tribute:

> Do not raise memorials to him: to all this he attached so little importance. If you want to honour the name Vladimir Ilyich, build crèches, kindergartens, houses, schools, libraries, medical centres, hospitals, homes for the disabled, and, most of all let us put his precepts into practice.[396]

Lenin dedicated his life to the emancipation of working people, not just in Russia but throughout the world, and he fought to build a revolutionary party to help organise for it. Above all he placed his belief in the ability of working people to cast off the chains of their oppressors and exploiters.

The upheavals that shook Russia in 1917—the strikes and mutinies in opposition to the First World War, the clamour for self-determination by the oppressed nationalities, the rising of the women workers and the fight for land and freedom by Russia's poor peasants—would all have happened without him. Lenin's genius was in seeing how the mass movements for change could be drawn together into a single force capable of transforming society. His legacy was a party that while organising a sizeable minority of the workers, managed to win the support of the majority of the people for a revolution to end capitalist rule in Russia.

Without Lenin and the Bolsheviks it is inconceivable that a coalition of workers, soldiers and peasants would have taken power in 1917. The absence of revolutionary leadership and such a bold socialist workers' party in all the other revolutionary upheavals that have challenged capitalism throughout the last 100 years, explains why 1917 is unique. Times change but we can still learn from the past. That is why it is such a tragedy that Lenin's real legacy has been hidden or distorted by what passes for bourgeois scholarship. It is important to set the record straight.

1917 shows the latent energy, creativity and power of working people. "Revolutions are festivals of the oppressed and exploited" Lenin wrote. "At no other time are the mass of the people able to come forward so actively as creators of a new social order, as at a time of revolution. Then ordinary people are capable of performing miracles, if judged by the limited, philistine yardstick of gradual progress".[397]

Revolutionary situations offer great opportunities for the rapid spread of revolutionary ideas and organisation. But the task of building socialist organisation can't wait until a popular upsurge happens. It is too late to begin building an army in the heat of battle. Success depends on that happening well in advance. The Bolsheviks were able to grow and lead the October revolution because before 1917 they spent 15 years building a fighting socialist organisation. By February that year it had over 20,000 active members, a collective tradition and real roots inside the Russian working class and among the rank and file of the armed forces. In seven months it was able to grow to become a party of 400,000.

Yet today among those who consider themselves radical opponents of capitalism, the attitude to Lenin and the Bolshevik tradition is mainly negative. Even those who accept the chasm between Lenin and Stalin and acknowledge that Bolshevik-type organisation made sense in Tsarist Russia query its relevance now. The argument that Russia in 1917 is different from societies today and so nothing of much significance can be learned from dead Russians passes for common sense. Yet it fails to distinguish between what was specific to Russia at the start of the 20th century and what remains generally applicable about Lenin's conception of revolutionary organisation.

Lenin argued workers can liberate themselves only through revolutionary struggle from below but in doing so will confront a number of obstacles. The first is a highly centralised state run by unelected hierarchies overseen from above by members of the ruling class. In times of mass revolt when these hierarchies are challenged, restoring order in the state machine becomes the top priority for our rulers. And in all but one of the many mass revolts described in this chapter the ruling class succeeded in doing so—though often with great difficulty.

In 1914 the Tories allied with the Orange bosses of Ulster and the British Army High Command to threaten the then Liberal government with civil war if it tried to implement its policy of Home Rule for Ireland. In the 1920s Trotsky wrote, "the present British parliament forms a monstrous distortion of the principles of bourgeois democracy. Without revolutionary force one can hardly obtain in Britain even an honest division of parliamentary constituencies or the abolition of the monarchy or the House of Lords".[398]

Little has changed since. When Jeremy Corbyn was elected leader of the Labour Party, an unnamed general threatened that if Corbyn ever became prime minister and sought to "downgrade Britain's nuclear capabilities" the military "would not stand for it". While socialists defend parliamentary democracy against the far right we have to be clear that the freedoms it offers are strictly limited and that the ruling class will dispense with them if their rule is seriously challenged.

Lenin insisted that confronting and smashing this centralised state requires internationalist political organisation that can pull together all the struggles and give them an overall direction and purpose. To be effective, revolutionary organisation has to be rooted in the day-to-day battles of the masses and be capable of intervening in a coherent unified manner. Lenin was adamant that the Bolsheviks should not just wage economic struggle but should act and intervene politically.

For Lenin, avoiding political questions meant surrendering the field of battle to rival political forces that were happy to operate within the framework of the existing system. It meant ignoring the need to convince oppressed groups that their liberation is ultimately dependent on the overthrow of the capitalist system.

The other major obstacle workers face is what Lenin called the uneven consciousness. Some workers have backward ideas—they vote Tory, hold racist views and break strikes. A minority of workers hold revolutionary ideas and oppose oppression and exploitation. This element grows enormously in periods of revolt. But most of the time most workers are somewhere in between, holding a mixture of contradictory ideas about themselves and the world around them. This explains the attraction of reformist ideas and reformist political organisation and it is the reason why revolutionaries have to engage in political argument to combat the idea of gradualism at the same time as they fight to raise the militancy and confidence of the working class.

Through the practical experience of building a socialist party in Russia, Lenin developed a form of organisation through which the revolutionary minority could be drawn together and armed with the arguments, the experience and methods of struggle required to pull wider forces around them. Lenin's party was flexible. It was able to transform itself to fit changing conditions. The necessarily clandestine party of 1902 was different from the combat party of 1905 and the open mass party of 1917. But it was a party that could win the mass of workers and lead them to victory in the revolution.

All these facets of Leninism are relevant now. The problems they address are not peculiar to Tsarist Russia in 1917 but are to be found in 21st century Britain, where workers consciousness is uneven, where a centralised state rules British society behind a shallow veneer of parliamentary democracy and where the separation of economics and politics explains the appeal of reformism to workers and helps the ruling class to get away with scapegoating migrants and Muslims.

So long as capitalism, based on the exploitation of the growing mass of workers, remains, so too does the relevance of Lenin's ideas and the party he built.

Lenin reloaded

Does Lenin have anything to say to the left today? The world is very different from the one he knew. His pamphlets and articles were written in exile, duplicated by hand and smuggled into Tsarist Russia by dedicated socialists under threat of persecution, arrest and death. Today communication is instantaneous. Ideas and information fly round the globe at the touch of a screen or the push of a button.

Yet if we could bring Lenin back to life, much of 21st century capitalism would be familiar to him. In 1918 he wrote an open letter to American workers. It could well have been written to them today in the wake of Trump's election: "America has become one of the foremost countries in regard to the depth of the abyss which lies between the handful of arrogant multi-millionaires who wallow in filth and luxury, and the millions who constantly live on the verge of pauperism".[399]

Lenin would recognise how modern imperialism is defined by the multi-polar rivalries of the competing super powers and their lesser associates, just as he described at the start of the First World War. Above all he would be struck by the universality of the modern working class, its wonderful diversity and its resilience. It has become increasingly fashionable on the left, as well as the right, to dismiss the working class and insist that radical politics based on its agency are a thing of the past. But as Lenin was fond of pointing out, "facts are stubborn things" and the facts about a growing, more powerful working class are indisputable.

Marx's clarion call at the end of the *Communist Manifesto*, "workers of the world unite", was written in 1848 when Europe was filled with revolutionary hope. But capitalism was new and the class of wage labourers that Marx and Engels appealed to was then tiny and confined to pockets of northern Europe and north America. In 1848 it numbered a few million, perhaps only two percent of the global population. Nevertheless Marx and Engels insisted capitalism, the new mode of production, was so revolutionary and dynamic it would come to dominate the whole world. And in doing so, they argued, it would create its own gravedigger, the proletariat—a universal class of producers on whose labour the entire system would depend.

History has vindicated them. By the year 2000 the working class of South Korea was larger than the entire world working class at the time of Marx's death in 1883. And in 2000 South Korea was only the 11th biggest economy in the world. Today, for the first time in human history, the majority of people participating in the global workforce are wage labourers, or to use Marx's term, proletarians: some 1.6 billion of them, an increase of 600 million since the mid-1990s.[400] In Lenin's day the working class was puny by comparison.

A recent book, *Southern Insurgency: The Coming of The Global Working Class*[401] charts emerging workers' movements in what Western academics call the Global South. The last few years have seen strikes and factory occupations in South Korea and the creative "umbrella protests" in Hong Kong. Ominously for the rulers of China and India, the author of *Southern Insurgency* shows how the same process is happening there, on a much bigger scale. Between 2012 and 2014 a wave of mass sit-down strikes paralysed the large car plants of northern India and have since hit other industries to such an extent that "strikes are becoming ubiquitous in India's special Export Processing Zones". Last year India saw the biggest general strike in world history.

New possibilities

The neo-liberal consensus of the last 30 years has been thrown into chaos. The victories for Trump and Brexit show it: the centre cannot hold. The emergence of what are called populist parties is an ambiguous response that can move either to the radical left or to the racist right, depending on the influence of socialists and socialist ideas.

That is why the Russian Revolution matters. It provides an alternative view of what is possible when society polarises and socialists organise to offer hope and unity in place of fear and division. It shows that the job of socialists is not to commentate but to look reality in the face and act accordingly; that real change won't happen without mass engagement, a battle of ideas and above all, independent working class political organisation. Across the world there is a revolt against the people at the top of society—the one percent. It can go left or right and it is the job of all of us who want a better, safer world to shape it and pull it in a socialist direction.

Imperialism has created the biggest refugee crisis since the Second World War with hundreds of thousands fleeing destruction, terror and famine. Fortress Europe, containing most of the richest nations on earth, has turned its back on the biggest crisis facing humanity. Instead of finding relief and shelter the dispossessed are left to freeze and starve in squalid, makeshift camps or drown in the Mediterranean. Such acts of murder and callous disregard indict the rich and powerful. And while our rulers' attempt to scapegoat the victims serves to fuel the growth of racism, the far right and the Nazis, it has also provoked great acts of solidarity from large numbers of ordinary people.

In the years ahead rising sea levels caused by climate change will see increasing numbers of refugees. It is not a refugee crisis, it is a capitalist crisis. But it is the poor who will suffer. The global corporations won't be reformed or regulated into thinking the future of humanity and the planet we live on matters more than their profits. Millions are enraged at corporate capitalism and its venal politicians; at how the rich's insatiable thirst for profit has created a global crisis and endless wars; and at how the free market is pushing the world ever closer to ecological disaster.

Angry people are looking for real alternatives, for something that can change the world. That's why in the 2016 primaries for the US presidential election, more young people voted for Bernie Sanders, who called himself a socialist, than for Hilary Clinton and Donald Trump combined. The need for another world becomes clearer with every passing minute but it will take more than electing left-wingers to do it for us; it will take mass involvement and revolutionary upheaval to overthrow the present setup.

For thousands of years people starved because there was not enough food. Capitalism is the only system of society in which people starve because there is too much food. Instead of the present crazy set up the world could be run on the basis of need instead of greed. Lots of people agree but still think the only way to get there is to elect the right people into positions of power so they can legislate change. That's what most Russian workers and peasants expected from their politicians after they toppled the Tsar in February 1917. But to get peace, bread and land they had to take power into their own hands.

Lenin's question, What is to be done? is still valid. All those who believed or hoped the rise of Syriza in Greece heralded a new kind of party that could straddle reform and revolution and unite the entire left, face the same problem that confronted the left inside social democracy in 1914. 1917 shows there is an alternative.

The future is not what it used to be

The deepening crisis of capitalism means more corruption and a less stable world. But it also brings a new generation of activists who want to change it. In 2017 many of them will ask what happened to the Russian Revolution, the most important and the most successful social movement in world history. The Russia of 1917, its despotic Romanov dynasty and its militant Petrograd Soviet seem like ancient history now. But what is crucial and relevant about the Russian Revolution is not its quaint historical detail, or the melodrama surrounding the corrupt Romanov court, but the compelling portrait it presents of ordinary women and men taking extraordinary action to stop a world war and achieve freedom.

Orthodox historians try to cover their contempt for social revolution and their eternal pessimism about revolutionary change under the cloak of "realism". The "realism" of 1914 brought catastrophic global conflict and would bring it again and again in the decades that followed. In 1917 by contrast, the women and men who took to the streets in Russia were reaching out to a much different and better world by challenging this brutal system. At the heart of the revolutionary process that swept Tsarism aside were the actions of ordinary Russians who, for a time, became the freest people in the whole world. A proper understanding of what began in 1917 is the best possible antidote to pessimism about the capacity of the working class to change both itself and the world.

1917 proved workers could break free from the stultifying idea of their own inferiority and take power. It is such an important example that socialists keep referring back to it, and it is such a dangerous example for the tiny minority who rule us that they and their predecessors have spent the last one hundred years trying to bury the truth about it.

We live in an age of extreme possibilities and extreme dangers. 1917 proved another world is possible and it showed how we might be able to win it. Those who rule over us are destroying large chunks of the world and its people because they think it serves their interests. They will do anything to stop a challenge to their wealth and power. Yet they cannot break their dependence on us: the billions who labour in the great concentrations of world industry, in the fields, offices, mines, hospitals, in the supermarkets, on the rail networks, in the banks, on the building sites and in the call centres. Without our class the rich and powerful are nothing. You can hear the echoes of our power in the recent Indian general strike or in the mass protests in South Korea.

Their system cannot guarantee a stable existence for us and revolt will flare up again and again in the present century just like the last one. The question is not will there be revolutions in the years that lie ahead but in which direction will the revolts go? Will they be defeated or can we unite into revolutionary organisation all those among the exploited and the oppressed that see and feel the horrors of the system and sense the possibility of overthrowing it?

Lenin said at the start of the 20th century: "In its struggle for power the working class has no other weapon but its organisation".[402] The ruling class organises its forces, selects and trains its leaders according to its principles, as do the reformist parties in their unending search for compromise. Only fools or the one percent would argue that revolutionaries should not organise too.

Notes

Chapter 1: Introduction

1 S A Smith in D H Kaiser (editor), *The Workers' Revolution in Russia of 1917*, (Cambridge, 1987), p61.

2 Founded in 1898, the RSDLP split into two wings in 1903: the Bolsheviks (majority in Russian) and the Mensheviks (minority). Between 1903 and 1912 both wings worked together, unified for a while, and then split again. In 1912 the division became permanent, though many socialists worked with both wings or tried to remain neutral in the dispute.

3 Lenin, *The War and Russian Social-Democracy*, Collected Works, Vol 21, (Moscow, 1964), p28.

4 Figes and Kolonitskii, *Interpreting the Russian Revolution: Language and Symbols of 1917*, (London, 1997), p173.

5 *The Bolsheviks and The October Revolution*: Central Committee Minutes of the RSDLP (Bolsheviks), August 1917-February 1918, (London, 1974), p97.

6 See M Empson, *Land and Labour: Marxism, ecology and human history*, (London, 2014), p297.

7 John Bellamy Foster, *Marx's Ecology: Materialism and Nature*, (Monthly Review Press, 2000), p243.

8 The term was used by Marx in relation to the European revolutions of 1848. The origin of the famous phrase is uncertain: Marx used it for the first time in an article of 1844, in which he observed that Napoleon had 'substituted permanent war for permanent revolution'.

9 Quoted in E H Carr, *The Bolshevik Revolution 1917-23*, Volume 3 (London, 1983), p29.

10 Up until 1914 social democracy was widely regarded as synonymous with socialism and even Marxism.

Chapter 2: Context: Russia at the start of the 20th century

11 Trotsky, *The History of the Russian Revolution*, Volume 1, (London, 1967), pp22-3.

12 C Porter, *Alexandra Kollontai: A Biography*, (Pontypool, 2013), p73.

13 P Mason, *Live Working or Die Fighting: How the Working Class Went Global*, (London, 2007), p219.

14 Mason, 2007, p219.

15 Anthony Brewer, *Marxist Theories of Imperialism*, (London, 1999), pp88-9.

16 L Huberman, *Man's Worldly Goods*, (London, 1937), pp263, 268.

17 J Newsinger, *The Blood Never Dried: A People's History of the British Empire*, (London, 2006), frontpiece

18 Trotsky, *1905*, (London, 1973), p53.

19 Marx, *Selected Works*, Volume 1, (London, 1942), p241.

20 Marx and Engels, *Collected Works* VII, (London, 1975), pp483, 489.

21 Lenin, *Collected Works*, Volume 21 (Moscow, 1964), p23.

22 E Crankshaw, *The Shadow of the Winter Palace: The Drift to Revolution 1825-1917*, (London, 1978), p342.

23 B D Wolfe, *Three Who Made a Revolution*, (London, 1966), p32.

24 Quoted in E H Carr, *The Bolshevik Revolution 1917-23*, Volume 1, (London,

1983), p15.

25 See N Harding, *Lenin's Political Thought*, Volume 1, (London, 1983), p46.

26 https://www.marxists.org/archive/marx/works/subject/hist-mat/18-brum/ch07.htm .

27 Letters of Marx and Engels, (Moscow, 1947), p341.

28 Tony Cliff, *Lenin Volume 1: Building the Party*, London 1975), p41.

29 Isaac Deutscher, *Stalin: A Political Biography*, (London, 1961), pp47-48.

30 Trotsky, quoted in Jane McDermid and Anna Hillyar, *Midwives of the Revolution*, (Athens Ohio, 1999), p51

31 McDermid and Hillyar, 1999), p52.

32 Plekhanov's final words in his speech to the founding Congress of the Second International in 1889. See www.marxists.org/archive/cliff/works/1957/01/plekhanov.htm

33 S H Baron, *Plekhanov: The Father of Russian Marxism*, (Stanford, 1966), p143.

34 Trotsky, *The Young Lenin*, (New York, 1972), pp181-2.

35 Lenin, *Collected Works*, Volume 1, pp338, 400.

36 Lenin, *Collected Works,* Volume 5, p491.

37 N S Krupskaya, *Memories of Lenin*, (London, 1970), p86.

38 McDermid and Hillyar, 1999, p57.

39 McDermid and Hillyar, 1999, p61.

40 Trotsky, *My Life*, (London, 1979), p157

41 Carr, 1983, Volume 1, p18.

42 Lenin, *Collected Works*, Volume 2, pp119-120.

43 Lenin, *Collected Works*, Volume 4, p315.

44 Lenin, 'What is to be done?' *Collected Works*, Volume 5, (Moscow, 1961), p514-5.

45 Lars Lih, *Lenin Rediscovered: What Is to Be Done? in Context*, (Chicago, 2008), pp9, 20, 27, 317.

46 See *Rosa Luxemburg Speaks*, (New York, 1980), pp112-130.

47 Lenin, *Collected Works*, Volume 16, p301-302.

48 Quoted in LarsLih, 2008, pVII.

49 Lars Lih, 2008, p13.

50 Lionel Kochan, *Russia in Revolution 1898-1918*, (London, 1966), p27.

51 *Rosa Luxemburg Speaks*, 1980, p164,

52 M Pokrovsky, *Brief History of Russia, Volume 2*, (London, 1933), p51.

53 Luxemburg, 1980, p166.

54 Luxemburg, 1980, pp167-8.

55 Cliff, *Lenin Volume 1: Building the Party*, (London, 1975), p61.

56 Lenin, *Collected Works*, Volume 8, (Moscow 1962), p37.

57 Figure from Pokrovsky, *Brief History of Russia*, Volume 2, (London, 1933), p109.

Chapter 3: 1905: Russia's great dress rehearsal and the years of reaction

58 Lenin, *The Revolutionary Upswing*, Collected Works, Volume 18, p108.

59 C Schorske, *German Social Democracy, 1905-17*, (London, 1985), p28.

60 Philip Foner, *History of the Labour Movement in the US*, Volume 4, (New York, 1965), p29.

61 Porter, 2013, p92.

62 Quoted in Porter, 2013, p92.

63 Lenin, *Collected Works*, Volume 8, 1962, pp111-113.

64 Lenin, *Collected Works*, Volume 8, 1962, pp537, 538.

65 Porter, 2013, p95.

66 Lenin, *Collected Works*, Volume 10, (Moscow, 1962), p119.

67 Lenin, *Collected Works*, Volume 10, p32.

68 Lenin, *Collected Works*, Volume 34, (Moscow, 1966), p359.

69 Lenin, *Collected Works*, Volume 34, p32.

70 Lenin, *Collected Works*, Volume 8, (1962), p146.

71 Trotsky, 1973, pp238-9.

72 Lenin, *Collected Works*, Volume 11, (Moscow, 1962), p173.

73 A Ascher, *The Revolution of 1905: Russia in Disarray*, (Stanford, 1988), p185.

74 *Rosa Luxemburg Speaks*, 1980, p176.

75 Trotsky, 197, p11.,

76 Trotsky, 1973, p310.

77 Leon Trotsky, *Stalin*, (London, 2016), pp768-9.

78 Trotsky, 1967, Volume 1, p159.

79 Trotsky, 1973, p102.

80 Trotsky, 1973, p136.

81 Trotsky, 1973, p7.

82 Lenin quoted in Porter, 2013, p111.

83 Figures from D Lane, *The Roots of*

Russian Communism, (Assen, 1969), p12.

84 Lenin, *Collected Works*, Volume 11, p354-5.

85 Lenin, *Collected Works*, Volume 11, p145.

86 Lenin, *Collected Works*, Volume 13, p42.

87 Lenin, *Collected Works*, Volume 25, p305.

88 Piatnitsky, quoted in J Molyneux, *Marxism and the Party*, (London, 1978), p69.

89 E Crankshaw, *The Shadow of the, Winter Palace*, (London, 1978), p453.

90 Lenin, *Collected Works*, Volume 17, p467.

91 Lenin, *Collected Works*, Volume 20, (Moscow, 1964), p328.

92 Lenin, *Collected Works*, Volume 20, p370.

93 Trotsky, 2016, p214.

94 Barbara Allen, *Alexander Shlyapnikov: the Life of an Old Bolshevik*, (Chicago, 2016), p34.

95 A Shlyapnikov, *On the Eve of 1917: Reminiscences from the Revolutionary Underground*, (London, 1982), p1.

96 Shlyapnikov, 1982, p5.

97 Shlyapnikov, 1982, p6.

98 Shlyapnikov, 1982, p7.

99 The city was called St Petersburg until August 1914 when the Tsar Nicholas had this German sounding name changed to the Russian Petrograd. However the local Bolsheviks refused to pander to national chauvinism, retaining the name of their Petersburg committee.

100 Shlyapnikov, 1982, p18.

101 L Trotsky, *War and the International*, (London, 1971), p88.

102 Trotsky, 1971, p155.

103 Trotsky, 2016, pp 207-8.

104 Lenin, *Collected Works*, Volume 23. p132.

Chapter 4: The outbreak of war and the collapse of official socialism

105 Pierre Broué, *The German Revolution 1917-23*, (London, 2006), p9.

106 *The War Correspondence of Leon Trotsky; The Balkan Wars 1912-13*, (New York, 1981), p15.

107 Trotsky, (1981), p15.

108 Paul Frohlich, *Rosa Luxemburg*, (London, 1994), p186.

109 Broué, 2006, p44.

110 Mason, 2007, p161.

111 *Vorwärts*, 25 July 1914, quoted in P Mason, (London, 2007), p160.

112 Broué, 2006, p44.

113 Trotsky, 1979, p243.

114 Stephen Cohen, *Bukharin and the Bolshevik Revolution*, (London, 1974), p22.

115 Lenin, *The War and Russian Social Democracy, Collected Works*, Volume 21, p23.

116 Lenin, *Collected Works*, Volume 21, p315.

117 Quoted in Mason, 2007, p162.

118 Quoted in J Schneer, *Ben Tillett*, (Kent, 1982), p192.

119 W Kendall, *The Revolutionary Movement in Britain*, (London, 1969), p88.

120 J Maclean, *Justice*, (newspaper of the BSP), 17 September 1914.

121 Lenin, *Collected Works*, Volume 21, p28.

122 Ken Weller quoted in Lesley Hoggart, *The War against War*, Socialist Review 85, (London, 1986), p33.

123 Ralph Milliband, *Parliamentary Socialism*, (London, 1972), p44.

124 *Forward*, August 1914, quoted in Kendall, 1969, pp110, 111.

125 Engels, quoted by Lenin, *Collected Works*, Volume 27, pp494-9.

126 C Harman, *A People's History of the World*, (London, 1999), p405.

127 Figures from E Hobsbawm, *The Age of Extremes*, (London, 1994), p51.

128 Lenin, *Collected Works*, Volume 21, p17.

129 Lenin, *The War and Russian Social Democracy, Selected Works*, Volume 1, (Moscow, 1970), pp656, 657.

130 McDermid and Hillyar, 1999, p179.

Chapter 5: February 1917: Soviets and the Provisional government

131 Trotsky, 1967, p109.

132 See A Solzhenitsyn, 1914, (London, 1972).

133 Trotsky, Volume 1, 1967, p41.

134 Figures taken from S A Smith, *Red Petrograd: Revolution in the Factories 1917-18*, (Cambridge, 1983), p45.

135 Lenin, *Collected Works*, Volume 23, 1964, p253.

136 At the outbreak of war in 1914

Nicholas II had the city's name changed to Petrograd because St Petersburg sounded too German.

137 Tony Cliff, *Lenin Vol 2: All Power to the Soviets*, (London, 1976), p82.

138 McDermid and Hillyar, 1999, pp148-9.

139 McDermid and Hillyar, 1999, p147.

140 F W Halle, *Women in Soviet Russia*, (London, 1933), p91.

141 McDermid and Hillyar, 1999, p154.

142 Trotsky, *History of the Russian Revolution Volume 1*, (London, 1967), pp111-112.

143 Quoted in McDermid and Hillyar, 1999, p7.

144 McDermid and Hillyar, 1999, p150.

145 N Sukhanov, *The Russian Revolution 1917: A Personal Record*, (Guildford, 1984), p18.

146 P Miliukov, *Political Memoirs*, (Ann Arbor, 1967), p406.

147 J Reed, *Ten Days that Shook the World*, (London, 1977), p10.

148 Mike Haynes, *Russia: Class and Power 1917-2000*, (London, 2002), p21.

149 Reed, 1977, p40.

150 Lenin, *The Tasks of the Proletariat in our Revolution, Collected Works*, Volume 24, p60.

151 *The Age of Permanent Revolution; A Trotsky Anthology*, edited by Isaac Deutscher, (New York, 1964), p89.

152 Trotsky, 2016, p237.

153 *Trotsky Anthology*, 1964, p90.

154 Sukhanov, 1984, p337.

155 Quoted in Haynes, 2002, p27.

156 Lenin, *Collected Works*, Volume 24, p39.

157 Norman Stone, *The Eastern Front*, (London, 1975), p218.

158 Quoted in Figes and Kolonitskii, 1997, p163.

159 S A Smith, *Red Petrograd: Revolution in the Factories 1917-18*, (Cambridge, 1983), p98.

160 Smith, 1983, p99.

161 Sukhanov, 1984, p227.

162 Porter, 2013, p241.

163 Trotsky, *Social Democracy and Revolution*, in *Witnesses to Permanent Revolution* (Leiden, 2009), p445.

164 The term was first used by Marx and Engels in relation to the 1848 European Revolutions.

165 Lenin, *Collected Works*, Volume 23, p297.

166 N Ascherson, *Lenin: The Man who Broke the System*, Observer Sunday Magazine, 5 April 1970.

167 Lenin, *Collected Works*, Volume 24, p23.

Chapter 6: April 1917: Re-arming the party

168 Lenin, *Collected Works*, Volume 21, p310.

169 Krupskaya, 1970, p287.

170 C Merridale, *Lenin on the Train*, (London, 2016), p192.

171 W Hahlweg, *Lenin's Ruck-khernach Russland 1917*, (Leiden, 1957), p25.

172 Lenin, *Collected Works*, Volume 23, p371.

173 Merridale, 2016, p210.

174 F Raskolnikov, *Kronstadt and Petrograd in 1917*, (London, 1982), p71.

175 Sukhanov, 1984, p272.

176 Trotsky, 2016, p250, 251.

177 Harman, 1999, pp420-421.

178 T Cliff, *Lenin Volume 2: All Power to the Soviets*, (London, 1976), pp131-2.

179 Lenin, *Collected Works*, Volume 24, pp22-23.

180 McDermid and Hillyar, 1999, p165.

181 Miliukov's Memoirs, in Merridale, 2016, p235.

182 Smith, 1983, p3.

183 McDermid and Hillyar, 1999, pp192-3.

184 Goodey, *Factory Committees and the Dictatorship of the Proletariat*, Critique 3, (London, 1974), p29.

185 Trotsky, 1967, Volume 1, p389.

186 Smith, 1983, pp253-255.

187 S A Smith, essay in *The Workers' Revolution in Russia; The View from Below*, edited Kaiser, (Cambridge, 1987).

188 D Koenker, essay in *The Workers' Revolution in Russia; The View from Below* 1987.

189 McDermid and Hillyar, 1999, pp166-7.

190 Figures from OH Radkey, *The Sickle under the Hammer*, (New York, 1968), pp278-9.

191 N Golovine, *The Russian Army in the World War*, (Yale, 1931), pp272-4.

192 Figures from Sukhanov, 1984, p534.

193 Trotsky, 2016, p265.

194 Trotsky, 2016, p304.

195 Figures from T Cliff, *Lenin Volume 2: All Power to the Soviets*, p150.

196 Smith, 1983, p101.

197 Trotsky, *History of the Russian Revolution*, Volume 2, (London, 1967), pp31, 32.

198 D Koenker, *Moscow Workers and the 1917 Revolution*, (Guildford, 1981), p94.

199 Lenin, *Collected Works*, Volume 25, p312.

200 Deutscher (ed), 1964, pp98-9.

201 WS Woytinsky, *Stormy Passage*, (New York, 1961), p306.

202 Sukhanov, 1984, p486.

203 Incidents taken from McDermid and Hillyar, 1999, pp196-70.

204 Krupskaya, 1970, p75.

205 Trotsky, 1967, Volume 2, p99.

206 Trotsky, 2016, p269.

207 Lenin, *On Soviet Socialist Democracy*, (Moscow, 1962), p62.

208 Marx, *The Communist Manifesto in the Revolution of 1848*, (London, 1973), p69.

209 Bukharin, *Imperialism and the World Economy*, (London, 1976), p128.

210 Lenin, *The State and Revolution*, (New York, 1998), p40.

211 Lenin, 1998, p101.

Chapter 7: The Kornilov coup and the road to workers' power

212 M Ferro, *October 1917, a social history of the Russian Revolution*, (London, 1980), p51.

213 Lenin, *Collected Works*, Volume 25, pp285-9.

214 Trotsky, 1967, Volume 2, p227.

215 D Mandel, *The Petrograd Workers and the Soviet Seizure of Power* (Macmillan, 1984), p140.

216 Trotsky, 1967 Volume 2, p225.

217 Trotsky, 1967, Volume 2, p 233.

218 Reed, 1977, p31.

219 Reed, 1977, p45.

220 Sukhanov, 1984, p534.

221 Sukhanov, 1984, p253.

222 Porter, 2013, p261.

223 Reed, 1977, p101.

224 The Bolshevik Party changed its name to the Russian Communist Party in March 1918.

225 Trotsky, 1979, pp342, 343.

226 The January and April figures were official party figures, while the August and October figures were party secretary Sverdlov's estimates reported to the central committee and based on local returns to his office.

227 Reed, 1977, p29.

228 Lenin, *Can the Bolsheviks Retain State Power?* Collected Works, Volume 26, p127.

229 Trotsky, *The Challenge of the Left Opposition: 1923-25*, (New York, 1975), p234.

230 Marx quoted in Lenin, *Collected Works* Volume 26, p127.

231 Tony Cliff and Chris Harman have, in separate articles, attributed this observation to Trotsky.

232 Reed, 1977, pp11-12.

233 Reed, 1977, p47.

234 Reed, 1977, p34.

235 Sukhanov, 1984, p578.

236 Sukhanov, pp595, 596.

237 Morgan Philips-Price, quoted in *Constructing the Socialist Order*, Socialist Review 102, (London, 1987), p20.

238 McDermid and Hillyar, 1999, pp75, 76.

239 Reed, 1977, p105.

240 The only casualties in Petrograd fell during the assault on the Winter Palace.

241 Sukhanov, 1984, pp627-629.

242 Trotsky, 1967, Volume 3, p270.

243 Robert Service, *The Bolshevik Party in Revolution 1917-23*, (London, 1979), pp62-63.

244 Service, 1979, p62.

245 Sukhanov, 1984, pp576, 648-9.

246 See Figes, *A People's Tragedy*, (London, 1996) and Richard Pipes, *The Russian Revolution, 1899-1919*, (London, 1990).

247 A Rabinowitch, *The Bolsheviks Come to Power*, (London, 2004), p311.

248 Rabinowitch, 2004, ppXX and XXI.

249 Service, (1979), p52, 53.

250 Ferro, 1980, pp272-274.

251 Reed, 1977, p28.

252 Reed, 1977, p104.

253 Reed, 1977, p133.

254 Porter, 2013, p267.

255 Quoted in Deutcher (ed), 1964, p108.

Chapter 8: War and revolution: the international impact

256 Lenin, quoted in Carr, Volume 3, 1983 p63.

257 Trotsky, 1973, Foreword written 1922, p8.

258 James Hinton, *The First Shop Stewards' Movement*, (London, 1973), pp21, 23.

259 James Connolly writing in *The Irish Worker*, 8 August 1914.

260 J Newsinger, *Them and Us: Fighting the Class War 1910-39*, (London, 2015), p54.

261 *The Leeds Convention*, Reprint of the *Daily Herald*, (Nottingham, 1976), p22.

262 H McShane and J Smith, *No Mean Fighter*, (London, 1978).

263 Hinton, 1973, p261.

264 Newsinger, 2015, p70.

265 A Rothstein, *The Soldiers' Strikes 1919*, (London, 1980), p94.

266 S Graubard, *British Labour and the Russian Revolution: 1917-24*, (Cambridge, Mass, 1956), p71.

267 Newsinger, 2015, p93.

268 R Challinor, *The Origins of British Bolshevism*, (London, 1997), p196.

269 K Allen, *1916: Ireland's Revolutionary Tradition*, (London, 2016), p69.

270 C Rosenberg, *1919*, (London, 1987), p31.

271 G Sheffield and J Bourne, *Douglas Haig: War Diaries and Letters 1914-18*, (London, 2005), p487.

272 R Hoffroge, *Working Class Politics in the German Revolution*, (Leiden, 2014), p49.

273 C Fuller, *The Mass Strike in the First World War*, International Socialism 145, (London, 2015), pp159-160.

274 D Gluckstein, *The Western Soviets: Workers' Councils versus Parliament 1915-20*, (London, 1985), p170.

275 V Serge, *Year One of the Russian Revolution*, (London, 1992), pp314-315, 325.

276 Quoted in Carr, Volume 3 (1983), pp135-6.

277 J Newsinger, *The Revolutionary Journalism of Big Bill Haywood*, (London, 2016), p29.

Chapter 9: Achievements of the revolution

278 A Kopp, *Town and Revolution*, (London, 1967), pp1, 2.

279 Y Akhapkin, *First Decrees of Soviet Power*, (London, 1970), p42.

280 J Reed, *Soviets in Action*, US magazine *The Liberator*, published October 1918 and reprinted in International Socialism Number 69, (London, May 1974), pp21-2.

281 Statistics from Smith, 1983, pp23, 24.

282 Smith, 1983, p26.

283 A Kollontai, *Selected Articles and Speeches* (Moscow, 1984).

284 L Trotsky, *Problems of Everyday Life*, (New York, 1973), pp63, 65.

285 A Kollontai, *Communism and the Family*, www.marxists.org/archive/kollontai/1920/family.htm

286 L Trotsky, *Women and the Family*, (London, 1974), p54.

287 Porter, 2013, p174.

288 D Healey, *Homosexual Desire in Revolutionary Russia*, (Chicago, 2001), p141.

289 A Kollontai, *On the History of the Movement of Women Workers in Russia*, www.marxists.org/archive/Kollontai/1919/history.htm.

290 *Is Soviet Russia fit to be Recognised*, Liberty Magazine 1933, reprinted in *Women and the Family*, (New York, 1970).

291 S Rowbotham, *Women, Resistance and Revolution*, (London, 1974), p141.

292 Quoted by M Haynes in *Brief Encounters*, Socialist Review, issue 177 (London, 1994), p14.

293 Marx and Engels, *The German Ideology*, (London, 1985), p95.

294 McDermid and Hillyar, 1999

295 Quoted in R Kingsbury and M Fairchild, *Factory, Family and Women in the Soviet Union*, (New York, 1935), pXXII.

296 Porter, 2013, p304.

297 Quoted in C Rosenberg, Socialist Review issue number 211, (London, 1997), p29.

298 Lenin, *Soviet Power and the Status of Women, Collected Works*, Volume 30, (Moscow, 1977), p30.

299 Lenin, *Collected Works*, Volume 36, p175.

300 J Smith, *The Bolsheviks and the National*

Question 1917-23, (London, 1999), p29.

301 J Smith, 1999, p29.

302 See D Crouch, *The Bolsheviks and Islam*, International Socialism Journal 110, (London, 2006), p43.

303 Crouch, 2006, p45.

304 Figures from D Crouch, *Bolsheviks and Islam*, Socialist Review, Issue 280, (London, 2003).

305 T Krausz, *Reconstructing Lenin*, (New York, 2015), p278.

306 See D Crouch, *The Seeds of National Liberation*, International Socialism 94, (London, 2002).

307 Reed, 1979, p39.

308 Reed, 1979, p40.

309 C Rosenberg, *Education under Capitalism and Socialism*, (London, 1991), p53.

310 S Behrman, *Shostakovich: Socialism, Stalinism and Symphonies*, (London, 2010), pp9, 10, 30.

311 Trotsky, 1967, Volume 3, p323.

Chapter 10: Consolidating Soviet power

312 *Rosa Luxemburg Speaks*, 1980, p25.

313 Reed, 1977, p121.

314 C Porter, 2013, p269.

315 For example see Robin Blackburn, *Fin De Siecle: Socialism After the Crash*, NLR 185, (London, 1991).

316 Serge, 1992 pp79-106.

317 O H Radkey, *The Sickle under the Hammer*, (New York, 1963), p66.

318 Rabinowitch, 2004, p96.

319 Trotsky, *On Lenin*, (London, 1971), p105-6.

320 For full details of this and the voting figures see Cliff, *Lenin Volume 3: Revolution Besieged*, pp32-34.

321 www.marxists.org/archive/kautsky/1918/dictprole/ch07.htmKautsky.

322 Rosa Luxemburg, quoted in Hal Draper, *Women and Class*, (Alameda, California, 2011) p287.

323 Trotsky, *Terrorism and Communism*, (London, 1975), p1.

324 *Rosa Luxemburg Speaks*, 1980, p203.

325 *Rosa Luxemburg Speaks*, 1980, pp77-78.

326 marxists.org/archive/kautsky/1914/09/war.htm.

327 Lenin, *Collected Works*, Volume 28, (Moscow, 1965), p108.

328 Quoted in J P Nettl, *Rosa Luxemburg*, (Oxford, 1969), p425.

329 *Rosa Luxemburg Speaks*, 1980, p25.

330 Luxemburg, *The Dreyfus Affair and the Millerand Case*, (www.marxists.org/archive/luxemburg/1899/II/dreyfus-affair.htm).

331 Quoted in C Porter, 2013, p339.

332 Lenin, *Collected Works*, Volume 28, p264.

333 Lenin, *Collected Works*, Volume 25, p393.

334 Reed, 1977, pp20, 21.

335 Lenin, *Collected Works*, Volume 27, p21.

336 J Bunyan and H Fischer, *The Bolshevik Revolution 1917-18: Documents and Materials*, (Stanford, 1934), p523.

337 Figures from Bunyan and Fischer, pp523-524.

338 Serge, 1992, p173.

339 Broué, 2006, p102, 103.

340 Carr, 1983 Volume 3, p104.

341 Reed, 1977, p13.

Chapter 11: Revolution under siege: how the revolution was lost

342 D Hallas, *The Comintern*, (London, 1985), p25.

343 President G Bush senior, in his speech to the annual IMF/World Bank Meeting, 25 September 1990.

344 Quoted by Lindsey German in *Socialist Review* 149, (London, January 1992), p29.

345 Quoted in Carr, 1983, pp17, 18.

346 *Trotsky on China*, (New York, 1976), p297.

347 Serge, 1992.

348 R McNeal, *Bride of the Revolution: Krupskaya and Lenin*, (London, 1973), p259.

349 A Antonov-Ovseyenko, *The Time of Stalin: Portrait of a Tyranny*, (New York, 1980), pxvii.

350 Lenin, *Collected Works*, Volume 32, p48.

351 Lenin, *Collected Works*, Volume 32, p480.

352 V Serge, *From Lenin to Stalin*, (New York, 1980), p40.

353 For fuller details see M Lewin, *Lenin's*

Last Struggle, (London, 1975).

354 M Lewin, *The Making of the Soviet System*, (London, 1985), p199.

355 A Shlyapnikov, *On the Eve of 1917*, (London, 1982), pVIII.

356 Victor Serge, *Memoirs of a Revolutionary 1901-41*, (London, 1967), ppXV, XVI

357 Marx and Engels, *Selected Works*, Volume 1, (Moscow, 1965), p100.

358 S Cohen, *Rethinking the Soviet Experience*, (Oxford, 1985), p62.

359 I Deutscher, *Stalin*, (London, 1961), p328.

360 M Empson, *Marxism and Ecology: Capitalism, Socialism and the Future of the Planet*, (London, 2016), p28.

361 A Callinicos, *The Revolutionary Ideas of Karl Marx*, p183.

362 K Murphy, *The Light that Hasn't Failed*, International Socialism Journal 110, (London, 2006), p155.

363 C Read, *From Tsar to Soviets*, (London, 1996), p292.

364 Ferro, 1980, p37.

365 Lenin, *Collected Works*, Volume 26, p294.

366 Trotsky, *On Lenin*, (London, 1971), pp151, 118.

367 Serge, 1992, p79.

368 J Rees, *In Defence of October*, International Socialism 52, (London, Autumn 1991), pp32, 33.

369 R Pipes, *The Russian Revolution*, (London, 1990), p790.

370 W Bruce Lincoln, *Red Victory*, (New York, 1989), p86.

371 Quoted in W Bruce Lincoln, p317.

372 Murphy, 2006, pp162, 164.

373 See M Gilbert, *The Holocaust*, (London, 1978), p9.

374 Quoted in the introduction to V Serge, *Revolution in Danger*, (London, 1997), pv.

375 Serge, 1997, pv.

376 W H Chamberlin, *The Russian Revolution*, Volume 2, (New York, 1987), p461.

377 Trotsky, 1975, p3.

378 Figures from M Trudell, *The Russian Civil War*, International Socialism 86, (London, 2000), p113.

379 E H Carr, *The Bolshevik Revolution*, Volume 2, (London, 1983), pp194-200.

380 C Read, *From Tsar to Soviets*, p112.

381 McDermid and Hillyar, 1999, p200.

382 Marx, quoted in D Hallas, *The Meaning of Marxism*, (London, 1971), p36.

383 K Murphy, *Can We Write the History of the Russian Revolution*, International Socialism Journal 116 (London, 2007), p47.

384 V Serge, *Memoirs of a Revolutionary*, (London, 1975), p147.

385 M Haynes, *Was there a Parliamentary Alternative in Russia 1917?*, International Socialism 76 (London, 1997), p59.

386 Luxemburg, 1980, pp29-30.

387 Kerensky's Address to the Army and Navy, cited in Merridale, 2016, p245.

388 Browder and Kerensky, *Russia's Provisional Government, 1917: Documents*, Volume 2, (Stanford, 1961), p942.

389 Luxemburg, 1980, p395.

Chapter 12: Conclusion: When all things are possible

390 K Marx, *Political Writings*, Volume 3, (London, 1974), p82.

391 N Bukharin, *The Economics of the Transformation Period: 1920*, (London, 1979), pp66-7.

392 F Fukuyama, *The End of History? The National Interest*, (New York, 1989), p3.

393 P Fryer, *The Hungarian Tragedy*, (London, 1956), p46.

394 P Foot, *The Vote: How it was won and how it was undermined*, (London, 2005), p441.

395 J Shenker, *The Egyptians: A Radical Story*, (London, 2016), pp2, 3.

396 *Pravda*, January 1924.

397 Lenin, *Collected Works*, Volume 9, p113.

398 *Trotsky's Writings on Britain*, Volume 2 (London, 1974), p68.

399 Lenin, *Collected Works*, Volume 28, p63.

400 Population and employment statistics here are from ILO report, 2013.

401 I Ness, *Southern Insurgency; The Coming of the Global Working Class*, (London, 2016).

402 Lenin, *One Step Forward, Two Steps Back*, in *Collected Works* Volume 7, p415.

Further reading

The Russian Revolution has remained controversial throughout the hundred years since it happened and an enormous amount of literature has been generated, much of it hostile and inaccurate, written from the standpoint of those who want to bury the revolution.

The champions of capitalism belittle revolutions as glitches and hiccups of history, not its great turning points—though capitalism was itself the product of revolutionary violence against the feudal order it replaced. In 2017 there will doubtless be more tales of how the Bolsheviks seized power behind the backs of the masses and Lenin established a totalitarian state, morphing seamlessly into Stalin's murderous dictatorship.

The Bolshevik revolution provoked fear and fury among the ruling classes of the West. Britain and her allies tried their damnedest to forestall it. Winston Churchill, who came to admire Mussolini's fascists, told the British war cabinet in 1919 it might need to rebuild the German army to fight the spread of Bolshevism.

In 1920 American auto tycoon Henry Ford, ruthless opponent of trade unions and socialism and a vicious anti-semite, published his notorious book, *The International Jew: the World's Foremost Problem*. It claimed the Bolshevik revolution was part of a Jewish plot for world domination—a foretaste of Hitler's *Mein Kampf*. Like his rich German counterparts who funded the rise of the Nazis, Ford was happy to do business with Hitler's regime.

During the McCarthy witch-hunts of the 1950s US academia was turned against Russia; its former ally against Hitler became its new cold war adversary. At the time the president of the US Historical Association warned, "total war, whether it be hot or cold, enlists everyone and calls upon everyone to assume his part".[5] Dissident historians were purged

---

5   P Novick, *That Noble Dream: The 'Objectivity Question' and the American Historical*

and the truth about what actually happened in 1917 became a major casualty as fear and conformity dominated the USA and its universities. From the Cold War era came totalitarianism theory: a crude attempt to equate any challenge to Western capitalism with Nazism.

With the collapse of Russia and its state capitalist satellites in 1989-91 a new neo-liberal offensive was launched against the legacy of the October Revolution. Kevin Murphy, who won the Deutscher Memorial Prize for new research into the revolution, made this point in 2007: "If it were simply a question of sources, the standard textbook interpretation of the Russian Revolution would be moving to the left, towards the classical Marxist account, but instead we see the opposite, a shifting to the right and the repackaging of old arguments that often contradict the sources they are based on".[6]

Some material written long ago, such as W H Chamberlin's two volume history, *The Russian Revolution*, has stood the test of time, while more recent publications including Hungarian Tamas Krausz's *Reconstructing Lenin: An Intellectual Biography*, published in 2015, and Canadian Lars Lih's *Lenin Rediscovered: What Is to Be Done? in Context*, published in 2008, draw on historical records made available only in the 1990s to demolish the argument that Stalinism was the outcome of Lenin's Marxism.

Below is a full bibliography of books and articles sourced or quoted; some merit further mention.

Tony Cliff's study of Lenin, published in four volumes between 1975 and 1979, is available again and is highly recommended along with his four-volume study of Trotsky published between 1989 and 1993. Tamas Krausz's *Reconstructing Lenin* presents a Lenin that is relevant now. Krausz shows how in *State and Revolution*, written months before the October insurrection, Lenin sought, "to rediscover and re-energise the elements of the Marxist tradition that mainstream European social democracy was intent on burying".[7]

Alexander Rabinowitch was one of the social historians who challenged both the USSR's authorised version of 1917 and the anti-Bolshevik narrative of the cold war historians. Professor of Russian history at

Profession, (Cambridge, 1988), pp281-319.

6 K Murphy, *Can We Write the History of the Russian Revolution?* ISJ 116, (London, 2007), p35.

7 T Krausz, *Reconstructing Lenin: An Intellectual Biography*, (New York, 2015), p360.

Indiana University, his *The Bolsheviks Come to Power*, written in the 1970s and republished in 2004, is one of the best of these histories.

Steven Smith's *Red Petrograd: Revolution in the Factories 1917-18* is a detailed account of how Russian workers deposed the Tsar and overthrew capitalism. It easily demolishes the lie that what happened in 1917 was not a workers' revolution but a coup by which Lenin and the Bolsheviks seized power. Kevin Murphy's 2005 book, *Revolution and Counter-revolution: Class Struggle in a Moscow Metal Factory*[8] pays tribute to Rabinowitch and Smith's earlier work as well as others who challenged the cold war stereotype.

Lenin himself recommended John Reed's eyewitness account, *Ten Days that Shook the World*. Historian A J P Taylor liked it too: "Reed's is not only the best account of the Bolshevik revolution, it comes near to being the best account of any revolution. He was too good a journalist to write propaganda but he made no secret where his sympathies lay. He had a further quality, which completed the others. He was a great writer".[9]

Warren Beatty's Hollywood movie *Reds*, available on DVD and YouTube, is well worth watching. Made in the 1970s, it is sympathetic to the revolution and focuses on the remarkable Reed, the early years of the workers' government and its impact in the USA. Nikolai Sukhanov's *The Russian Revolution 1917: A Personal Record* is useful. Sukhanov joined the Mensheviks in 1917 and was one of the representatives of the then moderate Petrograd Soviet in its negotiations with the capitalist politicians. An opponent and critic of Bolshevism, Sukhanov's honesty makes him a good witness to the key moments of 1917.

E H Carr's *The Bolshevik Revolution 1917-23* is scrupulous on the facts and gives a good account of the history of Bolshevism but says little on the role of the working class. It was an important work. When it appeared at the height of the Cold War, the main orthodoxy peddled by the Western establishment argued Stalinism stemmed from Lenin's Bolsheviks and revolution in general. The other, Moscow, orthodoxy was of a land of socialism, peace and progress, where there were only happy workers and peasants. The combined weight of these two great lies was immense and challenged by only a tiny handful of socialists at the time. Carr was not a Marxist but his factual account helped rebut both.

---

8   K Murphy, *Revolution and Counter Revolution: Class Struggle in a Moscow Metal Factory*, (2005).

9   A J P Taylor's introduction to *Ten Days that Shook the World*, (London, 1977), p.viii.

1917: Russia's Red Year is a brand new graphic novel of the world's greatest year so far. Written by John Newsinger and illustrated by Tim Sanders, it gives a concise account of the events in Russia and their impact abroad. Engagingly written with great illustrations, it is, in the words of cartoonist Steve Bell, "a ripping good read".

The revolution and the early years of the Soviet government had a profound impact on women's lives, and not just in Russia. For this and the role of women in the revolution I recommend Jane McDermid and Anna Hillyar's *Midwives of the Revolution: Female Bolsheviks and Women Workers in 1917*; Cathy Porter's *Alexandra Kollontai: A Biography*; Judith Orr's *Marxism and Women's Liberation*; and Emma Davis's forthcoming book on Kollontai.

Dan Healey's *Homosexual Desire in Revolutionary Russia* is extensively researched and contrasts the positive attitude and approach to LGBT+ people in Lenin's revolutionary Russia, with the Tsarist regime and the suffocating religious orthodoxy that preceded it, and the reactionary Stalinist regime that usurped it in the late 1920s.

Barbara Allen's *Alexander Shlyapnikov, 1885-1937: Life of an Old Bolshevik* is an important new biography of the most prominent of the Bolshevik worker-intellectuals. A key link between the underground party members in Russia and its exiled leadership during the turbulent period after the 1905 revolution, Shlyapnikov was a party stalwart willing to challenge the likes of Lenin and Trotsky. Allen's material on the Bolsheviks prior to 1917 and the arguments inside the party before, during and after the revolution make this a fascinating read. It is also worth reading Shlyapnikov's own memoirs, *On the Eve of 1917*.

For the period immediately after the October revolution, Victor Serge's *Year One of the Russian Revolution*, French socialist Alfred Rosmer's *Lenin's Moscow* and Arthur Ransome's *Six Weeks in Russia 1919* and his *The Crisis in Russia 1920* all convey the enormous difficulties that confronted the new regime. Ransome, known for his children's adventure stories, was in Russia for long spells between 1913 and 1920 and wrote for the *Daily News* and *The Manchester Guardian*. He came to know Russia well and learned the language. Unlike Serge, Rosmer and Reed, Ransome had no previous commitment to socialism but what he saw left its mark on him.

For the global impact of 1917 as well as the later isolation and degeneration of the revolution read Tony Cliff's *Lenin* Volumes 3 and 4; Chris

Harman's *How the Revolution Was Lost* and John Rees's *In Defence of October*. Mike Hayne's *Russia: Class and Power 1917-2000* is a very readable account of 20th century Russia, while Tony Cliff's pioneering work *State Capitalism in Russia*, originally published in 1948 as *The Nature of Stalinist Russia*, cleared the path of rediscovery to the 1917 revolution.

Lenin was a prolific writer and his *Collected Works* stretch to 45 volumes. Ian Birchall's *Rebel's Guide to Lenin* is a good, short introduction but as Birchall says; "If you only ever read one book by Lenin, *State and Revolution* is the one."

Catherine Merridale's recent *Lenin On The Train* is fascinating, despite its shortcomings. Published in 2016 it is a semi-fictional account of Lenin's return from exile in April 1917, by train through war-torn Germany via Denmark, Sweden and Finland to Petrograd. Despite its hostility to the Bolshevik government it gives a good detailed account of the February events in Petrograd.

I have left the best to last: Trotsky's *History of the Russian Revolution*. Isaac Deutscher called it, "arguably the most remarkable European book of the twentieth century". No praise is too high for Trotsky's epic. Unsurpassed in its historical understanding and literary style, no one who reads it could ever argue history is boring or Marxism is only concerned with economics.

Trotsky's theory of uneven and combined development is crucial for understanding both the Russian Revolution and the modern world. The concept was first presented in his two earlier books, *Results and Prospects* and *1905*.

A new edition of Trotsky's *Stalin* came out in 2016. This was the book he was writing when he was assassinated in Mexico by one of Stalin's agents. The new edition brings together all of the material available from the Trotsky archives at Harvard University, making it the most complete version yet published. It contains a chapter on 1917 that gives a great condensed account of Russia's red year. Trotsky's autobiography *My Life* will also benefit the reader and Esme Choonara's *A Rebel's Guide to Trotsky* is a good short introduction to his ideas.

This present book was written to celebrate the centenary and highlight its relevance. It draws on these and other books and tries to make the greatest year in working class history come alive for a new audience and new times. That means challenging those who made their careers out of trashing the revolution and holding Lenin responsible for Stalin.

Bibliography

Acton, E: *Rethinking the Russian Revolution*, London, 1990.

Allen, B C: *Alexander Shlyapnikov 1885-1937: Life of an Old Bolshevik*, Chicago, 2016.

Allen, K:*1916: Ireland's Revolutionary Tradition*, London, 2016.

Antonov-Ovseyenko, A: *The Time of Stalin: Portrait of a Tyranny*, New York, 1980.

Behrman, S: *Shostakovich: Socialism, Stalinism and Symphonies*, London, 2010.

Birchall, I: *A Rebel's Guide to Lenin*, London, 2005.

The Bolsheviks and the October Revolution: Central Committee Minutes of the RSDLP (Bolsheviks) August 1917-February 1918, London, 1974.

Broué, P: *The German Revolution: 1917-23*, London, 2006.

Browder, R and Kerensky, A : *Russia's Provisional Government 1917: Documents*, Volume 2, Stanford, 1961.

Bukharin, N: *Imperialism and World Economy*, London, 1972.

Bukharin: *The Economics of the Transformation Period*: 1920, London, 1979.

Callinicos, A: *The Revolutionary Ideas of Karl Marx*, London, 1983.

Callinicos: *The Revenge of History*, London, 1991.

Campbell, Sally: *A Rebel's Guide to Rosa Luxemburg*, London, 2011.

Carr, E H: *The Bolshevik Revolution*, Volumes 1-3, London, 1983.

Challinor, R: *The Origins of British Bolshevism*, London, 1977.

Chamberlin, W H: *The Russian Revolution*, Volumes 1 and 2, New York, 1987.

Choonara, E: *A Rebel's Guide to Trotsky*, London, 2007.

Cliff, T: *State Capitalism in Russia*, London, 1974.

Cliff: *Lenin Volume 1: Building the Party*, London, 1975.

Cliff: *Lenin Volume 2: All Power to the Soviets*, London, 1976.

Cliff: *Lenin Volume 3: Revolution Besieged*, London, 1978.

Cliff: *Lenin Volume 4: The Bolsheviks and World Revolution*, London, 1979.

Cliff, *Trotsky Volume 1: Towards October 1879-1917*, London, 1989.

Cliff, *Trotsky Volume 2: The Sword of the Revolution 1917-23*, London, 1990.

Cliff and Gluckstein, D: *The Labour Party: A Marxist History*, London, 1988.

Cohen, S: *Bukharin and the Bolshevik Revolution*, London, 1974.

Cohen: *Rethinking the Soviet Experience*, Oxford, 1985.

Crankshaw, E: *The Shadow of the Winter Palace*, London, 1978.

Crouch, D: *The Seeds of National Liberation*, International Socialism Journal (ISJ) 94, London, 2002.

Crouch: *The Bolsheviks and Islam*, ISJ 110, London, 2006.

Darlington, R: *Radical Unionism: The Rise and Fall of Revolutionary Syndicalism*, Chicago, 2013.

Degras, J: *The Communist International 1919-43: Documents*, Volume 1, London, 1956.

Deutscher, I: *Stalin: A Political Biography*, London, 1961.

Empson, M: *Land and Labour: Marxism, Ecology and Human History*, London, 2014.

Empson: *Marxism and Ecology: Capitalism, Socialism and the Future of the Planet*, London, 2016.

Ferro, M: *October 1917, a Social History of the Russian Revolution*, London, 1980.

Figes, O: *The People's Tragedy*, London, 1996.

Foner, P: *History of the Labour Movement in the USA*, Volume 4, New York, 1965.

Foot, P: *The Vote*, London, 2005.

Fröhlich, P: *Rosa Luxemburg*, London, 1994.

Fryer, P: *The Hungarian Tragedy*, London, 1956.

Fuller, C: *The Mass Strike in the First World War*, ISJ 145, London, 2015.

Glatter, P: *1905: The Great Dress Rehearsal*, London, 1985.

Gluckstein, D: *The Western Soviets*, London, 1985.

Golovine, N: *The Russian Army in the World War*, Yale, 1931.

Goodey, C: *Factory Committees and the Dictatorship of the Proletariat*, Critique 3, London, 1974.

Harding, N: *Lenin's Political Thought*, London, 1993.

Hallas, D: *Trotsky's Marxism*, London, 1979.

Hallas: *The Comintern*, London, 1985.

Harman, C: *How the Revolution Was Lost*, International Socialism 30, London, 1967.

Harman: *The Lost Revolution*, London, 1982.

Harman: *A Peoples' History of the World*, London, 1999.

Haynes, M: *Was there a Parliamentary Alternative in 1917?* ISJ 76, London, 1997.

Haynes: *Russia: Class and Power 1917-2000*, London, 2002.

Healey, D: *Homosexual Desire in Revolutionary Russia*, Chicago, 2001.

Hinton, J: *The First Shop Stewards Movement*, London, 1973.

Hoggart, L: *The War against War*, Socialist Review 85, London, 1986.

Holt, A: *Selected Writings of Alexandra Kollontai*, London, 1984.

Kendall, W: *The Revolutionary Movement in Britain*, London, 1969.

Krausz, T: *Reconstructing Lenin*, New York, 2015.

Kochan, L: *Russia in Revolution 1898-1918*, London, 1966.

Kollontai, A: *Selected Articles and Speeches*, Moscow, 1984.

Kollontai: *Communism and the Family*, www.marxists.org/archive/kollontai/1920/family.htm .

Kollontai: *On the History of the Movement of Women Workers in Russia*, www.marxists.org/archive/Kollontai/1919/history.htm .

Krupskaya, N: *Memories of Lenin*, London, 1970.

Le Blanc, P: *Unfinished Leninism*, Chicago, 2014.

Lenin: *Collected Works*, Volumes 1-36, Moscow, 1960-66.

Lewin, M: *Lenin's Last Struggle*, London, 1975.

Lewin: *The Making of the Soviet System*, London, 1985.

Lih, Lars T: *Lenin Rediscovered: What Is to Be Done? in Context*, Chicago, 2008.

Lincoln, W Bruce: *Red Victory*, New York, 1989.

Lunacharsky, A: *Revolutionary Silhouettes*, edited Deutscher, London, 1967.

Rosa Luxemburg Speaks, New York, 1980.

Luxemburg: *The Mass Strike, The Political Party and the Trade Unions*, London, 1986.

Mandel, D: *The Petrograd Workers and the Soviet Seizure of Power*, London, 1984.

Marx, K: *Political Writings*, Volume 3, London, 1974.

Marx and Engels, F: *The German Ideology*, London, 1985.

Marx and Engels: *The Communist Manifesto*, New York, 1992.

Mason, P: *Live Working or Die Fighting*, London, 2007.

McDermid, J and Hillyar, A: *Midwives of the Revolution*, Athens Georgia, 1999.

McNeal, R: *Bride of the Revolution: Krupskaya and Lenin*, London, 1973.

McShane and Smith: *No Mean Fighter*, London, 1978.

Merridale, C: *Lenin on the Train*, London, 2016.

Milliband, R: *Parliamentary Socialism*, London, 1972.

Milton, N: *John Maclean*, London, 1973.

Molyneux, J: *Marxism and the Party*, London, 1978.

Murphy, K: *The Light that Hasn't Failed*, ISJ 110, London, 2006.

Murphy: *Can We Write The History of the Russian Revolution?* ISJ 116, London, 2007.

Ness, I: *Southern Insurgency: The Coming of the Global Working Class*, London, 2016.

Nettl, J P: *Rosa Luxemburg*, Oxford, 1969.

Newsinger, J: *The Blood Never Dried*, London, 2006.

Newsinger: *Fighting Back*, London, 2012.

Newsinger: *Them and Us: Fighting the Class War 1910-39*, London, 2015.

Newsinger: *The Revolutionary Journalism of Big Bill Haywood*, London, 2016.

Orr, J: *Marxism and Women's Liberation*, London, 2015.

Pipes, R: *The Russian Revolution*, London, 1990.

Pokrovsky: *Brief History of Russia*, Volume 2, London, 1933.

Porter, C: *Alexandra Kollontai: a Biography*, Pontypool, 2013.

Rabinowitch, A: *The Bolsheviks Came to Power*, London, 2004.

Radkey, O H: *The Sickle and the Hammer*, New York, 1963.

Ransome, A: *Six Weeks in Russia 1919*, London, 1992.

Ransome: *The Crisis in Russia 1920*, London, 1992.

Raskolnikov, F: *Kronstadt and Petrograd in 1917*, London, 1982.

Read, C: *From Tsar to Soviets*, London, 1966.

Reed, John: *Ten Days that Shook the World*, London, 1977.

Reed: *Soviets in Action*, International Socialism 69, London, 1974.

Rees, J: *In Defence of October*, ISJ 52, London, 1991.

Rosenberg, C: *Education under Capitalism and Socialism*, London, 1991.

Rosmer, A: *Lenin's Moscow*, London, 2016.

Rothstein, A: *The Soldiers' Strikes 1919*, London, 1980.

Rowbotham, S: *Women, Resistance and Revolution*, London, 1974.

Sagall, S: *Unlocking the Prison House*, Socialist Review 149, London, 1992.

Sanders, T and Newsinger, J: *1917: Russia's Red Year*, London, 2016.

Schneer, J: *Ben Tillett*, Kent, 1972.

Schorske, C: *German Social Democracy 1905-17*, London, 1985.

Serge, V: *Year One of the Russian Revolution*, London, 1992.

Serge: *From Lenin to Stalin*, New York, 1980.

Serge: *Revolution in Danger*, London, 1997.

Serge: *Memoirs of a Revolutionary 1901-41*, London, 1967.

Service, R: *The Bolshevik Party in Revolution, 1917-23*, London, 1979.

Shenker, J: *The Egyptians: A Radical Story*, London, 2016.

Sherry, D: *Empire and Revolution: A Socialist History of the First World War*, London, 2014.

Shlyapnikov, A: *On the Eve of 1917*, London, 1982.

Smith, J: *The Bolsheviks and the National Question 1917-23*, London, 1999.

Smith, S A: *Red Petrograd: Revolution in the factories 1917-18*, Cambridge, 1983.

Stone, N: *The Eastern Front*, London, 1975.

Strachan, H: *The First World War*, London, 2006.

Sukhanov, N N: *The Russian Revolution 1917: A Personal Record*, Princeton, 1984.

Trotsky: *1905*, London, 1973.

The War Correspondence of Leon Trotsky: The Balkan Wars 1912-13, New York, 1981.

Trotsky: *Terrorism and Communism*, London, 1975.

Trotsky: *War and the International*, London, 1971.

Trotsky: *History of the Russian Revolution*, Volumes 1-3, London, 1967.

Trotsky: *Problems of Everyday Life*, New York, 1973.

Trotsky: *Women and the Family*, London, 1974.

Trotsky: *On Lenin*, London, 1971.

Trotsky: *The Young Lenin*, New York, 1972.

Trotsky on China, New York, 1976.

Trotsky: *My Life*, London, 1979.

Trotsky: *Stalin*, London, 2016.

The Age of Permanent Revolution: A Trotsky Anthology ed. Deutscher, New York, 1964.

Trudell, M: *Prelude to Revolution*, ISJ 76, London, 1997.

Widgery, D: *Abortion: the Pioneers*, International Socialism 80, London, 1975.

Winter, J: *Socialism and the Challenge of War*, London, 1974.

Wright, S: *Russia: the Making of the Revolution*, London, 1984.

Index

1968 244

All Power to the Soviets (slogan) 15, 16, 126, 133, 138, 147, 160-1, 203
Allen, Barbara 71
All-Russian Congress of Muslims 192
All-Russian Congress of Soviets 150; First 16, 126, 127; Second 147-8, 150, 162-4, 199
All-Russian Congress of Working Women 189
America *see* USA
Annual Congress of the Commintern, Third 217
anti-semitism 24-26, 56, 193-4, 231 *see also* Jews
Antonov-Ovseyenko, Vladimir 155, 219-20
April Theses (pamphlet) 14-16, 114, 146
Arab Spring 246-7
Armand, Inessa 187, 189
armed forces 126-7, 144; *see also* soldiers and sailors
art 195-6
Ascherson, Neal 110
Aurora (battleship) 141, 155, 158
Austria 169, 178
Austro-Hungary 176

Balkan Wars 76-78
Berlin 167, 175-8
Bernstein, Eduard 40, 51, 175, 241, 242
Black Hundreds 56, 57, 60, 119
Blackburn, Robin 199
Bloody Sunday (1905) 54-58
Bolivia 243, 246
Bolsheviks 100, 110, 126, 144, 207, 233; accept Brest Litovsk 211; activism 74, 115-7, 119, 120, 121; and Constituent Assembly 201-2; and Duma 67-8, 72; and July Days 129-31; and Kronstadt uprising 235; and religion 192-4; and revolutionary defeatism 88-9; and soviets 58-62; and working class 60; back united front against coup 141-2; at Brest Litovsk 211-2; boycott Moscow State conference 139- 40; coalition negotiations 200-1; call for national rights 125-6; confusion 103; divisions in 223; gain majority in soviets 145-6; influence in factories 120, 123-5; influence in army 127; increase support 144-5; premature revolution 239-40; support Provisional government 106-7; under attack 132-5; women 117, 143-5, 188-9, 234
bourgeois revolution 27-8, 29, 60, 102, 104
bourgeoisie 29-30, 49, 97, 108
Boxer Rebellion 49
Brest Litovsk 210, 211-2, 213, 231
Britain 99, 118, 140, 151, 152, 165, 167, 169-74, 197, 213, 226, 245, 247; Great Unrest 84; Empire 25-6, 75-6; in Russian civil war 226-7; response to Revolution 169-74
Bukharin, Nikolai 137, 241-2
Bund, the 24-5
Bush, George senior 215

Callinicos, Alex 226
Can the Bolsheviks Retain State Power? (article) 148-9, 150-1
Canada 226
capitalism 241-2, 248, 254
Carr, E H (historian) 39, 234
Central Executive Committee of the Soviet congress 163
centrism 205-7
CGT union (France) 79, 81
Chagall, Mark 196

China 48-9, 217, 243, 252-3
Chinese Communist Party (CCP) 217
Churchill, Winston 172, 197, 227
civil war 16, 226-8, 233-4
Clements, Barbara Evans 37
Coalition government 201
Cohen, Stephen 225
Cold War 228, 245
collectivisation 224-5, 226
combined and uneven development 27-30, 32
Commintern *see* Communist International, Third
Communist International, Third (Commintern) 193, 216-7, 221
Communist Manifesto 252
Communist Party of Great Britain 217, 243-4
Communist Party of the Soviet Union 219, 224
Congress of Berlin 22
Congress of Soviets 146; Second 199
Connolly, James 78, 85, 168
Constituent Assembly 109, 125, 127, 151, 201-3, 206, 207, 227
Constitutional Democrats *see* Kadets
Cossacks 56, 57, 61, 94-5, 229, 232
Council of People's Commissars 163-4
Council of the Popular Militia 129
counter-revolution 151, 153, 198, 229, 230-4, 216, 229, 238
Crimean War 22

Dan, F I 115, 119-200
Darlington, Ralph 89
Declaration of Peace 164
Democratic Conference 149
Denikin, General 227
Deutscher, Isaac 33
Dictatorship or Democracy (publication) 203, 205
Down with the Provisional Government (slogan) 130
Down with the Ten Capitalist Ministers (slogan) 130
Down with the War (slogan) 127
dual power 101, 104-107, 108, 127, 143, 151, 167
Duma 57, 67-8, 69, 72, 96, 97, 100, 223

economism 40
economy 29, 46, 92, 233-4
education 194-5

Elections to the Russian constituent Assembly, 1917 (study) 202
Empson, Martin 225-6
End of History, The (book) 242
Engels, Friedrich 18, 32-3, 86
Europe 18-9, 21-2, 25, 52, 82, 84-5, 166-70, 178-9, 216, 217; *see also* individual countries
Eastern Europe 243-4, 235-6

factory committees 106, 118-23, 142, 145, 152, 153, 213 *see also* soviets
Farewell to the Working Class, The (book) 242
Ferro, Marc 228-9
Figes, Orlando 160
Finland 23-4, 61, 145, 178, 191, 210, 230
Five Year Plan 224-5, 236-7
France 25, 26, 87, 99, 118, 140, 152, 165, 168-9, 197, 213, 226
From Tsar to Soviets (book) 228
Fryer, Peter 244
Fukuyama, Francis 242

Gapon, Father Georgy 50, 54
George, David Lloyd 173-4, 179
German Independent Social Democratic Party (USPD) 175, 177
German Revolution 177, 206-7, 212
German Social Democratic Party (SPD) 63, 78-9, 80-1, 83, 84, 85, 86, 175, 176, 178, 203-4, 206, 207, 237, 238
Germany 25, 26, 75-6, 77, 78, 167, 174-8, 210, 216
Gorz, Andre 242
Graves, General Williams S 232
Guchkov, Minister of War 104

Haig, General 172-3
Hallas, Duncan 215
Hands off Russia (campaign) 173
Hardie, Keir 84, 85
Harman, Chris 114
Hasse, Hugo 78, 85
Healey, Dan 185-6
Henderson, Arthur 81, 84, 170, 172
Hilferding 175
Hillyar, Anna 38, 124
Hinton, James 167
Hobsbawm, Eric 199
Hungary 178, 243
Hyndman, H M 81-2

Imperialism and the World Economy (book) 137

Independent Social Democratic Party (USPD) 207

International Workers of the World (IWW) 53, 65, 179

Ireland 167, 174

Iskra (newspaper) 39, 41-42, 44

Italy 99, 178-9, 216, 237-8

Izvestia (newspaper) 130, 197

imperialism 25-6, 75-6, 253

industry 29

insurrection 149, 150, 152, 153; Moscow 62-4; October 154-62

internationalism 12, 75, 77, 84, 88, 109, 166, 212, 221, 226

Japan 213, 226

Jews 56, 231, 232 *see also* anti-semitism

July Days 15, 122, 128-131

Junius Pamphlet 88

Junker Mutiny 199

Kadets 49, 100, 103, 105, 143, 201

Kaiser, Wilhelm II 80, 84, 174, 177, 210, 212, 213

Kamenev, Lev 100, 106-7, 109, 113, 135, 148, 151, 219, 229; against seizing power 150; backs Provisional government 100-1; opposes insurrection 154

Kautsky, Karl 83-84, 85, 87, 175, 203-5

Kayurov, Benyamin 93

Keegan, Williams 215

Kerensky, Alexander 14, 15, 107, 118, 126, 128, 132, 141, 229, 239; forms new coalition 143; moves against revolution 154-5

Kienthal Conference (1916) 73

Koenker, Diane (historian) 124, 130

Kolchak, Admiral 227

Kollantai, Alexandra 23, 43, 54, 55, 102, 107, 116, 117, 132, 164, 184, 185, 187, 189, 207, 234

Kornilov, General Lavr 15, 127, 135, 140, 197, 201, 231

Koumintang (KMT) 217

Krasnov, General 229

Krausz, Tamas 194

Kronstadt 57, 60, 74, 127, 129-30, 141, 154, 161; uprising 235-6

Krupskaya, Nadezhda 37-8, 41, 116, 132, 135, 187, 219, 248

Labour Party (Britain) 81, 83, 84, 85, 170; Leeds Convention 170-1

Law, Bonar 174

League for the Emancipation of Labour 34, 36

League of Struggle for the Emanciptation of Labour 37

Left Opposition 224, 226

Left SRs (Social Revolutionaries) 138, 145, 163, 201, 218

Lena goldfields massacre 69

Lenin Rediscovered (book) 42

Lenin, Vladimir 79, 92, 182, 198, 217, 224, 236, 248-9, 250, 256; against Provisional government 113-5; and organisation 30, 38-40, 59-60, 70, 125, 146, 249, 251; and July Days 130-1, 132; and Plekhanov 34, 35-6; and Stalin 19, 218-20; call to seize power 148-51; early life 35; in hiding 135-6, 141; international revolution 221-3; on Bloody Sunday 55; on dual power 101; on Duma 67-8; on nature of the revolution 18, 26, 28-9, 107-10, 166; on organisation 59; on Red Terror 229; on soviets 58; on Soviet Power 205; on supporting Kerensky 141; returns to Russia 111-5; mass strikes 51; national oppression 56; new international 73; reads Declaration of Peace 164; revolutionary defeatism 79-80, 88-9, 100; self-determination 23, 147, 190-1

Leninism 251

Lenin's Last Struggle (book)

Letters from Afar 111, 113

Lewin, Moshe 223

Liebnicht, Karl 78, 79-80, 87, 175, 176, 177, 212, 238

Lih, Lars 42

Lincoln, W Bruce 231

Litveiko, Anna 119-20

Lockhart, Bruce 95

Lunacharsky, Anatoly 195

Luxembourg, Rosa 23, 43, 44, 64, 78, 79, 87-8, 197, 203, 204-5, 206, 207, 238-9, 240; on 1896 general strike 45-46; on German trade unions 64; on mass strike 52, 63

Lvov, Prince Georgy 13, 102, 132

MacDonald, Ramsey 81, 85, 171

Machine Gun Regiment 128, 129, 135

Maclean, John 82, 171-2

Manchester Guardian (newspaper) 232
Mandel, David (historian) 142
Martov, Julius 38, 39, 43, 44, 45, 100
Marx, Karl 18, 28, 241, 252; on peasantry 31, 241; on revolution 188, on the state 136-7
Marxism and Ecology (pamphlet) 225
Mason, Paul (historian) 24
Mass Strike, the Political Party and the Trade Union, The (pamphlet) 63
McDermid, Jane 38, 124
McNeal, Robert (biographer) 37
McShane, Harry 171-2
Mehring, Franz 78
Mensheviks 27-8, 29, 42, 57, 97, 100, 104, 109, 118, 125, 128, 131, 140, 153, 164, 239; and soviets 57, 58, 59, 104-5, 109, 123, 128, 159; coalition negotiations 200-201; differences with Bolsheviks 43, 44-5, 60, 67, 100, 115, 119, 125; lose support 143-4, 145, 163; on Soviet power 197, 198, 199, 200; opposition to Soviet government 198-200; support Provisional government 101, 102, 103-4, 132, 163, 239; walk out of Congress 163
Merridale, Catherine 112-3
Midwives of the Revolution (study) 188
Militarism, War and the Working Class (speech) 78
Military Revolutionary Committee 142, 153, 155, 159, 230; proclaim soviet power 157
Miliukov, Pavel 118, 126
Minsk Congress 30
Moscow 13, 45, 48, 57, 89, 96, 97, 120, 123, 130, 187, 198, 229, 231, 235; insurrection 62-4, 89; Soviet 97, 145; uprising (1905) 62-4, 65
Moscow State conference 139-40
Moscow Workers and the 1917 Revolution (book) 130
Murphy, Kevin 227-8, 231-2, 236
Muslims 192
Mussonlini, Benito 237-8
mutinies 55, 57, 67, 96, 227
My Life (book) 146

Narodniks 32-4
national oppression 22-3, 147, 190-1, 232-3; *see also* Finland
New Economic Policy (NEP) 220-1, 228, 236
Northern Underground 70, 71, 73, 102, 170

October Revolution 228-9
Okhrana (secret police) 71, 74, 95
On Strikes (article) 40
Ottoman Empire 21, 22

Pale of Settlement 24
Pankhurst, Sylvia 78
Paris 168-9; Commune (1871) 131, 182
Peace, Land and Bread-All Power to the Soviets (slogan) 16, 126, 147, 160,
peasantry 25, 30-2, 36, 98, 99, 108, 125, 127, 144, 224, 225, 232, 234, 235, 236
People's Will, The *see also* Narodniks 32-4
Pereverzev, Pavel 132
permanent revolution 18, 28, 52-3, 108-9, 218
Peter and Paul Fortress 155-6
Petrograd 92-6, 117, 123, 130, 152, 198, 229
Petrograd Popular Militia, Council of 129
Petrograd Soviet of Workers' Deputies 53, 97, 99, 101-2, 115, 142, 144, 145, 146, 150, 152, 153, 154
Phillips-Price, Morgan 143, 156-7
Piatnitsky, Osip 68
Pipes, Richard 95, 160, 230
Plekhanov, Georgi 34-6, 39, 63, 65, 85, 101
Poland 21, 49, 52, 55-6, 61, 83, 191
Portugal 245
Pravda (newspaper) 69-70, 72, 102, 103, 106, 117, 129, 132, 165
Provisional government 13-5, 16, 89, 97-100, 106-7, 113-4, 115, 123, 125-6, 127, 147, 150, 153, 157, 201-2, 239; attack Bolsheviks 132-3, 143, 139; crisis 118; deposed 157; in crisis 118; in Turin 178; Moscow State conference 139; opposition to 130 *see also* July Days
Putilov factory 50, 53, 123, 142

Rabinowitch, Alexander 160-1, 199, 200
Rabotnitsa (newspaper) 188
Radek, Karl 212
Radkey, O H 202
Raskolnikov, Fyodor 129
Read, Christopher 228
Red Army 230, 231, 232, 234
Red Guards 126, 127, 129, 142, 230
Red Terror 227, 229, 233
Reed, John 98-9, 143-4, 146, 152-3, 162-3, 164, 182-3, 194, 197, 213; on Finland 147; on soviets 208-9
reformism 204-5, 241, 251
religion 31, 192-3

repression 131-5
Results and Prospects (book) 66, 108
revisionism 51, 241
revolution 247, 248-9
revolutionary defeatism 80, 88-9
revolutionary movements 242-5, 246
revolutionary organisation 248-51, 256
    see also What Is to Be Done?
revolutionary paper 39, 41-2
revolutionary party 39, 40-4, 107
Right SRs (Social Revolutionaries) 163, 218;
    opposition to Soviet government
    198-200, 201, 202
Romanovs 13-4
Rosmer, Alfred 78
RSDLP *see* Russian Social Democratic Party
Ruhle, Otto 175
Russia pre-1917 26-30
Russian Empire 21-2, 48
Russian Revolution degeneration of 218-20,
    226
Russian Social Democratic Labour Party
    (RSDLP) 34, 42, 51, 54, 67, 100;
    Congress (1903) 42-3; split 44-5
Russo-Japanese War 48-50, 56, 57

sailors 49, 58, 89, 96, 150, 156, 162, 170, 177,
    198 *see also* Kronstadt
Samsonov, General 91
Schorske, Carl (historian) 52
Second International 27, 51-2, 73, 77, 82-3;
    Stuttgart Congress of (1907) 75
self-determination 17, 23, 28, 147, 190-1, 232,
    234, 248
Serbia 77, 246
Serge, Victor 179, 199, 211-2, 229-30, 236
Service, Robert 159, 162
Shenker, Jack 247
Shlyapnikov, Alexander 70-2, 102, 113, 193,
    219
Shlyapnikov: Life of an Old Bolshevik
    (book) 71
Smith, Steve 118-9, 124
Snowden, Phillip 85, 171, 173
social democracy 206, 207, 254; European
    19, 27, 51-2, 75, 237, 239; European
    leaders 12, 237-8; Russian 30, 40, 42, 44
    see also RSDLP and SPD
Social Peace 166-7
Social Revolutionaries (SRs) 99, 100, 102,
    103, 104-5, 125, 128, 131, 138, 143, 145,
    202; *see also* Left SRs and Right SRs

socialism 34, 81, 82, 104, 136, 138, 169, 182,
    207, 214, 215, 241
socialism in one country 216, 218, 223-6,
    224, 225
Socialist Party (Britain) 85
Socialist Party (France) 81
Socialist Party (PSI) (Italy) 83, 237
Socialist Party (USA) 83
soldatki 90, 93, 115, 124,
Soldatskaya Pravda (newspaper) 129
soldiers 63, 72, 89, 94, 97, 101, 105, 148, 152,
    172-3; *see also* Cossacks
*Southern Insurgency: The Coming of the
    Global Working Class* (book) 252-3
Soviet government 19, 162-4, 198-9, 209,
    and Consitituent Assembly 202-3; and
    war 209-11; reforms 181-2 183, 185,
    194-5; survives civil war 234
soviets 16, 57-62, 97, 106, 110, 121-2, 159;
    after the revolution 207-9; government
    opposition to 140; power 147-8;
    struggle inside 145-6; under Stalin 218
    see also individual Soviets *and* factory
    committees
Soviet Union *see* USSR
Spain 243
Spartakists 175
Spartakus (journal) 238
SPD *see* German Social Democratic Party
Spiridonova, Maria 34
St Petersburg 45, 50, 52, 53, 55, 57-8, 62, 65,
    76, 193
St Petersburg Soviet of Workers' Deputies
    51, 52, 60-1, 62
Stal, Ludmilla 114-5
Stalin, Josef 19, 106-7, 109, 113, 135, 148, 151,
    191, 221-2, 224; against seizing power
    150; and national oppression 191; backs
    Provisional government 100-1 *see also*
    socialism in one country
Stalinism 189-90, 215-6, 214-5, 218-20, 223
State and Revolution, The (pamphlet) 136-8,
    145
State capitalism 225, 226
state, the 241, 250 *see also State and
    Revolution, The* (pamphlet)
strikes 46-7, 53-4, 56-8, 61-2, 69, 96, 168-70;
    laundresses 116-7; mass 49, 52, 63-6,
    204; textiles (1896) 45-6, (1905) 93-4
Struve, Peter 36
Sukhanov, Nikolai 96-7, 134, 144, 154,
    158-9, 160

Supreme Soviet 218
Sverdlov, Yakov 202

Tasks of Revolutionary Social Democracy in the European War (resolution) 80
Tauride Palace 97, 115, 130, 156
Ten Days that Shook the World (book) 152, 164, 208
Testament 222
The Workers' Revolution in Russia: The View from Below (book) 124
Tillet, Ben 81
Towards a History of the Working Women's Movement in Russia (pamphlet) 187
trade unions 47-8, 50, 53, 59
Trotsky, Leon 15, 21, 27, 91, 101, 121, 127-8, 155-6, 196; appeals to Peter and Paul Fortress 155-6; at Brest-Litovsk 210; builds Red Army 231; exiled 219; joins Bolsheviks 146-7; letter to Provisional government 132-3; on 1905 65, 66; on alliance with China 217-8; on *April Theses* 146; on Balkan Wars 76-7; on Bolshevik confusion 103; on capitulation to war 80; on Cossacks 95; on family 187; on international revolution 166; on July Days 135; on Kautsky 204; on Krupskaya 38; on limitations of mass strike 64-5; on February Revolution 108-9; on revolutionary party 43, 44; on seizing power 149-50; on the insurrection 159; on women and revolution 184, 185; on Zasulich 33-4; return from exile 118
see also permanent revolution
Tsar Alexander I 23
Tsar Alexander II 25, 26, 33, 45
Tsar Alexander III 33, 35
Tsar Nicholas II 13, 22, 23, 33, 48, 49, 54-5, 56, 57, 61, 62, 65, 67, 89, 96, 97, 193, 233
Tsarism 26-7, 52, 96-7, 191

Ukraine 22, 29, 55, 116, 190, 198, 230, 231, 232
uneven consciousness 250-1
unions 47-8, 50

United Internationalists 163
United Socialist Party (SFIO) (France) 83
USA 16, 25, 87, 99, 151, 152, 165, 179-80, 197, 213, 217, 226-8
USSR 214-5, 226

Vyborg District 73, 93, 116, 142

War Communism 220, 236
War of Independence, Ireland 174
Webb, Beatrice 172
What Is to Be Done? (pamphlet) 40-5
White Guard 230
White Russians 16
White Terror 230-4; Finland 230
Wilson, General Sir Henry 174
Wilson, US President Woodrow 227-8
Winter Palace 157-8, 162
women 46, 118, 134-5, 169; and the revolution 183-90; and World War I 89-90; defend Soviet republic 234; in factory committees 124-5; in the insurrection 157; laundresses' strike 116-7; liberation 183-90; protest Provisional government 115-6; strikers 53, 56, 57; textile strike (1917) 92-4; textile strike (1896) 45-6
working class 31-2, 35, 36, 39-40, 42, 48, 50, 60, 67, 83, 108, 118-9, 122, 220, 235; women 89-90; worldwide revolts 242-8, 252-3, 255
World War I 87, 167, 210; opposition tp 84-8, 166

Year One of the Russian Revolution (book) 229

Zasulich, Vera 33-4, 39
Zetkin, Clara 78
Zhenotdel 189
Zimmerwald Conference (1915) 73
Zinoviev, Grigory 135, 148, 150, 151, 219; against seizing power 150; opposes insurrection 154
Zubatov, Security Police Colonel 48, 50